SCHOOL HOUSE BOOKS

Advanced Placement
English

AP

WRITER

by
Duane Earnest
English Instructor
Detroit Lakes Community
Senior High School

FIRST EDITION

SCHOOL HOUSE BOOKS
921 Pembina Trail
Detroit Lakes, Minnesota 56501

2

Acknowledgments

ThisThis book is dedicated to my wife, Julia Lucca Earnest, for her support and encouragement; to my three daughters: Crystal Bieter, who is an English teacher herself, Bridgette Earnest, who is a senior in college majoring in elementary education and minoring in English, and Erin Earnest, who is in her first year of college this year; and to my son-in-law Nick Bieter, who is finishing his law degree this year. They have all inspired me to be a better teacher.

I would also like to thank Lowell Niklaus, Mary Regelstad, and Rod Thompson, for their continued administrative support, as well as my fellow English teachers: Jack Archer, Jennifer Burnside, Sylvia Fleming, Mark Hassenstab, Sandy Koski, Dennis Kral, Elaine Meyer, Barb Oistad, and Rebecca Weets. They have all had a tremendous influence on my professional life.

And a special dedication to a master writing teacher, recently retired, Loren Crawford.

Author: Duane Earnest

Publisher: SCHOOL HOUSE BOOKS

Cover Art: Tim Wolfe
Text Cover: Nicholas and Crystal Bieter

ISBNISBN 1 - 928741 - 02 - 9

FIRST EDITION

© Copyright September 1999 by Duane Earnest.

No part of this publication may be reproduced, stored in a retrieval system, or transmitted by any form or by any means, electronic, mechanical, photocopying, recording, or otherwise, except as permitted in writing by the publisher.

For information write: SCHOOL HOUSE BOOKS
921 Pembina Trail
Detroit Lakes, MN 56501

All Rights Reserved. Printed in U.S.A.

AP Acknowledgments

AP and Advanced Placement are trademarks of The College Board, which has not participated in the development of or endorsed this publication. Publications from the AP College Board have been one of the sources of reference for writing this book.

Editor's Acknowledgments

Errors may creep into this book in spite of the care taken by everyone involved in its production. If errors are found, the editor takes full responsibility for them. Please report all errors to Plan Press, Inc. so that future editions will not compound them.

Student Acknowledgments

Thanks to the 1998-1999 Detroit Lakes Junior and Senior Advanced Placement strudents. They have provided invaluable help in developing creative activities, writing and field testing the practice tests and essays, etc.

Need an Answer Key?

School House Books also publishes an *ANSWERS/EXPLANATIONS* booklet with answer keys to all tests, explanations of the rationale behind each correct answer, and answers to the contest questions. Use the order form on page 358.

Permissions

Permissions have been given to use the following works:

Discovering Poetry by Elizabeth Drew. Copyright © 1933 by W. W. Norton & Company, Inc., renewed © 1960 by Elizabeth Drew. Reprinted by permission of W. W. Norton & Company, Inc.

A Mencken Chrestomathy by H. L. Mencken. Copyright © 1924 by Alfred A. Knopf, Inc. and renewed 1952 by H. L. Mencken. Reprinted by permission of the publisher.

Art work created by K.C. Skinner, a former Detroit Lakes student, has been used in this book with his permission.

The text for the back cover has been created by Nicholas and Crystal Bieter.

4

Table of Contents

Preface

Designed to teach writing from the perspective of a writer, this textbook encourages the love of reading and the meticulous use of language necessary for success in college.

Chapter One: Rewarding Free Reading

Designed to encourage wide reading, this chapter has arranged some of the most highly recommended writers by author's name, title, and time period. These works have appeared on various book club charts, publisher's lists , and tests created by The Advanced Placement program. Most have won various book awards. Reading a wide variety of works of literary merit like those on this list is the best way to ensure success on either of the English tests. The chapter ends with suggestions on how to reward this type of reading.

Chapter Two: Diction

This chapter emphasizes the writer's ability to absorb environment and record impressions with just the right word. Keeping lists of neat words and phrases, consciously or subconsciously, in a struggle to find just the right word, is an activity shared by all successful writers.

Chapter Three: Syntax

This chapter explains various ways writers take special care to create special arrangements of and relationships with words. Understanding the slight or delicate variations of syntax, and the effect it creates, or the purpose it fulfills is crucial to developing a command of the language for reading and writing.

Chapter Four: Close Reading

This chapter emphasizes the importance of accurate interpretations of the meaning of works. Part One assigns a paraphrasing — a word-for-word rewriting of a difficult passage — to learn to read with more objective accurateness.

Part Two in each exercise asks you to practice reading with more objective accurateness by taking a short multiple-choice quiz.

Part Three in each exercise asks you to practice writing with more exactness by taking an essay exam on the same passage.

Checklists

Every essay question assigned, throughout the *Writer,* has a specific checklist designed to guide the grading of that particular essay question.

Chapter Five: The Classroom Forty Minute Essay

This chapter deals with essays that ask for an analysis accompanied by an excerpt of a work of literature. In these assignments, you are expected to read the accompanying excerpt carefully — this usually means you have to read it three times — and refer to this passage directly or indirectly when answering the question. Learning to read the question and determine what the question is asking is the first step in reading the passage with an understanding that is necessary for clear writing. Finishing the essay within the forty minute time limits is a challenge that requires the type of practice that this chapter allows.

Chapter Six: Evaluating an Argument

This chapter helps students understand correct argument by asking the right questions to determine the effectiveness of argument written by others.

Chapter Seven: Writing an Argument

This chapter helps students develop personal stances on abstract issues through the correct use of observation, personal experience, and reading.

Chapter Eight: Comparison and Contrast

This chapter helps students make sense of something by comparing and contrasting to make a more informed choice or reach a more sound conclusion.

Chapter Nine: Contests of Knowledge

This chapter includes contests designed by students to improve reading comprehension, writing skills, and vocabulary retention.

Chapter Ten:
An Extended
Writing Project

This chapter maps out eight weeks of instruction for a term paper unit. After selecting an abstract issue that affects today's students; surveying the information available on the issue by reading selections written by people from the Suggested Reading List in chapter one that have an opinion on the topic; and developing an eventual personal stance on that issue, students are expected to produce a ten page paper on their findings.

Chapter Eleven:
Three Full Length
Multiple-Choice
Practice Tests

This chapter includes three 50-55 point multiple-choice tests, typical of either the English Literature or English Language examinations. The answers and explanations for the rationale behind each answer are found in a separate Teacher's Guide (item 6002) that can be purchased with the order form at the end of this *Writer*.

Chapter Twelve:
A Glossary
of Terms

This chapter is a glossary of terms that have been used on English Literature and English Language examinations from 1970 to 1999.

Chapter One:

Rewarding Free Reading

Chapter One: Rewarding Free Reading

It may seem strange to have a chapter on reading as the number one chapter in a writing textbook, but it is number one on purpose. Good writers are avid readers of good books. Rita Dove begins her preface to *Selected Poems* by saying, "When I am asked: 'What made you want to be a writer?' my answer has always been: 'Books.' First and foremost, now, then, and always, I have been passionate about books." This important correlation between reading and writing is confirmed by most established writers.

Writing teachers, recognizing this correlation, encourage students to read widely by incorporating the concept of free reading and writing into some of the assignments they require and some types of essay questions they ask. Many good writing teachers encourage students to read widely among newspapers and magazines, noting articles of literary merit and sharing these with the class. Many magazines carry essays by some of America's best writers on a variety of subjects. Some of these magazines include: *Harper's, The Atlantic, The New Yorker, The Saturday Review, Literary Cavalcade, The American Scholar, The Yale Review, Foreign Affairs, Christian Science Monitor, Life, The Saturday Evening Post, Holiday,* and *Colliers.* Sometimes brilliant articles are found in unexpected places. One magazine that I've discovered as a good source of essays is *Midwest Fly Fishing.* Also, all major newspapers are now on the Internet. Look for Commentary, Book Reviews, Magazine Section, etc. For instance, the Sunday Magazine Section of the *New York Times* almost always has an essay of quality. Emphasizing the quality reading of magazines and newspapers encourages life long learning habits.

To encourage the wide reading of good books, this *Writer* will suggest titles of good books in most of the pursuing chapters. This chapter includes six suggested reading lists to guide the selection of free reading choices. Arranged in alphabetical order by the author's last name, placed in time periods (Pre-1900 and the 20th Century), and listed with titles, these are the most complete suggested reading lists available anywhere.

These complete works represent a wide range of genres (autobiography, biography, collected criticism, collected essays, journalism, novels, plays, political writings, collected short stories, scientific writing, etc.) in a wide range of time periods (the Renaissance, the Restoration, the Romantic, the Victorian, and the Modern periods). Equally important, a concerted effort has been made to represent women writers fairly, and to represent all of the diverse cultures of our nation. Most importantly, these works have been selected because they are all worthy of scrutiny; their richness of thought and diverse manipulations of language challenge the reader; and their style is worthy of emulating.

Here are the Lists:

Pre-1900 Plays of Literary Merit

Aeschylus, *Oresteia. Agamemmon. The Libation Bearers. The Eumenides.*
Oliver Goldsmith, *The Vicar of Wakefield. She Stoops to Conquer.*
Victor Hugo, *Les Miserables.*
Ben Johnson, *Works* (A Collection of Plays and Poems)
Euripides, *Medea.*
Christopher Marlowe, *Dr. Faustus.*
Moliere, *Tartuffe. The Misanthrope.*
William Shakespeare, *As You Like It. Hamlet. Romeo and Juliet. The Turn of the Screw. Twelfth Night. Othello. King Lear. A Midsummer Night's Dream. Anthony and Cleopatra. The Merchant of Venice. Henry IV.*
Sophocles, *Oedipus the King. Oedipus Rex. Antigone.*

20th Century Plays
of Literary Merit

Edward Albee, *Who's Afraid of Virginia Woolf?*
Samuel Beckett, *Waiting for Godot. Krapp's Last Tape.*
Anton Chekov, *The Sea Gull. Uncle Vanga. The Three Sisters.*
  The Cherry Orchard.
Rita Dove, *The Darker Face of the Earth.*
Lorraine Hainsberry, *A Raisin in the Sun.*
Lillian Hellman, *The Children's Hour. The Little Foxes.*
  The Autumn Garden. Watch on the Rhine.
  Toys in the Attic.
Davis Henry Hwang, *M. Butterfly.*
Henrik Ibsen, *A Doll House.*
W. Inge, *Come Back, Little Sheba.*
Eugene Ionesco, *The Bald Soprano.*
Arthur Miller, *The Crucible. Death of a Salesman.*
  All My Sons.
Sean O'Casey, *Juno and the Paycock. The Shadow of a Gunman.*
  The Plough and the Stars.
Eugene O'Neill, *Beyond the Horizon.*
  Long Day's Journey Into Night. Iceman Cometh.
Harold Pinter, *The Caretaker. The Homecoming. Betrayal.*
  Old Times. The Birthday Party. Landscape.
  The Dumb Waiter.
Luigi Pirandello, *Naked Masks (Five Plays).*
George Bernard Shaw, *Pygmalion. Mrs. Warren's Profession.*
  Saint Joan.
Sam Shepard, *Buried Child.*
Richard Brinsley Sheridan, *The Rivals. The School for Scandal.*
Tom Stoppard, *Rosencrantz and Guildenstern Are Dead.*
Oscar Wilde, *The Importance of Being Earnest.*
Thornton Wilder, *Our Town.*
Tennessee Williams, *A Street Car Named Desire.*
  The Glass Menagerie, Summer and Smoke.
  Cat on a Hot Tin Roof. A Lovely Sunday for Creve Coeur.
August Wilson, *Fences. The Piano Lesson.*

Poetry Collections
or "Titles of Longer Poems"
of Literary Merit
Written Before 1900

William Blake, *The Complete Poetry and Prose of William Blake.*
Anne Bradstreet, Various Anthologies.
Robert Browning, *The Poetical Works of Robert Browning.*
       Complete from 1833 to 1868.
Lord Byron, *The Poetical Works of Byron.*
Geoffrey Chaucer, "Canterbury Tales."
Samuel Taylor Coleridge, "The Rime of the Ancient Mariner."
       "Cristabel." and "Kubla Khan."
       Poems of Samuel Taylor Coleridge.
Emily Dickinson, *Poems and Letters of Emily Dickinson.*
John Donne, *The Poetry of Johh Donne.*
Homer, *The Odyssey.*
Gerald Manley Hopkins, *A Hopkins Reader.*
John Keats, *Selected Poems.*
Robert Lowell, *Prometheus Bound.*
John Milton, *The Complete English Poetry Of John Milton.*
       L'allegro.
Edgar Allan Poe, *An Edgar Allan Poe Reader: Poems and Short*
       Stories. Essay and Reviews: Theory of Poetry.
Alexander Pope, "Rape of the Lock."
       The Complete Poetical Works of Alexander Pope.
William Shakespeare, *The Complete Works of William Shakespeare.*
Alfred Lord Tennyson, *Selections from Tennyson and Browning.*
       "The Charge of the Light Brigade."
Virgil, *The Aeneid.*
Walt Whitman, *Leaves of Grass.*
William Wordsworth, *The Complete Poetical Works*
       of William Wordsworth.
William Butler Yeats, *Collected Poems.*

Poetry Collections
or "Titles of Longer Poems"
of Literary Merit
Written in the Twentieth Century

African American Voices (A collection of writings by such
    authors as W. E. B. Dubois, Toni Morrison,
    Rita Dove, Richard Wright, and Ralph Ellison
    exploring the connections of circle, veil, water,
    and song that link past and present African
    American cultures)

W. H. Auden, *Reading from his Works (record).*
    Collected Shorter Poems, Selected Poems.
    The Dog Beneath the Skin. About the House.

Mayou Angelou, *Just Give Me a Cool Drink of Water 'fore I Diiie.*
    Oh Pray My Wings Are Going To Fit Me Well.
    And Still I Rise. Shaker Why Don't You Sing.

The Best American Poetry, Edited by Adrienne Rich

Elizabeth Bishop, *The Complete Poems. Geography III.*
    Questions of Travel.

Gwendolyn Brooks, *Beckonings. Bronzeville Boys and Girls.*
    Gwendolyn Brooks Reading Her Poetry (Record).

H. D. (Hilda Doolittle), *Collected Poems.*

Rita Dove, Poetry Collections: Pulitzer prize-winning
    "Thomas and Beulah" as well as "Museum" and
    "The Yellow House on the Corner"

T. S. Eliot, *The Complete Poems and Plays of T. S. Eliot.*
    Old Possum's Book of Practical Cats.
    Collected Poems 1909 - 1962.
    Murder in the Cathedral.
    "The Love Song of J. Alfred Prufrock,"
    "The Waste Land," *On Poetry and Poets* (Essays by
    T. S. Eliot).

Robert Frost, *Complete Poems.*

Joy Harjo, *In Mad Love and War.*

Seamus Heaney, *Selected Poems from 1966 to 1987.*

Garrett Hongo, *The Open Boat: Poems from Asian America*
    with and Introduction from Garrett Hongo.

A. E. Houseman, *The Collected Poems of A. E. Houseman.*

Langston Hughes, *The Block: Poems. Selected Poems.*

The Dream Keeper and Other Poems.
Phillip Larkin, *The Whitsun Weddings. The Less Deceived.*
D. H. Lawrence, *The Complete Poems of D. H. Lawrence.*
Lean Out the Window (Poetry Selections from Gwendolyn
         Brooks, James Joyce, Stephen Vincent Benet, Robert
         Frost, Elinor Wylie, Conrad Aitken, etc.)
Marianne Moore, *The Complete Poems of Marianne Moore.*
         Tell Me, Tell Me; Granite , Steel, and Other Topics.
         O To Be A Dragon.
Gloria Naylor, *Linden Hills.*
Wilfred Owen, *Collected Poems.*
Slyvia Plath, *Crossing the Water - Transitional Poems.*
         Ariel. The Colossus and Other Poems.
Adrienne Rich, Collection of Poems: *The Will to Change.*
         Diving Into the Wreck.
         A Wild Patience Has Taken Me This Far.
Leslie Marmon Silko, *Ceremony.*
Cathy Song, *Picture Bride.*
Six American Poets (Walt Whitman, Emily Dickinson,
         Wallace Stevens, William Carlos Williams,
         Robert Frost, and Langston Hughes).
Stopping for Death (A collection of poems about death, loss,
         and mourning, written by poets from all over the world
         including Alice Walker, Janet Frome, and
         Seamus Heaney).
Dylan Thomas, *Selections from the Writings of Dylan Thomas.*
         The Collected Poems.
Derek Walcott, *Collected Poems. Midsummer.*
         The Arkansas Testament.
Walt Whitman, *Leaves of Grass.*
Richard Wilbur, *A Game of Catch. Collected Poems.*
William Carlos Williams, *Selected Poems.*

Pre-1900 Works of Literary Merit

Joseph Addison, *The Sir Roger de Coverly Papers*
         from the Spectator.
Matthew Arnold, *On the Study of Celtic Literature.*
Louisa May Alcott, *Little Women.*
Jane Austen, *Pride and Predjudice. Sense and Sensibility.*

        Mansfield Park, Emma.
Sir Francis Bacon, *Essays.*
Ambrose Bierce, *The Devil's Dictionary.*
James Boswell, *The Life of Samuel Johnson.*
Charlotte Bronte, *Jane Eyre.*
Emily Bronte, *Wuthering Heights.*
Thomas Carlyle, *A History of the French Revolution.*
        Heroes and Hero-Worship.
Cervantes, *Don Quixote.*
Lord Chesterfield (Phillip Stanhope), *Letters.*
Kate Chopin, *The Awakening,* Two volumes of Short Stories:
        Bayou Folk and *A Night in Arcadie*
Samuel Coleridge, *Biographia Literaria.*
Stephen Crane, *The Red Badge of Courage.*
        Maggie: A Girl of the Streets.
Michel-Guillaume Jean de Crevecoeur
        Letters from as American Farmer.
Thomas Dequincy, *Tne English Mail-Coach, and Other Essays.*
        Confessions of an English Opium Eater.
Charles Dickens, *A Tale of Two Cities. Great Expectations.*
        Bleak House. Hard Times. Our Mutual Friend.
William O. Douglas, *Strange Lands and Friendly People* (Essays)
Frederick Douglass, *Life and Times of Frederick Douglass.*
        My Bondage and My Freedom.
Fyodor Dostoevski, *Crime and Punishment.*
        The Brothers Karamazov.
George Eliot, *Adam Bede. Silas Marner. The Mill on the Floss.*
        Middlemarch.
Queen Elizabeth I, speeches
Ralph Waldo Emerson, *Essays. Essays Second Series.*
        Representative Man. Self-Reliance. Nature.
        The Amnerican Scholar.
Henry Fielding, *Tom Jones.*
Benjamin Franklin, *The Autobiography.*
John Kenneth Galbraith *The Affluent Society.*
        The Age of Uncertainty.
Edward Gibbon, *The Decline and Fall of the Roman Empire.*
Oliver Goldsmith, *The Citizen of the World.* (Essay)
Thomas Hardy, *The Return of the Native. Far from the*
        Maddening Crowd. The Mayor of Casterbridge.
        Tess of the T'Urbevilles.
Nathaniel Hawthorne, *The Scarlet Letter. The Custom House.*

The House of Seven Gables. The Blithedale Romance.
Marble Faun, Twice-Told Tales.
William Hazlitt, *Essays.*
Thomas Hobbes, *Leviathan.*
Oliver Wendell Holmes, *The Autocrat of the Breakfast Table.*
William Howells, *The Rise of Silas Lapham.*
Thomas Jefferson, *The Life and Selected Writings of*
Thomas Jefferson. Jefferson's Letters.
Samuel Johnson, *The Lives of the Poets.*
Charles Lamb, *Tales From Shakespeare. Essays of Elia.*
John Locke, *A Letter Concerning Toleration.*
On Politics and Education.
Thomas Babington Macaulay, *History of England*
from the Succession of James II.
Niccolo Machiavelli, *The Prince.*
Herman Melville, *Moby-Dick.*
John Stuart Mill, *On Liberty.*
John Milton, *Areopagitica. Lycidas.*
Montaigne, *The Complete Essays of Montaigne.*
Thomas More, *Utopia.*
John Henry Newman, *The Idea of a University.*
Thomas Paine, *Common Sense. The American Crisis.*
The Rights of Man. The Age of Reason.
Francis Parkman, *The Oregon Trail. The Parkman Reader.*
Samuel Pepys, *Diary.*
Plato, *Dialogues, The Republic.*
Edgar Allan Poe, *The Fall of the House of Usher.*
The Pit and the Pendulum. The Purloined Letter.
Murders in the Rue Morgue. The Complete Tales
and Poems of Edgar Allan Poe.
Selected Prose and Poetry.
John Ruskin, *Selections and Essays.*
Richard Steele, Essays for *The Spectator.*
Robert Louis Stevenson, *Black Arrow. Dr. Jeckyll and Mr. Hyde.*
Harriet Beecher Stowe, *Uncle Tom's Cabin.*
Jonathan Swift, *Gulliver's Travels.*
Alexis de Tocqueville, *Democracy in America. Recollections.*
William Makepiece Thackery, *The History of Henry Esmond, Esq.,*
A Colonel in the Service of Her Majesty, Queen Anne.
Henry David Thoreau, *Walden.*
Leo Tolstoy, *War and Peace. Anna Karenina.*
Mark Twain, *The Adventures of Huckleberry Finn.*

*Life on the Mississippi. A Connecticut Yankee
in King Arthur's Court.*
Voltaire, *Candide.*
Mary Wollstonecraft, *Vindication of the Rights of Women.*

20th Century
Works of Literary Merit

Edward Abby , *Cactus Country.*
Chinua Achebe, *Things Fall Apart.*
James Agee, *A Death in the Family.*
Paula Gunn Allen, *As Long As the Rivers Flow.*
Julia Alverez, *How the Garcia Girls Lost Their Accents.*
       In the Time of the Butterflies.
Rudolfo Anaya, *Bless Me, Ultima.*
Maya Angelou, *I Know Why the Caged Bird Sings.*
       Gather Together in My Name.
       Singin' and Swingin' and Gettin' Merry Like Christmas.
       The Heart of a Woman.
Roger Angell, *Five Seasons: A Baseball Companion.*
       Late Innings: A Baseball Companion.
       Once More Around the Park. A Baseball Reader.
       Season Tickets, A Baseball Companion.
Gloria Anzaldua, *Borderlands - La Frontera (Prose and Poetry)*
Sherwood Anderson, *Winesburg, Ohio.*
Hannah Arendt, *Eichman in Jerusalem; A Report on the Banality
       of Evil. The Origins of Totalitarianism.
       On Violence. Thinking.*
Michael Arlen, *The View From Highway 1: Essays on Television.
       An American Verdict.*
Margaret Atwood, *Surfacing. The Handmaid's Tale. Cat's Eye.*
Isaac Asimov, *More Tales of the Black Widowers.
       The Best of Isaac Asimov.*
James Baldwin, *Go Tell It on The Mountain.
       Notes of a Native Son. Nobody Knows My Name.
       The Fire Next Time. The Price of a Ticket.
       Another Country.*
Walter Jackson Bate, *Coleridge. John Keats. Samuel Johnson.*

Simone de Beauvoir, *The Prime of Life.*
Nina Berberova, *The Italics Are Mine.*
Max Beerbohm, *Zuleika Dobson. Observations.*
Wendell Berry, *The Gift of Good Land.*
Saul Bellow, *Henderson is the Rain King.*
       The Adventures of Augie March.
Arnold Bennett, *The Old Wives Tale. Journals 1896 - 1910.*
Elizabeth Bowen, *The Death of the Heart. Collected Impressions.*
Paul Bowles, *The Sheltering Sky.*
Jacob Bronowski, *The Ascent of Man.*
Pearl S. Buck, *Tell the People* (Essays bout mass education
       in China).
Anthony Burgess, *A Clockwork Orange.*
William F. Buckley, *Keeping the Tablets: Modern American*
       Conservative Thought. Airborne: A Sentimental Journey.
       Atlantic High: A Celebration, Brothers No More.
John Burroughs, *Birds and Bees* (Essay on Natural Science).
Samuel Butler, *The Way of All Flesh.*
Rachel Carson, *The Edge of the Sea. The Rocky Coast.*
       The Sea Around Us.
Raymond Carver, Collections of short stories such as:
       Will You Please Be Quiet, Please?
       What We Talk About When We Talk About Love.
       Where I'm Calling From: New And Selected Stories.
Erskine Caldwell, *Tobacco Road.*
James M. Cain, *The Postman Always Rings Twice.*
Willa Cather, *Death Comes for the Archbishop .*
Mary Ellen Chase, *The Goodly Heritage* (Essays on Education).
John Cheever, *The Wapshot Chronicles.*
G. K. Chesterton, *Appreciations and Criticisms of Charles Dickens.*
       A Handful of Authors.
Winston Churchill, *Memories and Adventures.*
Sandra Cisneros, *House on Mango Street. Woman Hollering Crook.*
Judith Ortiz Cofer, *Silent Dancing.*
Colette (Sidonie-Gabrielle Colette),
       Mitsau, or, How Girls Grow Wise. My Apprenticeships.
       Cheri. Claudine's House. Gigi.
Joseph Conrad, *The Secret Agent. Nostromo. Heart of Darkness.*
       Lord Jim . The Mirror of the Sea (Essays about ships
       and sailors)
Vine Deloria, *Behind the Trail of Broken Treaties; An Indian*
       Declaration of Independence. American Indian Policies

in the Twentieth Century.

Anita Desai, *Fire on the Mountain. Clear Light of Day.*

Joan Didion, *Slouching Towards Bethlehem. The White Album.*

Annie Dillard, *The Writing Life. An American Childhood.*
Encounters with Chinese Writers. Teaching a Stone to Talk.
Living by Fiction. Holy the Firm. Pilgrim at Tinker Creek.
Tickets for a Prayer Wheel.

Isak Dinesen (the pen name of Karen Blixen),
Out of Africa.

E. L. Doctorow, *Ragtime.*

J. P. Donnleavy, *The Ginger Man.*

Rita Dove, *Through the Ivory Gate. The Poet's World.*

Elizabeth Drew, *Discovering Poetry.*

Theodore Drieser, *An American Tragedy. Sister Carrie.*

W. E. B. Dubois, *The Autobiography of W. E. B. DuBois, A Soliloquy on Viewing My Life. The Souls of Black Folk.*
The Writings of W. E. B. DuBois.

Lawrence Durell, *The Alexandria Quartet.*

Leon Edel, *Telling Lives. The Biographer's Art.*
Henry David Thoreau. Henry James.

Gretel Ehrlich, *The Solace of Open Spaces. Heart Mountain.*
Drinking My Dry Clouds; Stories from Wyoming.

Ralph Ellison, *Invisible Man.*

Nora Ephron, *Crazy Salad, Some Things About Women.*
Heartburn.

Louise Erdich, *Love Medicine. The Beet Queen. Tracks.*
The Crown of Columbus.

William Faulkner, *The Sound and the Fury. As I Lay Dying.*
Light in August.

James T. Farrell, *The Studs Lonigan Trilogy.*

M. F. K. Fisher (Mary Francis Kennedy Fisher)
Serve it Forth. Consider the Oyster. How to Cook a Wolf.
The Gastronomical Me. Among Friends.
Maps of Another Town. As They Were.

F. Scott Fitzgerald, *The Great Gatsby. Tender is the Night.*

Janet Flanner (Genet), *JFK's World: Uncollected Writings
1932 - 1975. Paris Journal.*

Ford Maddox Ford, *The Good Soldier. Parade's End.*
Return to Yesterday.

E. M. Forster, *A Passage to India. Howard's End.*
A Room With a View. Aspects of the Novel.

John Fowles, *The Magus.*

Paul Fussell, *The Great War and Modern Memory.*
Paul Gallico, *Farewell to Sport* (Essays).
Henry Louis Gates, Jr., *Colored People.*
     Thirteen Ways of Looking at Black Men.
Clifford Geertz, *Works and Lives. The Anthropologist as Author.*
Ellen Goodman, *At Large. Keeping in Touch. Close to Home.*
     Making Sense.
Nadine Gordimer, *The Soft Voice of the Serpent and Other Stories.*
     The Lying Day. A Guest of Honor. July's People.
Robert Graves, *I, Claudius.*
Jack Green, *Loving.*
Graham Greene, *The Power and the Glory.*
Nikki Giovanni, *Racism 101.*
Dashiell Hammett, *The Maltese Falcon.*
Joseph Heller, *Catch-22.*
Lillian Hellman, *Pentimento. Scoundrel Time.*
     An Unfinished Woman.
Ernest Hemingway, *The Sun Also Rises. A Farewell to Arms.*
     Death in the Afternoon (Essays bout Bull Fighting).
Edward Hoagland, *Balancing Acts : Essays.*
Richard Hughes, *A High Wind in Jamaica.*
Zora Neal Hurston, *Jonah's Gourd Vine. Mules and Men.*
     Their Eyes Were Watching God.
Aldous Huxley, *Brave New World. Point Counter Point.*
Kazuo Ishiguro, *A Pale View of Hills. The Remains of the Day.*
Henry James, *Washington Square. The Wings of the Dove.*
     The Ambassadors. The Golden Bowl . Tropic of Cancer.
     Partial Portraits. Daisy Miller.
James Joyce, *Ullysses, A Portrait of the Artist as a Young Man.*
     From Here to Eternity. Finnegan's Wake.
     The Critical Writings of James Joyce.
Pauline Kael, *State of the Art.*
Evelyn Fox Keller, *A Feeling for the Organism: The Life and Work*
     of Barbara McClintock.
Helen Keller, *The Story of My Life. Midstream: My Later Life.*
William Kennedy, *Ironweed.*
Martin Luther King, Jr., *I Have a Dream. Love Your Enemy.*
Maxine Hong Kinston, *The Woman Warrior. China Men.*
Joy Kogawa, *Obasan.*
Arthur Koestler, *Darkness at Noon.*
Jack Kerouac, *On the Road.*
Rudyard Kipling, *Kim.*

Lewis P. Lapham, *Money and Class in America: Notes and Observation. Imperial Masquerade.*
D. H. Lawrence, *Sons and Lovers. The Rainbow. Women in Love. Aaron's Rod. The Letters of D. H. Lawrence.*
T. E. Lawrence, *Seven Pillars of Wisdom.*
Harper Lee, *To Kill a Mockingbird.*
Gerda Lerner, *The Creation of Feminine Consciousness: From the Middle Ages to Eighteen-seventy. The Grimkae Sisters from South Carolina; Rebels Against Slavery. Why History Matters; Life and Thought.*
Sinclair Lewis, *Main Street .*
Andy Logan, *The Man Who Robbed the Robber Barons.*
Jack London, *The Call of the Wild.*
Barry Lopez, *Crossing Open Ground.*
Norman Mailer, The *Naked and the Dead.*
Nancy Mairs, *Carnal Acts: Essays. Plaintext : Essays. Ordinary Time: Cycles in Marriage, Faith, and Renewal.*
Bernard Malamud, *The Natural. The Assistant. The Fixer. The Tenants.*
Malcolm Lowry, *Under the Volcano.*
Katherine Mansfield, *The Short Stories of Katherine Mansfield.*
Bobbie Ann Mason, *The Rookers.*
Peter Matthiessen, *At Play in the Fields of God. The Cloud Forest; A Chronicle of the South American Wilderness. African Silences.*
W. Somerset Maugham, *Of Human Bondage .*
Cormac McCarthy, *All the Pretty Horses.*
Mary McCarthy, *Memories of a Catholic Girlhood.*
Carson McCullers, *The Heart is a Lonely Hunter.*
John McPhee, *Coming Into the Country.*
Margaret Mead, *Blackberry Winter: My Earlier Years Coming of Age in Samoa.*
H. L. Mencken, *A Mencken Chrestomathy.*
Jessica Mitford, *Daughters and Rebels. The American Way of Death*
N. Scott Momanday, *House Made of Dawn.*
Samuel Eliot Morison, *A Concise History of the American Republic.*
Jan Morris, *Conundrum. Destinations: Essays from Rolling Stone.*
Toni Morrison, *The Bluest Eye. Beloved. Sula.*
Bharati Mukherjee, *Jasmine, The Holder of the World. Leave It To Me.*
Iris Murdoch, *Under the Net.*

Vladimir Nabokov, *Lolita. Pale Fire.*

V. S. Naipaul, *A House for Mrs. Biswas. A Bend in the River.*

Joyce Carol Oates, *American Appetites.*

Sean O'Casey, *I Knock at the Door* (Autobiography).

Flannery O'Connor, *Wise Blood. A Good Man is Hard to Find.*
      The Violent Bear It Away.
      Everything that Rise Must Converge.

John O'Hara, *Appointment in Samarra.*

Tillie Olsen, *Mother to Daughter, Daughter to Mother:*
      Mothers on Mothering: A Day Book and Reader.
      Silences. Tell Me a Riddle.

George Orwell, *1984. Animal Farm. Shooting an Elephant.*
      The Collected Essays. Journalism and Letters of George
      Orwell. Such, Such Were the Joys.

Cynthia Ozick, *Art and Ardor. Metaphor and Memory.*
      The Pagan Rabbi. Blood Shed. Levitation.
      The Cannibal Galaxy. The Messiah of Stockholm.

John Dos Passos, *U.S.A.* (trilogy)

Walter Pater, T*he Renaissance. Studies in Art and Poetry.*

Alan Paton, *Cry the Beloved Country.*

S. J. Perelman, *The Best of S. J. Perelman* (Humorous Essays)

Walker Percy, *The Moviegoer.*

Sylvia Plath, *Diary.*

Anthony Powell, *A Dance to the Music of Time.* (series)

Katherine Anne Porter, *Ship of Fools.*

Santha Rama Rau, *Gifts of Passage.*

Arnold Rampersad, *Arthur Ashe. Days of Grace. A Memoir.*
      The Life of Langston Hughes.

Majorie Kinnan Rawlings, *Cross Creek.*

Jean Rhys, *Wide Saragasso Sea.*

Richard Rodriguez, *Hunger of Memory: The Education of*
      Richard Rodriguez. An Autobiography.
      Days of Obligation: An Argument With My Mexican
      Father.

Philip Roth, *Portnoy's Complaint* .

Sharman Apt Russell, *Frederick Douglass.*
      The Humpbacked Flute Player.

Salman Rushdie, *Midnight's Children.*

Carl Sagen, *Contact.*

J. D. Salinger, *The Catcher in the Rye.*

Scott Russell Sanders, *Aurora Means Dawn.*
      The Floating House.

George Santayana, *Soliloquies in England.*
Arthur M. Schlesinger, *A Thousand Days.*
    The Almanac of American History. Arthur Meier.
Albert Schweitzer, *Out of My Life and Thought* (Auto Essay)
Richard Seltzer, *The Name of Hero: A Novel.*
Leslie Marmon Silko, *Ceremony.*
Red Smith, *Press Box: Rec Smith's Favorite Sports Stories.*
    The Red Smith Reader.
Susan Sontag, *Against Interpretation, and Other Essays.*
    Aids and Its Metaphors. I, Etcetera.
    Illness as a Metaphor. A Susan Sontag Reader.
Shelby Steele, *The Content of our Character: A New Vision of*
    Race in America.
Wallace Stegner, *Angle of Repose.*
John Steinbeck, *The Grapes of Wrath.*
May Swenson, *The Complete Poems to Solve.*
    In Other Words: New Poems.
William Styron, *Sophie's Choice.*
Amy Tan, *The Joy Luck Club.*
Booth Tarkington, *The Magnificent Amberson's.*
Ronald Takaki, *Democracy and Race: Asian Americans*
    and World War II.
    A Different Mirror: A History of Multicultural America.
    Issei and Nisei: The Settling of Japanese America.
    India in the West: South Asians in America.
Paul Theroux, *The Black House. Chicago Loop.*
    The Family Arsenal. Girls at Play.
    Half Moon Street. The Mosquito Coast.
Lewis Thomas, *Etcetera, Etcetera: Notes of a Word Watcher.*
    The Fragile Species. Late Night Thoughts on Listening
    to Mahler's Ninth Symphony.
George Trevelyan, *Illustrated History of England.*
Calvin Trillin, *American Stories. Enough is Enough (and*
    Other Rules of Life).
Lionel Trilling, *The Liberal Imagination.*
Anne Tyler, *Dinner at the Homesick Restaurant.*
    The Accidental Tourist. Breathing Lessons.
Dylan Thomas, *Letters to Vernon Watkins.*
Barbara Tuchman, *The Guns of August. The First Salute.*
    A Distant Mirror: The Calamitous 14th Century.
John Updike, *The Afterlife and Other Stories.*
    Assorted Prose.

Gore Vidal, *The Decline and Fall of the American Empire.*
>*The Centaur,. Live from Golgatha. Bech is Back.*
Kurt Vonnegut, *Slaughterhouse Five.*
Alice Walker, *The Color Purple.*
Robert Penn Warren, *All the King's Men.*
Evelyn Waugh, *A Handful of Dust. Scoop. Brideshead Revisited.*
Eudora Welty, Collection of Short Stories: *A Curtain of Green.*
>*The Wide Net. The Golden Apples.*
>Novels: *The Ponder Heart. Losing Battles.*
>*The Optimist's Daughter. One Writer's Beginnings.*
Cornel West , *Jews and Blacks: Let the Healing Begin.*
>*Race Matters. Restoring Hope.*
Nathaniel West, *The Day of the Locust.*
Edith Wharton, *The Age of Innocence. The House of Mirth.*
E. B. White, *The Essay of E. B. White. One Man's Meat.*
>*Quo Vadimus. Poems and Sketches.*
>*The Second Tree From The Corner.*
>*The Point of My Compass.*
John Edgar Widemen, *Brothers and Keepers.*
Terry Tempest Williams, *The Secret Language of Snow.*
Thornton Wilder, *The Bridge of San Luis Rey.*
George Will, *The Leveling Wind: Politics, the Culture, and*
>*Other News 1900 - 1994.*
>*Men at Work: The Craft of Baseball.*
>*The Morning After: American Successes and Excesses.*
Garry Wills, *Inventing America: Jefferson Declaration of*
>*Independence.*
>*The Kennedy Imprisonment: A Meditation on Power.*
>*John Wayne America: The Politics of Celebrities.*
Edmund Wilson, *Apologies to the Iroquois.*
>*Axel's Castle; a Study in Imaginative Literature of*
>*1870 - 1930.*
Virginia Woolf, *To the Lighthouse.*
Thomas Wolfe, *Look Homeward Angel.*
>*Of Time and the River. The Web and the Rock*
>*You Can't Go Home Again. The Hills Beyond*
Virginia Woolf, *Moments of Being. A Writer's Diary.*
>*Mrs. Dalloway. The Common Reader.*
>*To the Lighthouse. The Wave.*
Richard Wright, *Native Son.*
Malcolm X , Speeches.
Anzia Yezierska, *How I Found America.*

Test Questions that Reward Free Reading

Free Reading can be best tested with the essay questions like the following, administered in a 40 minute in-classroom setting, or as a culminating activity, resulting in a two-week, five page paper.

Question One

Choose a character and write an essay in which you:
> A. Briefly describe the standards of the fictional society in which the character exists and
> B. Show how the character is affected by and responds to those standards.

Question Two

Choose two works and show how the significance of their respective titles is developed through the author's use of such devices as contrast, repetition, allusion, and point of view.

Question Three

Write an essay about the opening scene of a drama or the first chapter of a novel which introduces some of the major themes of the work you choose.

Question Four

Choose a work of literature written before 1900. Present arguments for or against the work's relevance for a person today. Your own position should emerge.

Question Five

In many plays a character has a misconception of himself or his world. Destroying of perpetuating this illusion contributes to the central theme of the play. Choose a play with a major character to whom this statement applies and write an essay in which you consider the following:
> A. What is the character's illusion and how does it differ from reality as represented in the play you have chosen?
> B. How does the destruction or perpetuation of the illusion develop a theme of the play?

Question Six

The conflict created when the will of an individual opposes the will of the majority is the recurring theme of many novels, plays, and essays. Select the work of an essayist who is in opposition to his or her society; or from a work of literary merit, select a fictional character who is opposition to his or her society. Analyze the conflict and discuss the moral and ethical implications for both the individual and society.

Question Seven

Choose an implausible or strikingly unrealistic incident or character in a work of fiction or drama of recognized literary merit. Explain how the incident or character is related to the more realistic or plausible elements in the rest of the work.

Question Eight

Choose a complex and important character in a novel or a play who might — on the basis of the character's actions alone — be considered evil or immoral. Then explain both how and why the full presentation of the character in the work makes us react more sympathetically than we otherwise might.

Question Nine

A recurring theme in literature is "the classic war between passion and responsibility." For instance, a personal cause, a love, a desire for revenge, a determination to redress a wrong, or some other emotion or drive may conflict with moral duty. Choose a literary work in which a character confronts the demands of a private passion with his or her responsibilities. Show clearly the nature of the conflict, its effect upon the character, and its significance to the work.

Question Ten

The meaning of some literary works is often enhanced by sustained allusions to myth, the Bible, or other works of literature. Select a literary work that makes use of such a sustained reference. Explain the allusion that predominates in the work and analyze how it enhances the work's meaning.

Question Eleven

Choose a work of literary merit that confronts the reader or audience with a scene or scenes of violence. Explain the significance of the violence in those scenes and analyze how these scenes contribute to the meaning of the complete work.

Question Twelve

From a novel or play of literary merit, select an important character who is a villain. Then, in a well-organized essay, analyze the nature of the character's villainy and show how it enhances meaning in the work.

Question Thirteen

A critic has said that one important measure of a superior work of literature is its ability to produce in the reader a healthy confusion of pleasure and disquietude. Select a work that produces this "healthy confusion." Then write a well-organized essay that analyzes the sources of the "pleasure and disquietude" experienced by the reader of the work and show how it enhances meaning in the complete work.

Question Fourteen

Some works of literature use the element of time in a distinct way. The chronological sequence of events may be altered, or time may be accelerated or altered. Choose a novel, an epic, or a play of recognized literary merit that manipulates time in an unusual way and show how this contributes to the effectiveness of the work as a whole.

Question Fifteen

Some novels and plays seem to advocate changes in social or political attitudes or in traditions. Choose a novel or play that seems to have this purpose. Briefly describe the particular attitudes or traditions that the author wants to change. Then analyze the techniques that the author uses to influence the reader's or audience's view.

Question Sixteen

Choose a distinguished novel or play in which some of the most important events are mental or psychological; for example, awakenings, discoveries, or changes in consciousness. Then write a well-organized essay that explains the importance of the events and analyzes how the author manages to give these internal events the sense of excitement, suspense, and climax usually associated with external action.

Question Seventeen

In questioning the value of literary realism, Flannery O'Connor has written, "I am interested in making a good case for distortion because I am coming to believe that it is the only way to make people see." Choose a literary work in which distortion helps the reader see. Then write a well-organized essay in which you "make a good case for distortion," as distinct from literary realism. Analyze how the important elements of the chosen work are "distorted" and explain how these distortions contribute to the effectiveness of the work.

Question Eighteen

Choose a novel or a play that depicts a conflict between a parent (or parental figure) and a son or daughter .... Analyze the sources of the conflict and explain how the conflict contributes to the meaning of the work.

Question Nineteen

Nadine Gordimer is known for her ability to show, as one critic put it, "the infinite variety of human character, the rich and surprising drama inherent in human personality and in the clash of personality." Choose a novel or play in which this type of deep characterization is portrayed. Then explain both how and why the full presentation of the character in the work adds to the meaning of the work as a whole.

Question Twenty

Nadine Gordimer has been compared to Virginia Woolf for her ability to capture moments in people's lives that reveal significant emotions. Critic Robert F. Haugh called it "the illuminating moment, the quick perceptive glance of the author which sparkles like a gem." Select a novel or play in which moments are captured which reveal significant emotions. Then analyze how these moments are made to "sparkle like gems" and explain how these "perceptive glances" contribute to the meaning of the work.

Question Twenty-One

In a novel or play, a confidant (male) or a confidante (female) is a character, often a friend or relative of the hero or heroine, whose role is the be present when the hero or heroine needs a sympathetic listener to confide in. Frequently the result is, as Henry James puts it, that the confidant or confidante can be as much "the reader's friend as the protagonist's." However, the author sometimes uses this character for other purposes as well. Choose a novel or play in which the confidant or a confidante performs a significant role. Then analyze the various ways this character functions in the work and explain how this character contributes to the overall meaning of the work.

Question Twenty-Two

In some works of literature, a character who appears briefly, or does not appear at all, is a significant presence. Choose a novel or play and show how such a character functions in the work. You may discuss how the character affects action, theme, or the development of other characters.

Question Twenty-Two

Writers often highlight the values of a culture or a society by using characters who are alienated by society or culture because of creed, gender, race, or class. Choose a novel or play in which such a character plays a significant role and show how that character's alienation reveals the surrounding society's assumptions and moral values.

Question Twenty-Three

The British novelist Fay Weldon offers these remarks about happy endings: "The writers, I do believe, who get the best and most lasting response from readers are the writers who offer a happy ending through moral development. By a happy ending, I do not mean mere fortunate events — a marriage or a last minute rescue from death — but some kind of spiritual reassessment or moral reconciliation, even with the self, even at death." Choose a novel or play that has the type of ending described by Fay Weldon. Then, in a well-written essay, identify the "spiritual reassessment or moral reconciliation" evident ion the ending and explain its significance to the work as a whole.

Question Twenty-Four

Novels and plays often include scenes of social occasions such as weddings, funerals, and parties. Such scenes may be used to reveals character values or the standards of the society in which they live. Select a novel or play that has such a scene. The write a focused essay which discusses the contribution that the scene make to the meaning of the work as a whole.

Question Twenty-Five

In his essay "Walking," Henry David Thoreau offers the following assessment of literature: "In literature it is only the wild that attracts us. Dullness is but another name of tameness. It is the uncivilized free and wild thinking in *Hamlet* and *The Illiad*, in all scriptures and mythologies, not learned in schools, that delights us." From the works you have studied in school, choose a novel, play, or epic poem that you may have initially thought was conventional and tame but that you now value for its "uncivilized free and wild thinking." Write an essay which describes this "uncivilized and wild thinking" and how this thinking is central to the value of the work as whole. Support your ideas with specific references to the text you have chosen.

Checklist for the Essay Testing the Free Reading Choice

STEP 1: Check each item listed below which accurately describes the positive aspects of the essay being graded. Add one point for each item checked from the list. This side describes the basic requirements for a well-written essay. (Grader one should check column one. Grader two should check column two):

___-___1. The writer selects a suitable novel or play in which the literary element addressed in the question is significant to the work as a whole.
___-___2. The writer presents a reasonable explanation of the purpose and meaning of the work.

___-___3. The writer effectively establishes how the literary element addressed in the question is significant to the work as a whole.
___-___4. The writer effectively explains how the literary element is significant to the work as a whole.

___-___5. The writer makes apt and specific reference to the text.
___-___6. The writer avoids plot summary not relevant to the explanation of the significant literary element.

___-___7. The writer discusses the literary work with sophistication, insight, and understanding.

___-___8. The writer displays consistent control over the language unique to the discussion of literature.

___-___9. The writer's diction, sentence structure, organization, and grammar aid in communicating a clear message.

MAXIMUM SCORE RESULTS: Grader 1 _____
MAXIMUM SCORE RESULTS: Grader 2 _____

STEP 2:   Check each item below which accurately describes the negative aspects of the essay being graded. This side describes how the essay may not be as good as the higher-scoring essays. (Grader one should check column one. Grader two should check column two):

___-___1. The writer's selection of a work of literary merit is not as appropriate as those of the higher-scoring essays.

___-___2. The writer's explanation of the meaning of the work is less thorough, less specific, or less perceptive than those of the higher-scoring essays.

___-___3. The writer's explanation of the significance of the literary element addressed in the question may be vague, underdeveloped, or misguided.

___-___4. The writer's explanation of how the literary element is significant to the work as a whole may be less convincing, mechanical, or inadequately related to the work as a whole.

___-___5. The writer's reference to the text lacks the specificity of the higher scoring essays.

___-___6. The writer simply paraphrases the meaning of the work with little reference to the significance of the literary element addressed in the question.

___-___7. The writer says nothing beyond the easy and obvious to grasp.

___-___8. The writer misuses the literary term(s) necessary to the discussion of literature or omits them partially or entirely.

___-___9. The essay contains distracting errors in grammar and mechanics.

RESULTS:

Grader 1: _____ - _____ = _____
        Step 1 Score   Step 2 Score

Grader 2: _____ - _____ = _____
        Step 1 Score   Step 2 Score

Grader 1 Score + Grader 2 Score = _____

Above sum / divided by 2 =

Score for essay

Chapter Two:

DICTION

Chapter Two: Diction

One thing shared by all writers is their love for and frustration with words. The following activities are the types of things writers reflect upon, record in their minds, and eventually include in their writing. Make a section in your journal for each of the following categories and add words to each category as you discover them through reading, listening, observing and sensing life around you.

Experiment with improving your style by adding more of these interesting words to your own writing; however, heed Daniel Defoe's warning: The perfect style is one "in which a man speaking to five hundred people, of all common and various capacities, Idiots and Lunatics excepted, should be understood by them all."

People:

Black-smocked smiths, smattered with smoke — Retiree - chinless and slouched, gray-faced, and slack of jaw — The Mathematician - enamored so of form, of calculation — gnomes — grandfather, sleepless in the room upstairs — alchemist — garrison — gastrologist — hipster — octogenarian — deep-eyed children — apostle — citizen — artisan — applicant — amorous leader beautiful and young — good child — I am two fools, I know — executors — the elf-child — the demon offspring — inhabitant — gossips — recent successors — magnificent potentate — illustrious creature — iron-souled truthmonger —

Add more of your own as you discover them through reading, listening, observing and sensing life around you:

_____

_____

Behaviors:

highfalutin' — his talking destroyed her — whipping —

Add more of your own as you discover them through reading, listening, observing and sensing life around you:

_____

_____

Things:

zamboni — unruffled sheets — bramble — thunderbolt — seance — the clear intensity of dawn — escalator — ancient nomadic snowmen — seafoam — elmy hedge — A noiseless patient spider — the bars and the gates and the degradation — dappled things — vacant eye — a liquor never brewed — epoch — lineage — perplexities — divine and mysterious truth — dusky grief — the ethereal medium of joy — contemplation — recollections — impetus — bric-a-brac — golden summits — cars, once steel and green, now old — cattail fluff — meads - forever crowned with flowers — foiled sleep — the muddy shallows —

Add more of your own as you discover them through reading, listening, observing and sensing life around you:

_____

_____

States of Being:

monotonous — homogenized — sultry — adoration — abdication — lamentation — abduction — visionless — sombre — dissension and strife — whey-faced anonymity — relative clumsiness — unvanquished — apparent failure — apparently with no surprise — approaching death — ardent in love and cold in charity — arrogance repressed — as difference blends into identity — when emotions too far exceeds it cause — the range of choice — ultimatums — I got religion and steadied down — impossibly alone — At lucky moments we seem on

the brink. (W. H. Auden) — Apparently with no surprise —
Constantly risking absurdity — much madness is divinest sense
— the marriage of true minds — the world is too much with
us, late and soon — the dreary burden of a heart unyielded,
because unvalued and unsought — a surer ground of mutual
happiness bathed in sunshine — a vague restlessness — obsti-
nately silent — radiance of her goodness — a safety in deri-
sion — in shadowy quarantine — one thin frail line of friendship — beyond earshot of others, furtively — the sad waters
of separation — eternal truth, almighty, infinite — charm - the
measure of attraction's power — four great walls have hemmed
me in — fruit of loneliness —

Add more of your own as you discover them through reading,
listening, observing and sensing life around you:

_____

_____

Places:

unrippled lakes — the fresh ruffles of the surf — bristled and
sallow fields — the august and ancient square — a sky suddenly mid-February blue — bison-dotted plain — the dim
frozen fields of night — the empty garden beds — the lonely
beach — shimmering meadows — snowy pastures — the
desert's drought and sand — the stony ridges — marshlands
— shuddering dock — summer-fevered skies — antlered for-
ests — lonesome grove — when the deep blue of heavens
brightens into stars — resting ships —

Add more of your own as you discover them through reading,
listening, observing and sensing life around you:

_____

_____

Neat Verbs:

dizzied — wimples — a-begging — momentary glance —
sprawl — drowsing — spiced — abate — loitered —
splotched — warbled — rattled — bequeathed — embroider

ing — had long since recognized — bespattered — speckled
— succor the afflicted — summer baked the water clear —
baffled — snarled and rattled — cease your labors — gently
dip, but not too deep — wreathe my dear friend's brow —

Add more of your own as you discover them through reading,
listening, observing and sensing life around you:

_____
_____
_____
_____
_____
_____
_____

Neat Adjectives:

whitewashed — misty — sage-grown — measureless — rev-
erend — luxurious — unravished — frazzled — palpable and
mute — disdain — authentic — shadow-like — recluse, lav-
ish richness of golden fancy — sober-hued — noiselessly —
whimsical bubbles of air — doleful — the burning brazen sky
— billowy — bliss — capricious — a darkening brilliance —
odoriferous — dappled —

Add more of your own as you discover them through reading,
listening, observing and sensing life around you:

_____
_____

Puns:

"Time wounds all heels."
Add more of your own as you discover them through reading,
listening, observing and sensing life around you:

_____
_____

Neat Quotes:

"Happiness (is) a shallow emotion reserved for people who lacked brains."

Add more of your own as you discover them through reading, listening, observing and sensing life around you:

_____

_____

Oxymorons:

In his book of essays, *Cold Comfort - Life at the Top of the Map* , Barton Sutter describes the smell of Duluth as a nice "bitter-sweet blend of industrial pollution and evergreens."

"Ants, although admirable, are rather aggravating." (Walter R. Brooks).

Annie Dillard says this about her childhood: "I got in trouble throwing snowballs, and have seldom been happier since." (*American Childhood*)

Here are some others:
— a vague restlessness excited and troubled him — fatally attractive — varied and constant — admiration and regret — dazzling uncertainty — We are the silences that speak — the scholarly and the illiterate, the envied and the ugly, the fierce and the docile — sensuous coldness — opulent dryness — mysterious clarity — alluring purity —

Add more of your own as you discover them through reading, listening, observing and sensing life around you:

_____

_____

Neat Titles:

Cold Comfort - Life at the Top of the Map by Barton Sutter
"The Anatomy of Happiness" Ogden Nash
Still Waiting for a Dull Moment

Add more of your own as you discover them through reading,
listening, observing and sensing life around you:

Metaphors:

"I would be pleased if this book . . . pointed the way to
some odd, forsaken place that makes the tuning fork beneath
your breastbone hum."
(Barton Sutter)

The asphalt was a hot, blackish river.

. . . both those sick pale faces were bright with the dawn
of a new future.

Add more of your own as you discover them through reading,
listening, observing and sensing life around you:

Alliteration:

Sordid secrets — weary waiting world — He clasps the crag
with crooked hands — failed to fulfill my fantasies — dank
death the rubble of the ruined house — the rubble or the ruined house — faces, forms, and phantoms — save or slay —
woodland ways — midsummer morning — wasting sickness
worn — country cousins — foreign freighter — the great Mississippi, the majestic, the magnificent Mississippi — fair fugi-
tive — frightfully friendly — lily-livered — dreary and deso-
late — toilsome, thoughtful — wounded, wasted, wronged —
truest test — the sound of singing floated faintly audible —

the Lady with the Lamp — horrors of the hospital — not as facile fancy painted her — regret and remorse — sympathy and sense — dominion and decrees — careless content —

A Limerick by Carolyn Wells

A tutor who tooted a flute
Tried to teach two young tooters to toot.
    Said the two to the tutor,
    "Is it harder to toot, or
To tutor two tooters to toot?

"Did thy sapphire shallop slip?" (Grace Hazard Conkling)

Add more of your own as you discover them through reading, listening, observing and sensing life around you:

_____

_____

Sounds:

1. Follow the steps below to write a paragraph with sounds as the focus:
    A. Begin with a topic sentence that indicates your intentions to do something with sound.
        Example: "Most places have as much to hear as to see:"
    B. Name the objects that produce the sound.
        Examples: bells — horns — gulls — waves — boat horn — rubber tires — river — dogs — pig
    C. Add descriptions of the sounds, using onomatopoeia as much as possible.
        Example: The voiceful windings of a river — the unnatural barking of the dogs — the tongueless echo in the pastoral vale —
        Onomatopoeia is the use of words that sound like the sound heard.
        Examples: swash — smack — whirring — hover — thundering — whine — burbling —

> yakking — all full of chitter noise — squeals
> D. End with an interpretation sentence that explains
>   the effect the sounds has on you.
>   Example: "The rich mixture of these sounds
>   is so suggestive that it has been
>   known to drive some people crazy."

Write your own paragraph:

_____

_____

2. Read poetry to hear sounds.

"On break, I usually read Conrad Aitken's poetry aloud. It
was pure sound unencumbered by sense. If I ever caught a
poem's sense by accident, I could never use that poem again."

                                          Annie Dillard

Find some Conrad Aitken poetry that has good sound value.
Write the words down and recite the line aloud.

_____

_____

Rhymes:

"As a rule, man's a fool." (Joseph Capp) — mile-wide tide —
Beside the rail, despite the gale — Can a mere human brain
stand the stress and the strain? —

Add more of your own as you discover them through reading,
listening, observing and sensing life around you:

_____

_____

Sights:

Streaks of white light — all the sails hang limp — an avalanche of lumber

Add more of your own as you discover them through reading, listening, observing and sensing life around you:

_____

_____

Smells:

The jungly smell of winter — the block was bluish with diesels — the odor of metal lingers in your nose all day

Add more of your own as you discover them through reading, listening, observing and sensing life around you:

_____

_____

Personification:

"Across the sky the daylight crept." (Coventry Patmore) — "All day the waves assailed the rock." (Emerson) — The summer trees were crying — The dusk captured the street — The birches that stand in their beggars row — The birches that dance at the top of the hill — A day bloated with statistics — Freckled August, drowsing warm and blond — The car is heavy with children —

Add more of your own as you discover them through reading, listening, observing and sensing life around you:

_____

_____

Litotes (Understatement):

After we knew that we were dead we sat down and cried a little. (Louis Dubek)

Add more of your own as you discover them through reading, listening, observing and sensing life around you:

_____

_____

Hyperbole:

Mark Twain

"Speech on the Weather"

The following speech was given by Mark Twain at the New England Society's seventy-first annual dinner. Read the speech carefully. Then write a well-organized essay in which you analyze how Mark Twain effectively uses various kinds of extreme diction, oxymorons, farfetched facts, parallels of extremes, and other types of hyperbole to reveal his mixed emotional sentiments about New England weather.

Just before Mark Twain spoke, the following toast was made:

"The Oldest Inhabitant — The Weather of New England."

> Who can lose it and forget it?
> Who can have it and regret it?
>
> Be interposer 'twixt us Twain.
>
> Merchant of Venice

To this Samuel L. Clemens (Mark Twain) replied as follows:

I reverently believe that the Maker who made us all makes everything in New England but the weather. I don't know who makes that, but I think it must be raw apprentices in the weather-clerk's factory who experiment and learn how, in New England, for board and clothes, and then are promoted to make weather for countries that require a good article, and will take their custom elsewhere if they don't get it. There is a sumptuous variety about the New England weather that compels the stranger's admiration — and regret. The weather is always doing something there; always attending strictly to business; always getting up new designs and trying them on the people to see how they will go. But it gets through more business in spring than in any other season. In the spring I have counted one hundred and thirty-six different kinds of weather inside of four and twenty hours. It was I that made the fame and fortune of that man that had that marvelous collection of weather on exhibition at the Centennial, that so astounded the foreigners. He was going to travel all over the world and get specimens from all the climes. I said, "Don't you do it; you come to New England on a favorable spring day." I told him what we could do in the way of style, variety, and quantity. Well, he came and he made his collection in four days. As to variety, he confessed that he got hundreds of kinds of weather that he had never heard of before. And as to quantity — well, after he had picked out and discarded all that was blemished in any way, he not only had weather enough, but weather to spare; weather to hire out; weather to sell; to deposit; weather to invest; weather to give to the poor. The people of New England are by nature patient and forbearing, but there are some things which they will not stand. Every year they kill a lot of poets for writing about "Beautiful Spring." These are generally casual visitors, who bring their notions of spring from somewhere else, and cannot, of course, know how the natives feel about spring. And so the first thing they know the opportunity to inquire how they feel has permanently gone by. Old Probabilities has a mighty reputation for accurate prophecy, and thoroughly well deserves it. You take up the paper and observe how crisply and confidently he checks off what today's weather is going to be on the Pacific, down South, in the Middle States, in the Wisconsin region. See him sail along in his joy and pride of his power till he gets to New England, and then see his tail drop. He doesn't know what the weather is going to be in New England. Well, he mulls over it, and by and by he gets out something like this: Probable northeast to southwest winds, varying to the southward and westward and eastward, and points between, high and

Chapter
Three:

SYNTAX

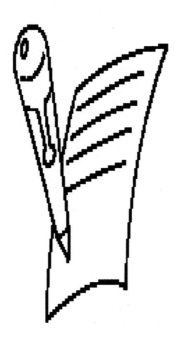

Chapter Three: SYNTAX

All writers take special care in creating a special arrangement of and relationship with words. Understanding the slight or delicate variations of syntax, and the effect it creates, or the purpose it fulfills is crucial to understanding a passage. Make a section in your journal for each of the following categories of syntax and add examples to each category as you discover them through reading, listening, observing and sensing life around you.

Experiment with improving your style by adding more of these interesting sentence structures to your own writing; however, heed Daniel Defoe's warning: The perfect style is one "in which a man speaking to five hundred people, of all common and various capacities, Idiots and Lunatics excepted, should be understood by them all."

Parentheses:

The parentheses are used to whisper a witty aside to the reader. Note how the parenthesis makes the remark seem more confidential than the comma would in the following examples:

"When a nimble Burman tripped me up on the football field and the referee (another Burman) looked the other way, the crowd yelled with hideous laughter."   George Orwell

"Tourists . . . swarm all over the Statue of Liberty (where many a resident of the town has never set foot), they invade the Automat, visit radio stations, St. Patrick's Cathedral, and they window shop."   E. B. White

"Twice has she condescended to give me her opinion (unasked too!) on this subject."   Jane Austen

"In a trice (which, in Bangladesch, is two and a half hours) we were back in our hired cab."   P. J. O'Rourke

"The hoses were set much alike between distance and tenderness of spray (and quite surely a sense of art behind this compromise, and a quiet deep joy, too real to recognize itself), and the sounds therefore were pitched much alike."
                                                          James Agee

"The words promised that I would not (yet) be alone."
                                                          John Berger

"Most of the recent propaganda about pit bulls — the crazy claim that they 'take hold with their front teeth while they chew away with their rear teeth' (which would imply, incorrectly, that they have double jaws) — can be traced to literature published by the Humane Society of the United States during the fall of 1987 and earlier."   Vicki Hearne

Punctuate the following sentence correctly:

One may speak the same language but in such a way that one's antecedents are revealed or one hopes hidden.
                                                          James Baldwin

Add more of your own as you discover them through reading, listening, observing and sensing life around you:

_____

_____

The Dash:

The dash is a sentence interrupter used to announce a series, or elaborate on a previously stated general idea. When this second strategy is used, the meaning of the sentence changes drastically. In fact, many times good writers will use a dash to create an anomaly, a departure from the expected, an abnormality. Note how the dashes in the following examples create an unexpected meaning or satire.

"The chamber of commerce was in the Motijheel Commercial Area, right around the corner — and therefore thirty or forty minutes away — from the Biman airline office."

P. J. O'Rourke

"There is a sumptuous variety about the New England weather that compels the stranger's admiration — and regret. "

Mark Twain

"In Moulmein, in Lower Burma, I was hated by large numbers of people — the only time in my life that I have been important enough for this to happen to me."

George Orwell

"The black and bottomless pool gleams in the shining rock — a sinister paradox, to a fanciful mind."

Edward Abbey

"It is now fast become a tradition — if one can use that word to describe a habit about which I feel a certain amount of shame-facedness — for our household to watch the Miss America contest on television every year."

Gerald Early

Punctuate the following sentence correctly:

"The day happened to be magnificent the finest of the year"

Add more of your own as you discover them through reading, listening, observing and sensing life around you:

_____

_____

The Colon:

The colon is used to announce. Notice how the opening statement in the following examples prepare the reader for an announcement which flows smoothly after the colon.

"I looked it up in the *Oxford English Dictionary*. It went like this:

> Fault: Deficiency, lack, want of something . . ."

Meena Alexander

"I was right about the tar: it led to within half a mile of the shore."

E. B. White

"My voice splintered in my ears into a cacophony: whispering cadences, shouts, moans, the quick delight of bodily pleasure, all rising up as if the condition of being fractured had freed the selves jammed into my skin, multiple beings locked into the journeys of one body."

Meena Alexander

"All government, in its essence, is a conspiracy against the superior man: its one permanent object is to police him and cripple him."

H. L. Mencken

Punctuate the following sentence correctly:

"By the time we had reached the top of the long ridge on which my cousin had set his traps the morning had slipped toward noon and our count had risen to seven animals three raccoons three skunks and the pregnant fox."

T. H. Watkins

Add more of your own as you discover them through reading, listening, observing and sensing life around you:

_____

_____

The Semicolon:

The semicolon is used to separate different but related sentences. Notice how the semicolons in the following examples also create balanced expressions.

"But the poor lady was wrong; it was not a swan that they had hatched; it was an eagle."

Lytton Stratchey

"I have in my own life a precious friend, a woman of sixty-five who has lived very hard, who is wise; who listens well; who has been where I am and can help me understand it; an who represents not only an ultimate ideal mother to me but also the person I'd like to be when I grow up."

Judith Viorst

Punctuate the following sentence correctly:

"In a rural family practice such as mine much of every work-day is taken up with disease I look forward to the prenatal visit with Barb to the continuing relationship with her over the next months to the prospect of birth."

Add more of your own as you discover them through reading, listening, observing and sensing life around you:

_____

_____

Mark Twain

from *Life on the Mississippi*

Read the following excerpt by Mark Twain. Then write a well-organized essay that explains how Twain's use of semicolons to masterfully connect specific descriptions of similar or exactly opposite things helps create his attitude toward steamboatmen.

When I was a boy there was but one permanent ambition among my comrades in our village on the West Bank of the Mississippi River. That was to be a steamboatman. We had transient ambitions of other sorts but they were only transient. When a circus came and went, it left us all burning to become clowns; the first Negro minstrel show that ever came to our section left us all suffering to try that kind of life; now and then we had a hope that, if we lived and were good, God would permit us to be pirates. These ambitions faded out, each in its turn; but the ambition to be steamboatmen always remained.

Once a day a cheap, gaudy packet arrived upward from St. Louis, and another downward from Keokuk. Before these events, the day was glorious with expectancy; after them, the day was a dead and empty thing. Not only the boys but the whole village felt this. After all these years I can picture that old time to myself now, just as it was then: the white town drowsing in the sunshine of a summer's morning; the streets empty or pretty near so; one or two clerks sitting in front of the Water Street stores, with their splint-bottomed chairs tilted back against the walls, chins on breasts; a sow and a litter of pigs loafing along the sidewalk, doing a good business in watermelon rinds and seeds; two or three lonely little freight piles scattered above the "levee"; a pile of "skids" on the slope of the stone-paved wharf, and the fragrant town drunkard asleep in the shadow of them; two or three wood slats at the head of the wharf but nobody to listen to the peaceful lappings of the wavelets against them; the great Mississippi, the majestic, the magnificent Mississippi, rolling its mile-wide tide along, shining in the sun; the dense forest away on the other side; the "point" above the town, and the "point" below bounding the river-glimpse and turning it into a sort of sea, and withal a very still and brilliant and lonely one. Presently a film of dark smoke appears above one of those remote "points"; instantly a Negro drayman, famous for his quick eye and prodigious voice, lifts up the cry, "S-t-e-a-m-boat a-comin'!" and the scene changes! The town drunkard stirs, the clerks wake up, a furious clatter of drays follows, every house and store pours out a human contribution, and all in a twinkling the dead town is alive and moving. Drays, carts, men, boys, all go hurrying from the many quarters to a common center, the wharf. Assembled there, the people fasten their eyes upon the coming boat as upon a wonder they are seeing for the first time. And the boat is rather a handsome sight, too. She is long and sharp and trim and pretty; she has two tall, fancy-topped chimneys, with a gilded device of some kind swung between them; a fanciful pilot house, all glass and "gingerbread," perched on top of the "texas" deck behind them; the paddle-boxes are gorgeous with a picture or gilded rays above the boat's name; the boiler deck, the hurricane deck, and the texas deck are fenced and ornamented with clean white railings; there is a flag gallantly flying from the jackstaff; the furnace doors are open and the fires glaring bravely; the upper decks are black with passengers; the captain stands by the big bell, calm, imposing, the envy of all; great volumes of the blackest smoke are rolling and tumbling out of the chimneys — a husbanded grandeur created with a bit of pitch pine just before arriving at the town; the crew are grouped on the forecastle; the broad stage is run far out over the port bow and an envied deckhand stands picturesquely on the end of it with a coil of rope in his hand; the pent steam is screaming the gauge cocks; the captain lifts his hands, a bell rings, the wheels stop; then they turn back, churning the water to foam, and the steamer is at rest. Then such a scramble as there is to get aboard and get ashore, and to take in freight and to discharge freight, all at the same time; and such a yelling and cursing as the mates facilitate it all! Ten minutes later the steamer is under way again, with no flag on the jackstaff and no black smoke issuing from the chimneys. After ten or more minutes the town is dead again and the town drunkard asleep by the skids once more.

Parallelism:

Parallelism is the repetition of similar beginnings to create balanced expressions. This is done when the writer wants to express a pair or series of ideas. Making each item parallel — making each item look alike grammatically — provides emphasis and establishes rhythm and balance.

One of the most powerful aspects of John F. Kennedy's Inaugural Address was his use of parallel expressions. Notice how the repeated verbs in following two sentences create parallelism.

"Let every nation know, whether it wishes us well or ill, that we shall <u>pay any price, bear any burden, meet any hard ship, support any friend, oppose any foe</u> to assure the survival and the success of liberty."

"Together let us<u> explore the stars, conquer the deserts, eradicate disease, tap the ocean depths, and encourage the arts and commerce.</u>"

Notice how the repetition of the infinitive (to plus a different verb) in following sentence creates parallelism.

"To that world assembly of sovereign states, the United Nations, our last best hope in an age where the instruments of war have far outpaced the instruments of peace, we renew our pledge of support — <u>to prevent it from becoming merely a forum for invective</u> — <u>to strengthen its shield of the new and the weak</u> — <u>and to enlarge the area in which its writ may run.</u>"
For each of the following sentences, provide parallel expressions that logically complete the thought:

1. Propaganda is a systematic effort to influence people's opinions, to _____ ,
or_to _____ .

2. He spends most of his evenings sitting on the couch, watching TV, and _____ .

Prepositions:

Commonly Used Prepositions

about	between	over
above	beyond	past
across	but	since
after	by	through
against	concerning	throughout
along	down	to
amid	during	toward
among	except	under
around	for	underneath
at	from	until
before	in	unto
behind	into	up
below	like	upon
beneath	of	with
beside	off	within
besides	on	without

Prepositions are used by good writers to interrupt or end the sentence with lively description. Note the examples:

" The train smells of oil and soot and orange peels and lurches groggily as we rock our way inland."   Joy Kogawa

"I remember a horse I rode for a while named Targhee whose Hocks were scarred from tangles in barbed wire when he was a colt and who spooked a lot in high grass."   Barry Lopez

"In the city we see entropy in the rundown subways and worn-out sidewalks and torn-down buildings, in the increasing disorder of our lives."   K. C. Cole
"Inside, on the shelf next to the ice-cube-tray compartment, is a row of tall stemmed dessert glasses, each one filled with its own golden dollop of butterscotch pudding." Sue Hubbel

Add more of your own as you discover them through reading, listening, observing and sensing life around you:

_____

_____

The Appositive:

An appositive is another noun, set off by double commas or dashes, that renames the subject. The appositives are underlined in the examples. Notice how they add additional information to the person, place, or thing just mentioned.

"Wooden-headedness, the source of self-deception, is a factor that plays a remarkably large role in government."

Barbara Tuchman

"I came upon her late one evening on a deserted street in Hyde Park, a relatively affluent neighborhood in an otherwise mean, impoverished section of Chicago."

Brent Staples

"Mama's house — a place built for children — where anything that could be broken had already been broken by my grandmother's early batch of offspring."

Judith Ortiz Coffer

Combine each of the following groups of related sentences or phrases together by making one new sentence with an appositive:

1. "Name calling is a propaganda technique in which negatively charged names are hurled against the opposing side or competitor. By using such names, propagandists try to arouse feelings of mistrust, fear, and hate in their audience."

Ann McClintock

2. "Guns are a particularly sensitive topic for parents, and many of us feel uncomfortable when our children lust for the plastic ones."

Jean Marzollo

Add more of your own as you discover them through reading, listening, observing and sensing life around you:

_____

_____

Participle Phrases:

Participle phrases beginning with a word ending in "ing."
Notice how the participle phrases in the following examples
add more information to the noun of the sentence.

"We found a sleepy hillside and sprawled out on it, <u>soaking
up the early-spring sunshine.</u>"   Gretel Ehlrich
"On the broad lobby desk, <u>lighted and bubbling,</u> was a ten-
gallon aquarium containing one large fish . . ."
                                    Annie Dillard

"Madame Bovary was hovering over the cosmetics counters,
<u>clutching the current issue of *Cosmopolitian*</u>"
                          Francine du Plessix Gray

"<u>Hiking the tree-lined streets of our St. Louis borough en route
to school,</u> I felt common names spring up in my mouth, <u>wav-
ing their leafy syllables.</u>"   Naomi Shihab Nye

"My friend Danny Chapman, the Ringling Bros. clown, had a
sliding, circus sort of face, marked by the sun, wind, pain, bad
luck and bad dealings, the standard lusts and equivocations,
like a stone the water had slid over for sixty years."
                                 Edward Hoaglund

Add more of your own as you discover them through reading,
listening, observing and sensing life around you:

_____

_____

Absolute Phrases:

An absolute phrase includes a noun immediately followed by
a participle — a verb form ending in "ing" or in the past tense
which describes the noun — and a prepositional phrase or two
or other types of adjective phrases. The absolute phrase is
underlined in the examples that follow.

"One day he brought home a <u>baby girl, wrapped up inside his
brown western-style greatcoat.</u>"
                            Maxine Hong Kingston

"In the village structure, spirits shimmered among the <u>live creatures, balanced and held in equilibrium by time and land.</u>"
Maxine Hong Kingston

"He wore these <u>pants, printed with rainbow-colored spurs.</u>"
Naomi Shihab Nye

"Actually, he wore a clown's tight rubber <u>wig, painted white.</u>"
Annie Dillard

"Blurred with <u>moss, knobby with barnacles,</u> its shape is hardly
recognizable anymore."
Anne Morrow Lindbergh

"We sit in rows like strangers in a theater, <u>coats rumpled in
our laps,</u> crossing and uncrossing our legs, waiting for the show
to start."
Scott Russell Sanders

Add more of your own as you discover them through reading, listening, observing and sensing life around you:

_____

_____

Cumulative Sentences:

A cumulative sentence is one in which the emendations are
added after the main clause is completed. In the following
example, the main sentence — the underlined portion — comes
first, and is followed by a number of descriptive phrases.

"<u>I could live two days in a den,</u> curled, leaning on mouse fur,
sniffing bird bones, blinking, licking, breathing musk, my hair
tangled in the roots of grasses."   Annie Dillard

Underline the main sentence in the following examples of cumulative sentence structure:

"While she ate, I watched the clouds of blue butterflies — spring
azures — squeezing into nearly opened blackberry blossoms
to lay their eggs."   Sue Hubbel

"We held our breaths, imagining a crash as the parts clanged together, or a terrible disaster if the piece were to slip loose."
                                        Naomi Shihab Nye

"The Greek woman is short and heavy, waistless, and is wearing a black dress, a black scarf pulled low around her eyes, a black sweater, thick black stockings, black shoes."
                                        Alice Bloom

Combine the following three related sentences to make one cumulative sentence.

1. "My truck is named Dodge. The name came with it. I don't know if it was named after the verb or the man who invented it."   Barry Lopez

Add more of your own as you discover them through reading, listening, observing and sensing life around you:

_____

_____

Periodic Sentences:

A periodic sentence is one in which the emendations are added after the main clause is completed. In the following example, the main sentence — the underlined portion — comes last, and is preceded by a number of descriptive phrases.

"Curled, leaning on mouse fur, sniffing bird bones, blinking, licking, breathing musk, my hair tangled in the roots of grasses, I could live two days in a den."   Annie Dillard

Underline the main sentence in the following examples of periodic sentence structure:

"By the last day of the tour, when a limousine picked me up at my Beverly Hills hotel for my last round of satellite TV interviews, I knew I had to stop."   Randy Shilts

"In our constitution and the works of law, philosophy, social thought, and science, in its every day uses in the service of justice and clarity, what I call the father tongue is immensely noble and indispensably useful."   Ursula K LeGuin

"Long before I am near enough to talk to you on the street, in a meeting, or at a party, you announce your sex, age, and class to me through what you are wearing."   Alison Lurie

"Ten years ago, when I first noticed the symptoms that would be diagnosed as MS, I was probably looking my best."
Nancy Mairs

"Three thousand miles to the west, where I live now, on a much-traveled hill road winding eastward from the coast, there is a standing pipe called the Lombardi Spring."
Adrienne Rich

Add more of your own as you discover them through reading, listening, observing and sensing life around you:

_____

_____

Strung-along Sentences:

A strung-along sentence is one in which the emendations are added in the middle, separating the main clause into two parts. These emendations can come in the form of absolute phrases, participle phrases, prepositions, gerunds, etc. and can be punctuated with a colon, a comma, a double comma, a dash, parentheses, etc. Here is an example:

"I have the impression that many people, if they think of this city at all, consider Duluth a cold kind of joke, a Peoria of the North, the last outpost on the northernmost edge of the middle of nowhere."   Barton Sutter

Emend simple sentence patterns to create more mature constructions. Think of the basic elements of the sentence, the subject, verb, and object. Add words to describe these basic elements. The result is an immediately more mature and graceful sentence.   Examples:

Basic sentence: John participated in football.
Emendation: John, the 145 pound weakling, cautiously participated in the barbaric game of football.

Basic sentence: Emerson believes that adversity is a blessing.
Emendation: Emerson, a respected essayist and philosopher, believes that adversity, even incredible misfortunes, can turn into blessing.

Basic sentence: Our society has prejudices.
Emendation: Our society, both as a country and internationally, has prejudices — preconceptions, narrowmindedness, intolerance, and even blatant bigotry — that we need to overcome.

Basic sentence: These people have a variety of personalities.
Emendation: Although not representing the average person, these people tend to possess a strong insight based on the variety of their personalities.

Basic sentence: This can occur on a smaller level, too.
Emendation: This influence of man on nature can also commonly occur on a smaller, less scientific level.

Now you try some:

Basic sentence: Love strikes when least expected.
Emendation:

Basic sentence: Every culture has a differing view on morality.
Emendation:

Basic sentence: Often religion becomes a convenience.
Emendation:

Basic sentence: Most literature supports a belief in creation.
Emendation:

Basic sentence: A friend portrays good listening habits.
Emendation:

Conciseness:

Most of the suggestions thus far have been ways to make longer sentences by combining or emending shorter ones. At the same time, it must be cautioned that every word added must add a new meaning in the sentence. Note the conciseness of the following two examples:

> "Above and below the ship, this blue." (John Blight)
> "After the sea, the harbor." (Edgar Daniel Kramer)

Many times the end result of "emendation" is wordiness, rather than gracefulness. Correct the following emendations by taking out all unnecessary words.

Cross out all unnecessary words.

The only way, pure and simple, to remain satisfied and content with the government, politics, and politicians is to remain, as always, involved by reading and perusing newspapers, exercising your voting rights, etc. and simply not letting the politicians own you.

The rise upward of most modern successful champions is almost, but not always, accompanied hand in hand by proud arrogance and awfully disdainful behaviors.

Love, in retrospect, is a very strong, powerful emotional feeling that does not spontaneously occur each and every day of the year.

In a way everybody — every man, woman, and child — every person — fear, to some degree, greatly or not, some aspect of death that affects their own life personally.

A uniquely unusual young man in his teens named Joe enjoyed savoring the essence — the mouth-watering smell — of slow-cooked bacon during a fancy luxury continental breakfast at the local, drab, leaky-roofed hotel, while wearing bell-bottoms and a polyester plaid shirt.

Repetition:

The conciseness exercise implies that every repeated word is unnecessary. We all know that is not true. Sometimes repeated words are necessary for emphasis. Sometimes repetition is needed in the topic sentences so that they echo the thesis more clearly. But perhaps the most graceful use is the subtle repetition of an idea. In the essay "Dull and Out of It" from *Cold Comfort, Life at the Top of the Map* , Barton Sutter refers to Duluth as "the last outpost on the northernmost edge of the middle of nowhere." Elsewhere in his collection of essays called *Cold Comfort*, he refers to Duluth as "the northern edge of the known universe." Notice how Suttor's changed description of the repeated idea adds to his description of Duluth's remoteness. Can you make other phrases that would similarly describe the isolation of Duluth?

Variety:

Make your essay more varied by beginning in more ways than Subject first.

A. Begin with an adverb:

Begin a sentence with an adverb — a word that describes the action of the sentence. Here are some examples:

"Exactly why the Germans banished intelligence is a vast and largely unanswered question."   Neil Postman

"Now, three years later, after the last bad fall, she had managed to forget the fatigue and lonliness and, in these free-wheeled excursions back through time, to capture happiness."
          Russell Baker

"Suddenly the whole room broke into a sea of shouting, as they saw me rise."   Langston Hughes

"How much we need, and how arduous of attainment is that steadiness preached in all rules for holy living. How desirable and distant is the ideal of the contemplative, artist, or saint — the inner inviolable core, the single eye."
          Anne Morrow Lindbergh

"Mainly I try to remind them that the road ahead is a long one and that it will have more unexpected turns than they think."
William Zinsser

"Never in my life have I gotten the attention of a waiter, unless it was an off-duty waiter whose car I'd accidently scraped in a parking lot somewhere."   Barbara Ehrenreich

Practice this by doing the exercise which follows.

Begin with the word "Normally" followed by an adjective that names a personality trait, then describe a behavior you find yourself doing that contradicts that trait.

Example: Normally rather restrained, I found myself speaking to everyone I met.
Use words like the following to fill in the blank: combative, energetic, belligerent, enterprising, adventurous, venturesome, resourceful, alert, lethargic, studious, reflective, conversable, cordial, debonair, sportive, frivolous, rattlebrained, flighty, auspicious, flippant, reliable, trustworthy, unfailing, steady, uncertain, clamorous, imperious, ambitious, insistent, apprehensive, solicitous, phobic, timorous, diffident, tremulous, fainthearted, penitent, conscience-smitten, rational, judicious, flexible, etc. The list is never-ending. You can probably pick better ones.)

Your turn:
Normally _____, I found myself _____
_____.

B. Begin with an adjective:

Any of the words listed on the previous page are adjectives since they describe people. Begin a sentence with one of those words or with any word that describes some other person, place or thing in the same sentence. Other neat adjectives can be found in the chapter on diction. Here are some examples:

"Subdued, resigned, Papa's life — all our lives — took on a pattern that would hold for the duration of the war."
Jeanne Wakatsuki Houston

"This frail boy bent under his load said more to me about poverty than a dozen poor fathers."   Gordon Parks

"These hopeless end-of-the-line visits with my mother made me wish I had not thrown off my own past so carelessly."
                                                                    Russell Baker

"Vague as this definition may be, I believe most people are aware of periods in their lives when they seem to be 'in grace' and other periods in their lives when they feel 'out of grace,' even though they may use different words to describe these states."   Anne Morrpw Lindbergh

"Long gone are the days of the "gentleman's C," when students journeyed through college with a certain relaxation, sampling a wide variety of courses — music, art, philosophy, classics, anthropology, poetry, religion — that would send them out as liberally educated men and women."   William Zinsser

"An unscrupulous theatrical producer has figured out that it is relatively easy to turn a buck by producing a play that fails."
                                                                    Neil Postman

Now try some of your own.

_____

_____

D. Begin with an infinitive:

Here are some examples:

"To explain what I am getting at, I find it helpful to refer to two films, which taken together embody the main lines of my argument."   Neil Postman

"To provide some verification of this, I conducted a survey a few years back on the subject of the Iranian hostage crisis."
                                                                    Neil Postman

Now try some of your own.

_____

_____

E. Begin with a subordinate clause:

Commonly used Subordinate Conjunctions

after, although, as, as much as, because, before, how, if, in order that, inasmuch as, provided, since, than, that, though, unless, until, when, where, while.

Here are some examples:

"Although there was no evidence of subversion, soon after the bombing of Pearl Harbor, President Franklin D. Roosevelt authorized the expulsion of West Coast Japanese-Americans — many of them born in this country — from their homes and businesses."   Jeanne Wakatsuki Houston

"When she was young, with life ahead of her, I had been her future and resented it."   Russell Baker

"When you are inside the jungle, away from the river, the trees vault out of sight."   Annie Dillard

Now try some of your own.

_____

_____

F. Begin with a gerund.

Begin with a verb form (ending in "ing") that acts as the subject of the sentence. Here are some examples:

Acting responsibly is an important concept to consider when discovering freedom.

"Looking at it, holding it, thinking of things to do with it displace other activities once thought essential."
                    Neil Postman

Now try some of your own.

_____

_____

G. Begin with a participle phrase.

Here are some examples:

"Breathing hard, balancing a tin of water on his head, a small boy climbed toward us."   Gordon Parks

"Sitting at her bedside, forever out of touch with her, I wondered about my own children, and their children, and children in general, and about the disconnections between children and parents that prevent them from knowing each other."
                                        Russell Baker

Now try some of your own.

_____

_____

H. Begin with a list of noun phrases.

Here are some examples:

"The wretched prisoners huddling in the stinking cages of the lock-ups, the grey, cowed faces of the long term convicts, the scarred buttocks of the men who had been flogged with bamboos — all these oppressed me with an intolerable sense of guilt."   George Orwell

"Each whorl, each faint knob, each criss-cross vein in its eggshell texture, is as clearly defined as on the day of creation."
                                Anne Morrow Lindbergh

Now try some of your own.

_____

_____

_____

_____

_____

Short and Simple Sentences:

For variety and a change in pace, shorter sentences are needed. One way to do this is to combine a few two or three word sentences into one. This is called a short and simple sentence. Examples follow.

"He ruminates, he dreams, he remembers."

Malcolm Cowley

No minors, no food, no pets.

"The baby frets. The maid sulks."

Joan Didion

Another way to shorten sentences is to write a simple sentence with compound parts. The result is a fast-paced sentence with parallel parts. Examples follow.

"The M.P., the soldiers, the turnkey, and the girl on the beach are white."   John McPhee

"Nature has no sense of humor: In its beauty, as in its ugliness, or in its neutrality, there is no laughter."

Joyce Carol Oates

"The student comes to his desk. On it, neatly arranged by the instructor, he finds his laboratory manual, a dissecting board, instruments, and a mimeographed list."

Walker Percy

"Its as simple — and as threatened — as that."

Adrienne Rich

"The facts are a mess. They are filled with gaps, chuckholes, switchbacks, and dead ends — just like life."

Scott Russell Sanders

Yet another way to shorten sentence structure is to add to realted shorter sentences together with a comma.

"They were alone, no one had seen them." Fyodor Dostoevsky

Add more of your own as you discover them through reading, listening, observing and sensing life around you:

_____

_____

Inverted Sentences:

The following sentences are called inverted because the natural order is switched. This is usually down for emphasis, but always creates variety. Note the list of examples that follow

Had he and I but met. — Had we but world enough, and time. — I ought before this to have reply'd. — Backward we look regretful, forward we glance with regret. — Before my face the picture hangs. — Bite deep and wide, o axe, the tree. — By the side of a murmuring stream a gentleman sat. — The earth with thunder torn. — at dawn of night, when sunset summer on autumn shone — Forward the crackling lashes send. — from a frightened face I flee. —

Add more of your own as you discover them through reading, listening, observing and sensing life around you:

_____

_____

Smash Those Cliches: (The final section on diction emphasizes the necessity of using all the neat words discovered in reading and listed on the previous pages.)

By the time most writers put their thoughts on paper, the writing is already in its third or fourth draft because it's been written that many times in the mind. Nevertheless, when it finally takes form on paper for the first time, there's still so much going on that the draft is usually full of mechanical errors and cliches. The first step in the rewrite should be to smash the cliches; the first step in rewriting is to take those old worn out expressions and change them, give them life by making them your own.

Helen Keller did this in her speech to the Lions International Convention in Cedar Point, Ohio, on June 30, 1925. Her smashed cliche about opportunity knocking was a powerful tactic in her plea to get Lions Club members to accept her and other blind people as members. Here's her opening lines: "Dear Lions and Ladies, I suppose you have heard the legend that represents opportunity as a capricious lady who knocks at every door but once, and if the door isn't opened quickly, she passes on, never to return. And that is how it should be, lovely desirable ladies won't wait. You have to go out and grab them.

I am your opportunity . . . . "

Here are some other ways to smash cliches:

"He's all thumbs" is a cliche that means he is awkward. You can rewrite that old, worn-out expression as "He's got butterfingers." This is a fresher way of saying the same thing.

"Don't add insult to injury" is a cliche that asks someone to avoid making something bad worse. You can rewrite that old, worn-out expression as "Don't add sugar to the cavity." This is a fresher way of saying the same thing.

"All work and no play makes Jack a dull boy" is a cliche that means too much work, without a balance of leisure, is unhealthy. You can rewrite that old, worn-out expression by repeating the beginning and changing the ending. Since the reader expects the same old ending, the surprise ending says the same idea in a fresh way. For example, you can change the same cliche to say "All work and no play makes Jack an accountant."

Try smashing some of the following cliches:

Ace in the whole (a surprise weapon that produces success) — Actions speak louder than words (what you do is more important than what you say) — Add fuel to the flame (to spread trouble) — Wash one's dirty linen in public (to make public something embarrassing that should be kept secret) — A little knowledge is a dangerous thing (A person who knows a little about something, may think she knows it all and make bad mistakes) — All in a day's work (something unpleasant but bearable as part of a routine) — He's got too many irons in the fire. — At the drop of a hat (without waiting) — She's a big frog in a small pond (An important person in a small position) — This should be a piece of cake (really easy) — It's a dog-eat-dog world — Don't count your chickens before they hatch. — Your getting too big for your breeches. — She's a fair-weather friend.

Jerry Klein
"Small Town Summer"

Exercise: An Essay Test on Syntax

The essay that follows, written for the *Peoria Journal Star* in Illinois describes summer in small-town America. Read the selection carefully. Then write a well-organized essay that analyzes how the various sentence structures illustrated in this chapter (as well as some unusual syntax not listed here) are used by the Jerry Kline to convey a typical American experience. Here is the srticle:

Now, in that slow, sweet time between the Fourth of July and Labor Day, summer makes its deepest, most profound impression upon the huiman psyche with an old-fashioned cadence and rhythm. To those who live in the cities, it may be nothing more than a succession of oppressive days of baked brick and steaming asphalt, hot nights when violence seethes below the surface, when the humid blanket dampens the spirit and the heat is an awesome, almost malevolent force. And yet summer in small-town America remains a magic, treasured time.

Here there are the houses set far back on their spacious front yards, cool and shady streets where ancient elms, sycamores and oaks muffle the sounds of children and traffic passing — sun-dappled by day, soft and beguiling at dusk, beckoning and mysterious tunnels by night.

One has the feeling that things have not changed here, thst the cars might well be square-nosed with wire wheels and softly blipping engines and that within these houses people might be listening to Fibber McGee and Molly or playing cards around their pedestal oak tables. An illusion, obviously, but things change slowly here and life is circumscribed by the grain elevator, the church, the park and the thin strip of downtown with its 1890's Victorian building fronts. And summer flows past as lazily as the creek wandering between its tree-shaded banks at the edge of town.

Already the afternoons drone with the cicadas, rising and falling in their peculiar intensity as if cued by some unseen director. It is a drowsy, somnolent sound, an invitation to such time-passing activities as throwing a tennis ball against the front porch steps and fielding the grounders, or sitting out in front of the tavern watching the flow of life at the little supermarket across the street.

Out beyond the cool oasis of town, the corn is a green-black sea, rising steadily toward high tide, and farther on, almost like mirages, the distant farmhouses and barns have the appearance of ships at anchor on the placid surface.

Noon whistles and church bells mark the passing of the day. A breeze flaps through the cottonwoods and then dies away. Clothes hang from the backyard lines as still and unmoving as if they are part of a painting. Porch swings stand empty. Later, when the night wind comes, they might creak softly, a welcome retreat for people sated with television and wanting a fresh breath of air. Real country air.

In the heat of the afternoon, the swimming pool in the park is churned into foam by scores of thrashing bodies. Hardly room to stand, much less to swim. Nearby, the little bandstand with its 50 or so seats stands empty.

At dusk, a three-piece countrywestern group will appear and play old songs. There will be a girls' league night softball game, too, with half a hundred people or more crowding the bleachers or sitting along the first base line in their colorful lawn chairs. The town policeman will stop and watch and the young men will cruise past in their cars. And there will be activity down at the tavern on main street, where men in their seed hats grip frosty glasses of beer and talk about the corn and the beans and the need for some rain — and quick.

Night comes slowly and the fireflies wink along the darkening streets and trimmed lawns like a sky full of stars brought down to earth for the season. The wind that springs up has the rich earthy smell of fertile cornfields and maybe distant pigs as well. In the park, the concert has ended. The softball games ends with a shout of triumph from one team and the lines of players passing one another, touching hand and repeating that sporting litany, "Good game, good game, good game . . . ."

Then the lights go out. The tavern down the street empties and an almost surreal silence falls across the town. Only the crickets and the night insects now, and the winking fireflies. In the distance there is a low rumple of thunder. The farmers listen and hope for rain. The younger people hope for another sunny day tomorrow. For them, summer stretches on almost forever. For the older folks, this small-town summer is too short and fall comes too soon.

Chapter Four:

Close Reading—

Summarizing
and
Paraphrasing

Chapter Four:
Close Reading —
Summarizing
and
Paraphrasing

Every essay about literature requires an accurate interpretation of the meaning of the work. Sometimes this may require a brief rewriting of the author's viewpoint in your own words. This is what I refer to as summarizing. Paraphrasing — a word-for-word rewriting of the original text in your own words, which results in a passage as long or longer than the original text — is a reading strategy to be used to make sense of shorter, but more complex passages. To use paraphrasing as a measure of your writing ability — to do nothing but paraphrase a passage on an essay exam — would result in sure failure. Since part of most serious term paper requirements is to read widely — a minimum of 600 pages, for example — to use paraphrasing as the sole means of writing for this assignment would be impossible. Essay exams and term papers require that you analyze, interpret, and embed quotes to support your interpretation. Summarizing should be limited to the introduction and perhaps the topic sentences of term papers and AP essay exams. However, paraphrasing can help you learn how to accurately interpret the meaning of more difficult readings — the type of shorter, but complex and obscure passages used on the AP English, PSAT, and SAT multiple-choice tests. Part One in each exercise asks you to practice reading with more objective accurateness by paraphrasing each excerpt.

Part Two in each exercise asks you to practice reading with more objective accurateness by taking a short multiple-choice quiz. Practice taking these in fifteen minute segments or combine four passages to make one complete test. For more practice and guidance with multiple-choice exams, read the multiple-choice chapters in the *Practical Guide the the Advanced Placement English Language and Composition Examination* or the *Practical Guide the the Advanced Placement English Literature and*

Composition Examination. These Guides have three full-lengths tests and are available in second editions through School House Books, Inc. (See Order Form at the back of this *Writer.*

Part Three in each exercise asks you to practice writing with more exactness by taking an essay exam. Practice these in forty-minute segments or combine three questions to make a complete test.

Francis Bacon

Of Studies

Exercise One: Part One

Read the selection carefully. Then, to learn to read with more objective accurateness, practice paraphrasing by making a word-for-word rewriting of Bacon's excerpt.

Here is the passage:

Studies serve for delight, for ornament, and for ability. Their chief use for delight is in privateness and retiring; for ornament is in discourse; and for ability, is in the judgement and disposition of business; for expert men can execute, and perhaps judge of particulars, one by one; but the general counsels, and the plots and marshalling of affairs come best from those that are learned. To spend too much time in studies is sloth; to use them too much for ornamentation is affectation; to make judgment wholly by their rules is the humor of a scholar. They perfect nature, and are perfected by experience; for natural abilities are like natural plants, that need pruning by study; and studies themselves do give forth directions too much at large, except they be bounded in by experience. Crafty men condemn studies, simple men admire them, and wise men use them; for they reach not their own use; but that is a wisdom without them and above them, won by observation. Read not to contradict and confute, nor to believe and take for granted, nor to find talk and discourse, but to weigh and consider. Some books are to be tasted, others to be swallowed, and some few to be chewed and digested; that is, some books are to be read only in parts; others to be read but not curiously; and some few to be read wholly, and with diligence and attention. Some books also may be read by deputy, and extracts made of them by others; but that would only be in the less important arguments and the meaner sorts of books; else distilled books are, like common distilled water, flashy things. Reading maketh a full man; conference a ready man; and writing an exact man. And therefore, if a man write little, he had need have a great memory; if he confer little, he had need have a present wit; and if he read little, he had need have much cunning, to seem to know that he doth not. Histories make men wise; poets, witty; the mathematics, subtle; natural philosophy, deep; moral, grave; logic and rhetoric, able to contend: *Abeunt studia in mores!* * Nay there is no stand or impediment in the wit but may be wrought out by fit studies; like as diseases of the body may have appropriate exercises. Bowling is good for the stone and reins, shooting for the lungs and breast, gentle walking for the stomach, riding for the head, and the like. So if a man's wit be wandering, let him study the mathematics; for in demonstrations, if his wit be called away never so little, he must begin again. If his wit not be apt to distinguish or find differences, let him study the schoolmen; for they are *cymini sectores!*** If he not be apt to beat over manners, and to call up one thing to prove and illustrate another, let him study the lawyer's cases. So every defect of the mind may have a special receipt.

* *Abeunt studia in mores!* Studies develop into manners! (Ovid)
***cymini sectores*, hair-splitters

Exercise One: Part Two

After completing the paraphrase, answer the multiple choice questions that follow. The suggested time for each quiz is fifteen minutes.

1. Bacon presented his ideas in logical order but without paragraphs. Sentence one and two could be paragraph one because they speak of

> (A) studies as essential excercise for the mind
> (B) reading
> (C) the assigned use for each of the studies
> (D) the abuse of each of the studies
> (E) reading, conference, and writing

2. The word "affectation" in the line "to use (studies) too much for ornament is affectation" can best be interpreted to mean all of the following EXCEPT:

> (A) artificial behavior adopted to impress others
> (B) a pretense
> (C) any type of mannerisms contrived for effect
> (D) a fond or tender feeling
> (E) a disguise

3. The antecedent for "they" in the line "They perfect nature, and are perfected by experience" is

> (A) studies
> (B) sloth
> (C) scholars
> (D) counsels
> (E) judges

4. In the line beginning, "Read not to contradict and confute," Bacon emphasizes that reading is best served when combined with

> (A) disagreement
> (B) confrontation
> (C) thinking
> (D) assumption
> (E) conversation

5. The balance of the memorable sentence, "Some books are to be tasted, others to be swallowed, and some few to be chewed and digested," is created by the author's careful creation of all of the following rhetorical and stylistic devices EXCEPT:

    (A) parallel syntax

    (B) metaphoric language

    (C) argument by generalization

    (D) ambiguity

    (E) cause and effect relationship

6. When Bacon follows this statement with "that is," he is creating meaning through the use of

    (A) paraphrase

    (B) repetition

    (C) understatement

    (D) syllogism

    (E) abstraction

7. In the phrase, some books are meant "to be read wholly, and with diligence and attention," the word "diligence," is best meant to mean

    (A) heedfulness

    (B) regardfulness

    (C) carefulness

    (D) cognizance

    (E) slovenliness

8. All of the following are true statements of Bacon's organization EXCEPT:

    (A) Sentence three, four, and five could be paragraph two because the topic of these sentences is the attitude of three kinds of men toward studies.

    (B) What could be paragraph three deals with reading.

    (C) The topics of paragraph four are conferencing and writing.

    (D) Paragraph four also deals with the different ways to chew, taste, swallow, or digest studies.

    (E) The final paragraph makes the assertion that studies are to the mind what exercise is to the body.

9. All of the following are amplified examples of how appropriate exercise is good for the body EXCEPT:

  (A) "There is no stand or impediment in the wit but
        may be wrought out by fit studies"
  (B) "Bowling is good for the stone and reins"
  (C) "Shooting (is good) for the lungs and breast"
  (D) "Gentle walking (is good) for the stomach"
  (E) "Riding (is good) for the head"

10. All of the following are assertions followed by an explanation of how studies function as exercise to the mind EXCEPT:

  (A) "If a man's wit be wandering, let him study the
        mathematics"
  (B) "In demonstrations, if his wit be called away never
        so little, he must begin again"
  (C) "If his wit not be apt to distinguish or find differ-
        ences, let him study the schoolmen"
  (D) " If he not be apt to beat over manners, and to call
        up one thing to prove and illustrate another,
        let him study the lawyer's cases"
  (E) "Every defect of the mind may have a special re-
        ceipt"

11. All of the following words are common words are used in
an unusual sense EXCEPT:

  (A) ornamemt
  (B) ready
  (C) flashy
  (D) moral
  (E) stone

12. The rhetorical purpose of this excerpt can best be described
as   (A) expository
  (B) speculative
  (C) narrative
  (D) descriptive
  (E) deductive

Exercise One: Part Three

After completing the multiple-choice exam, practice writing with more objective accurateness by taking an essay exam. Practice these in forty-minute segments or combine three questions to make a complete test.

Question One:
(Suggested Time: forty minutes)

Read the Francis Bacon passage a third time. Then write a well-organized essay which analyzes how Bacon develops the attitude of the speaker toward studies, the assumptions he makes about human nature, and the language devices Bacon uses to convince the reader of the rightness of his position.

Question Two:
(Suggested Time: forty minutes)

"There is no stand or impediment in the wit but may be wrought out by fit studies; like as diseases of the body may have appropriate exercises."

Francis Bacon

Write a carefully reasoned, persuasive essay which defends, challenges, or qualifies this assertion. Use evidence from your personal experience, observations, or reading to support your stance.

Use the checklist on the preceeding pages to grade these two essays.

The Essay—
Checklist for Attitude -

Francis Bacon
from *Of Studies*

STEP 1:   Check each item listed below which accurately describes the positive aspects of the essay being graded. Add one point for each item checked from the list. This side describes the basic requirements for a well-written essay. (Grader one should check column one. Grader two should check column two):

___-___1. The writer demonstrates an understanding of Francis Bacon's complex attitude toward studies.

___-___2. The writer analyzes the assumptions Francis Bacon makes about human nature, and the language devices he uses to convince the reader of the rightness of his position.

___-___3. The writer offers a convincing interpretation of the meaning and significance of the passage.

___-___4. The writer's use of quotes shows an appreciation of the author's style.

___-___5. The writer's explanations of the evidence are clear, concise and consistent with the meaning of the passage.

___-___6. The writer supports the discussion of each language device with apt and specific references to the text.

___-___7. The diction and sentence structure of this essay communicate a clear message.

___-___8. The implicit organization of this essay aids in communicating a clear message.

___-___9. The grammar aids in communicating a clear message.

MAXIMUM SCORE RESULTS: Grader 1 _____
MAXIMUM SCORE RESULTS: Grader 2 _____

STEP 2:   Check each item below which accurately describes the negative aspects of the essay being graded. This side describes how the essay may not be as good as the higher-scoring essays. (Grader one should check column one. Grader two should check column two):

___-___1. The writer's discussion of the Francis Bacon's views are less incisive than those of the highest scoring essays.

___-___2. The writer discusses the rhetorical and stylistic devices with limited purpose or accuracy.

___-___3. The writer's interpretation of the passage may be vague or pedestrian or incorrect.

___-___4. The writer's use of quotes is awkward, inappropriate, or uninteresting.

___-___5. The writer simply catalogues the rhetorical or stylistic devices without relating them to the creation of the author's (Speaker's or character's) attitude.

___-___6. Although adequate in quantity, the evidence in this writer is not as thorough, precise, or convincing as the top-scoring essays.

___-___7. Distracting errors in diction or syntax make the message unclear.

___-___8. The organization of this essay is less appropriate than those of the top-scoring essays.

___-___9. The writer makes consistent errors in grammar and/or other basic elements of composition.

RESULTS:

Grader 1: _____ - _____ = _____
               Step 1 Score   Step 2 Score

Grader 2: _____ - _____ = _____
               Step 1 Score   Step 2 Score

Grader 1 Score + Grader 2 Score = _____

Above sum
divided by 2 =

Score for essay

The Essay—
Checklist
Defend, Challenge,
or Qualify
Francis Bacon's *Of Studies*

STEP 1:   Check each item listed below which accurately describes the positive aspects of the essay being graded. Add one point for each item checked from the list. This side describes the basic requirements for a well-written essay. (Grader one should check column one. Grader two should check column two):

___-___1. The writer correctly defines Francis Bacon's assertion that "wit . . . may be wrought out by fit studies"

___-___2. The writer has reached some conclusions about the assertion.

___-___3. The writer supports his/her position with specific and accurate evidence from personal observations, experiences, and/or reading.

___-___4. The writer has connected the evidence to the thesis with some insights about human nature.

___-___5. The writer has convinced the reader of the validity of his/her assertion based on an effective use of persuasive devices (arguments, assumptions, logos, ethos, and pathos, etc.).

___-___6. The writer supports the discussion of each personal observation, experience, or reading with strong evidence (unified, specific, accurate, adequate, and representative).

___-___7. The diction and sentence structure of this essay communicates a clear message.

___-___8. The organization of this essay aids in communicating a clear message.

___-___9. The grammar aids in communicating a clear message.

MAXIMUM SCORE RESULTS: Grader 1 _____
MAXIMUM SCORE RESULTS: Grader 2 _____

STEP 2:   Check each item below which accurately describes the negative aspects of the essay being graded. This side describes how the essay may not be as good as the higher-scoring essays. (Grader one should check column one. Grader two should check column two):

___-___1. The writer does not explore the accuracy of the assertion as well as those of the top-scoring essays.

___-___2. Little attempt has been made to apply the aphorism or validate the assertion to modern society. The writer simply explains the author's (or article's) views or writes a wholly unrelated essay.

___-___3. The evidence is not well chosen, well used, or sufficient for the purpose.

___-___4. Superficial, confused or contradictory thinking are combined with an uninteresting or obvious thesis.

___-___5. The writer relies on illicit appeals or uses illogical thinking.

___-___6. Although adequate in number, the evidence in this essay is not as convincing as the top-scoring essay.

___-___7. A few lapses in diction or syntax may be present, but the message is clear.

___-___8. The organization of this essay is less appropriate than those of the top-scoring essays.

___-___9. The writer makes consistent errors in grammar and/ or other basic elements of composition.

RESULTS:

Grader 1: _____ - _____ = _____
                 Step 1 Score   Step 2 Score
Grader 2: _____ - _____ = _____
                 Step 1 Score   Step 2 Score
Grader 1 Score + Grader 2 Score = _____

Above sum
divided by 2 =

Score for essay

John Milton

from *Areopagitica*

Exercise Two: Part One

Read the selection carefully. Then, to learn to read with more objective accurateness, practice paraphrasing by making a word-for-word rewriting of Milton's excerpt.

Here is the passage:

I deny not, but that it is of greatest concernment in the Church and the Commonwealth, to have a vigilant eye how books demean themselves as well as men; and therefore to confine, imprison, or do sharpest justice on them as malefactors. For books are not absolutely dead things, but do contain a potency of life in them to be as active as that soul was whose progeny they are; nay, they do preserve as in a vial the purest efficacy and extraction of that living intellect that bred them. I know they are as lively, and as vigorously productive, as those fabulous dragon's teeth; and being sown up and down, may chance to spring up armed men. And yet, on the other hand, unless wariness be used, as good almost kill a good man as kill a good book. Who kills a man kills a reasonable creature, God's image; but he who destroys a good book, kills reason itself, kills the image of God, as it were in the eye. Many a man lives a burden to the earth; but a good book is the precious life-blood of a master-spirit, embalmed and treasured up on purpose to a life beyond life. 'Tis true, no age can restore a life, whereof perhaps there is no great loss; and revolutions of ages do not oft recover the loss of a rejected truth, for the want of which whole nations fare the worse.

We should be wary therefore what persecution we raise against the living labors of public men, how we spill that seasoned life of man, preserved and stored up in books; since we see a kind of homicide must be thus committed, sometimes a martyrdom, and if it extend to the whole impression, a kind of massacre; whereof the execution ends not in the slaying of an elemental life, but strikes at tht ethereal and fifth essence, the breath of reason itself, slays an immorality rather than a life.

Exercise Two: Part Two

After completing the paraphrase, answer the multiple choice questions that follow. The suggested time for each quiz is fifteen minutes.

1. When Milton begins with "I deny not . . ." he is
    (A) making concessions to his opponent
    (B) representing the important opposing arguments
        fairly
    (C) using a reasonable tone
    (D) making an attempt to embody some evidence of
        personal knowledge of the subject
    (E) using good sense, perspective, and taste in
        judgment

2. The word "malefactors," as used in the context of the opening, is most nearly synonymous with
    (A) criminals
    (B) complainers
    (C) grouches
    (D) repiners
    (E) malcontents

3. In the phrase "preserve as in a vial the purest efficacy and extraction of that living intellect that bred them," the author has created a(n)
    (A) metaphor
    (B) simile
    (C) antithesis
    (D) euphism
    (E) syllogism

4. What is the antecedent of "they" in the phrase " I know they are as lively . . .?"
    (A) dragon's teeth
    (B) living intellect
    (C) books
    (D) church
    (E) Commonwealth

5. In the line "I know they are as lively, and as vigorously productive, as those fabulous dragon's teeth; Milton refers to a Greek myth in which Cadmus slew a dragon and sowed its teeth from which sprang a lot of armed men. They fought each other until five remained. These five helped Cadmus build the city of Thebes. This practice of referring to an expected known story is called a(n)

    (A) analogy
    (B) allusion
    (C) personification
    (D) satire
    (E) understatement

6. All of the following represent figurative language EXCEPT:

    (A) "books demean themselves"
    (B) "have a vigilant eye "
    (C) " books . . . do contain a potency of life in them
    (D) " they are as lively. . . as vigorously productive, as
    (E) "good almost kill a good man as kill a good book"

7. When Milton says, "Who kills a man kills a reasonable creature, God's image; but he who destroys a good book, kills reason itself," he is

    (A) representing the opposing arguments fairly
    (B) amplifying perspectives through an analogy
    (C) quoting authorities
    (D) arousing desires useful to the persuader
    (E) arousing indignation for the opponent

8. In the last sentence of the first paragraph, Milton concludes that the worst crime people can commit is to

    (A) restore life
    (B) reject truth
    (C) persecute men
    (D) kill a man
    (E) embalm a book

9. All of the following words are examples of hyperbole EXCEPT:

    (A) "persecution"
    (B) "preserved"
    (C) "martyrdom"
    (D) "homicide"
    (E) "execution"

10. Milton's argument is based on a single analogy in which he compares and contrasts men with

    (A) the Commonwealth

    (B) the Church

    (C) malefactors

    (D) progeny

    (E) books

11. All of the following comparisons are made by Milton EX-CEPT:

    (A) "Books . . . contain a potency of life . . .as active as that soul whose progeny they are"

    (B) Books "preserve as in a vial . . . that living intellect that bred them"

    (C) "He who destroys a good book, kills reason itself"

    (D) "Wariness . . . kill(s) and man as kill(s) a book"

    (E) "A good book is the precious life-blood of a mas-ter-spirit"

Exercise Two: Part Three

After completing the multiple-choice exam, practice writing with more objective accurateness by taking an essay exam. Practice these in forty-minute segments or combine three questions to make a complete test.

Question One:
(Suggested Time: forty minutes)

In *Areopagitica,* John Milton addressed the Parliament of Great Britain, arguing for freedom of the press. Read the passage carefully. Then write a carefully reasoned essay evaluating Milton's defense for the "Liberty of Unlicensed Printing."

Question Two:
(Suggested Time: forty minutes)

In *Areopagitica,* John Milton addressed the Parliament of Great Britain, arguing for freedom of the press. Read the passage carefully. Then write a persuasive essay which dends, chal-lenges, or qualifies the relevance of Milton's stance in today's world. Use evidence from your personal experience, observa-tions, or reading to support your position.

The Essay—Checklist
for John Milton's
Areopagitica —
Evaluates his Assertion

STEP 1:   Check each item listed below which accurately describes the positive aspects of the essay being graded. Add one point for each item checked from the list. This side describes the basic requirements for a well-written essay. (Grader one should check column one. Grader two should check column two):

___-___1. The writer clearly identifies John Milton's assertions about freedom.

___-___2. The writer analyzes the balances of logos, pathos, and ethos used by John Milton in this passage.

___-___3. The writer has reached valid, pertinent, and relevant conclusions about John Milton's assertion.

___-___4. The writer has analyzed the validity of the assertion based on the passage's effective use of persuasive devices (arguments, assumptions, logos, ethos, and pathos, etc.).

___-___5. The thesis and topic sentences show a clear understanding of how the persuasive devices in the passage are used to sway the reader.

___-___6. The writer supports the discussion of each persuasive device with strong evidence (a minimum of three embedded bits of quotes per paragraph).

___-___7. The diction and sentence structure of this essay communicates a clear message.

___-___8. The organization of this essay aids in communicating a clear message.

___-___9. The grammar aids in communicating a clear message.

MAXIMUM SCORE RESULTS: Grader 1 _____
MAXIMUM SCORE RESULTS: Grader 2 _____

STEP 2: Check each item below which accurately describes the negative aspects of the essay being graded. This side describes how the essay may not be as good as the higher-scoring essays. (Grader one should check column one. Grader two should check column two):

___-___1. The writer simply identifies Milton's assertion (or the three devices, or both) with no discussion.

___-___2. The writer discusses the rhetorical and stylistic strategies with limited purpose or accuracy.

___-___3. The writer misreads the John Milton's assertion.

___-___4. The writer simply catalogues the persuasive devices without relating them to the authors' use of those devices to convince the reader.

___-___5. The connection between the evidence and the author's assertion is less clear than those of the top-scoring essays.

___-___6. Although adequate in number, the evidence in this essay is not as convincing as the top-scoring essay.

___-___7. A few lapses in diction or syntax may be present, but the message is clear.

___-___8. The organization of this essay is less appropriate than those of the top-scoring essays.

___-___9. The writer makes consistent errors in grammar and/or other basic elements of composition.

RESULTS:

Grader 1: _____ - _____ = _____
          Step 1 Score   Step 2 Score

Grader 2: _____ - _____ = _____
          Step 1 Score   Step 2 Score

Grader 1 Score + Grader 2 Score = _____

Above sum divided by 2 =

Score for essay

The Essay—Checklist
Defend, Challenge, Qualify
John Milton's *Areopagitica*

STEP 1:   Check each item listed below which accurately describes the positive aspects of the essay being graded. Add one point for each item checked from the list. This side describes the basic requirements for a well-written essay. (Grader one should check column one. Grader two should check column two):

___-___1. The writer correctly defines John Milton's defense for the "Liberty of Unlicensed Printing."

___-___2. The writer has reached some conclusions about relevancy of Milton's stance in today's world.

___-___3. The writer supports his/her position with specific and accurate evidence from personal observations, experiences, and/or reading.

___-___4. The writer has connected the evidence to the thesis with some insights about human nature.

___-___5. The writer has convinced the reader of the validity of his/her assertion based on an effective use of persuasive devices (arguments, assumptions, logos, ethos, and pathos, etc.).

___-___6. The writer supports the discussion of each personal observation, experience, or reading with strong evidence (unified, specific, accurate, adequate, and representative).

___-___7. The diction and sentence structure of this essay communicates a clear message.

___-___8. The organization of this essay aids in communicating a clear message.

___-___9. The grammar aids in communicating a clear message.

MAXIMUM SCORE RESULTS: Grader 1 _____
MAXIMUM SCORE RESULTS: Grader 2 _____

STEP 2: Check each item below which accurately describes the negative aspects of the essay being graded. This side describes how the essay may not be as good as the higher-scoring essays. (Grader one should check column one. Grader two should check column two):

___-___1. The writer does not explore the accuracy of the assertion as well as those of the top-scoring essays.

___-___2. Little attempt has been made to apply the aphorism or validate the assertion to modern society. The writer simply explains the author's (or article's) views or writes a wholly unrelated essay.

___-___3. The evidence is not well chosen, well used, or sufficient for the purpose.

___-___4. Superficial, confused or contradictory thinking are combined with an uninteresting or obvious thesis.

___-___5. The writer relies on illicit appeals or uses illogical thinking.

___-___6. Although adequate in number, the evidence in this essay is not as convincing as the top-scoring essay.

___-___7. A few lapses in diction or syntax may be present, but the message is clear.

___-___8. The organization of this essay is less appropriate than those of the top-scoring essays.

___-___9. The writer makes consistent errors in grammar and/ or other basic elements of composition.

RESULTS:

Grader 1: _____ - _____ = _____
           Step 1 Score   Step 2 Score

Grader 2: _____ - _____ = _____
           Step 1 Score   Step 2 Score

Grader 1 Score + Grader 2 Score = _____

Above sum
divided by 2 =

Score for essay

William Hazlitt

"Characteristics"

Exercise Three: Part One

Read the selection carefully. Then, to learn to read with more objective accurateness, practice paraphrasing by making a word-for-word rewriting of Hazlitt's excerpt.

Here is the passage:

To speak highly of one of whom we are intimate, is a species of egotism. Our modesty as well as our jealousy teaches us caution on this subject.

What makes it so difficult to do justice to others is, that we are hardly sensible of merit, unless it falls in with our own views and line of pursuit; and where this is the case, it interferes with our own pretentions. To be forward to praise others, implies either great eminence, that can afford to part with applause; or great quickness of discernment, with confidence in our own judgments; or great sincereity and love of truth, getting the better of our self-love.

Society is a more level surface than we imagine. Wise men or absolute fools are hard to be met with, as there are few giants or dwarfs. The heaviest charge we can bring against the general texture of society is, that it is common-place; and many of those who are singular, had better be common-place. Our fancied superiority to others is in some one thing, which we think most of, because we excel in it, or have paid most attention to it; whilst we overlook their superiority to us in something else, which they set equal and exclusive store by. This is fortunate for all the parties. I never felt myself superior to any-one, who did not go out of his way to affect qualities which he had not. In his own individual character and line of pursuit, every one has knowledge, experience, and skill: — and who shall say which pursuit requires most, thereby providing his own narrowness and incompetence to decide? Particular talent or genius does not imply general capacity. Those who are most versatile are seldom great in any one department: and the stupidest people can generally do something. The highest pre-eminence in any one study commonly arises from the concentration of the attention and faculties on that one study. He who expects from a great from a great name in politics, in philosophy, in art, equal greatness in other things, is little versed in human nature. Our strength lies in our weakness. The learned in books is ignorant of the world. He who is ignorant of books is often well-acquainted with other things: for life is of the same length in the learned and the unlearned; the mind cannot be idle; if it is not taken up with one thing; it attends to another through choice or necessity; and the degree of previous capacity in one class or another is a mere lottery.

There are few things in which we deceive ourselves more than in the esteem we profess to entertain for our friends. It is little better than a piece of quackery. The truth is, we think of them as we please — that is, *they* please or displease us. As long as we are in good humour with them, we see nothing but their good qualities; but no sooner do they offend us than we rip up all their bad ones (which we before made a secret of, even to ourselves) with double malice. He who but now was little less than an angel of light shall be painted in the blackest colours for a slip of the tongue, "some trick not worth an egg," for the slighest suspicion of an offense given or received. We often bestow the most opprobrious epithets on our best friends, and retract them twenty times in the course of a day, while the man himself remains the same. In love, which is all rhapsody and passion, this is excusable; but in the ordinary intercourse of life, it is preposterous.

It is well that there is no one without fault; for he would not have a friend in the world. He would seem to belong to a differents species.

Exercise Three: Part Two

After completing the paraphrase, answer the multiple choice
questions that follow. The suggested time for each quiz is fifteen minutes.

1. To speak highly of one of whom we are intimate, is ALL of
the following EXCEPT:

    (A) a part of the doctrine of selfcenteredness

    (B) a part of the doctrine of altruism

    (C) a species of egotism

    (D) an immodest practice

    (E) cautioned by our jealous nature

2. What makes it so difficult to do justice to others is, that we
are hardly sensible of

    (A) excellence in others

    (B) excellence in ourselves

    (C) honor in general

    (D) esteem in our vocation

    (E) pride in education

3. The word "pretentions" as it is used in the line "it interferes
with our own pretentions" is best interpreted to mean ALL of
the following EXCEPT:

    (A) claims

    (B) boastful self importance

    (C) pomposity

    (D) ostentation

    (E) demureness

4. All of the following are statements offered by Hazlitt meant
to be taken as facts to prove that "society is a more level surface than we imagine. "

    (A) Wise men or absolute fools are hard to find.

    (B) There are few giants or dwarfs.

    (C) the texture of society ic commonplace

    (D) Our fancied superiority to others is in some one
        thing, which we think most of"

    (E) We . . . set equal and exclusive store in the superi
        ority of others."

5. All of the following are meant to prove that people are basically narrowminded and incompetent EXCEPT:

    (A) Most people go out of their way to affect qualities that they don't have.

    (B) Everyone has knowledge, experience, and skill in their own individual character and line of pursuit.

    (C) Genius in one area imply genius in general capacity.

    (D) Those who are most versatile are seldom great in any one department.

    (E) The stupidest people can generally do something.

6. All of following are used as examples of the anomolies of human nature EXCEPT:

    (A) Our strength lies in our weakness.

    (B) The learned in books is ignorant of the world.

    (C) He who is ignorant of books is often well-acquainted with other things.

    (D) Life is of the same length in the learned and the unlearned.

    (E) The degree of previous capacity in one class or another is a mere lottery.

7. Which of the following best describes the tone of the speaker's voice in the passage?

    (A) critical

    (B) fearful

    (C) fascinated

    (D) incredulous

    (E) indifferent

8. Which of the following phrases best define Hazlitt's attitude toward human characteristics?

    (A) reverence for God's earthly creatures

    (B) self-satifaction with human dominion

    (C) disgust with the evil that mortals do

    (D) awe at the diversity oh human talents

    (E) admiration for the basic goodness of humans

9. The organization of the passage can be best described as

    (A) expository

    (B) narrative

    (C) descriptive

    (D) speculative

    (E) anecdotal

10. Which of the following stylistic devices are used most predominantly by Hazlitt in the passage?

    (A) elaborately structured metaphors
    (B) melodramatic episodes
    (C) argument by analogy
    (D) ambiguous references to mythology
    (E) deliberate creation of puzzling paradoxes

Exercise Three: Part Three

After completing the multiple-choice exam, practice writing with more objective accurateness by taking an essay exam. Practice these in forty-minute segments or combine three questions to make a complete test.

Question One: Agree or Disagree
(Suggested Time: forty minutes)

In "Characteristics," William Hazlitt claims that "we are hardly sensible of merit, unless it falls in with our own views and line of pursuit; and where this is the case, it interferes with our own pretentions. To be forward to praise others, implies either great eminence, that can afford to part with applause; or great quickness of discernment, with confidence in our own judgments; or great sincereity and love of truth, getting the better of our self-love." Write a persuasive essay which defends, challenges, or qualifies the relevance of Hazlitt's stance in today's world. Use evidence from your personal experience, observations, or reading to support your position.

Question Two: Agree or Disagree
(Suggested Time: forty minutes)

In "Characteristics," William Hazlitt claims that "We often bestow the most opprobrious epithets on our best friends, and retract them twenty times in the course of a day, while the man himself remains the same. In love, which is all rhapsody and passion, this is excusable; but in the ordinary intercourse of life, it is preposterous." Write a persuasive essay which defends, challenges, or qualifies the relevance of Hazlitt's stance in today's world. Use evidence from your personal experience, observations, or reading to support your position.

Question Three: Agree or Disagree
(Suggested Time: forty minutes)

In "Characteristics," William Hazlitt claims that "Simplicity of character is the natural result of profound thought." Write a persuasive essay which defends, challenges, or qualifies the relevance of Hazlitt's stance in today's world. Use evidence from your personal experience, observations, or reading to support your position.

Question Four: Agree or Disagree
(Suggested Time: forty minutes)

In "Characteristics," William Hazlitt claims that "Want of principle is power. Truth and honesty set a limit to our efforts, which impudence and hypocrisy easily overleap."" Write a persuasive essay which defends, challenges, or qualifies the relevance of Hazlitt's stance in today's world. Use evidence from your personal experience, observations, or reading to support your position.

Use the checklist on the following pages to grade any Defend, challenge or qualify question.

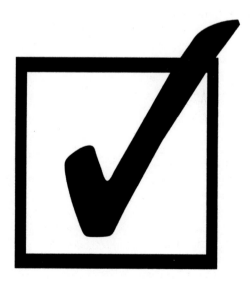

The Essay—Checklist for any Defend, Challenge, or Qualify Question

STEP 1: Check each item listed below which accurately describes the positive aspects of the essay being graded. Add one point for each item checked from the list. This side describes the basic requirements for a well-written essay. (Grader one should check column one. Grader two should check column two):

___-___1. The writer correctly defines the author's assertion.

___-___2. The write makes conclusions about relevancy of the author's stance in today's world.

___-___3. The writer supports his/her position with specific and accurate evidence from personal observations, experiences, and/or reading.

___-___4. The writer has connected the evidence to the thesis with some insights about human nature.

___-___5. The writer has convinced the reader of the validity of his/her assertion based on an effective use of persuasive devices (arguments, assumptions, logos, ethos, and pathos, etc.).

___-___6. The writer supports the discussion of each personal observation, experience, or reading with strong evidence (unified, specific, accurate, adequate, and representative).

___-___7. The diction and sentence structure of this essay communicates a clear message.

___-___8. The organization of this essay aids in communicating a clear message.

___-___9. The grammar aids in communicating a clear message.

MAXIMUM SCORE RESULTS: Grader 1 _____
MAXIMUM SCORE RESULTS: Grader 2 _____

STEP 2:   Check each item below which accurately describes the negative aspects of the essay being graded. This side describes how the essay may not be as good as the higher-scoring essays. (Grader one should check column one. Grader two should check column two):

___-___1. The writer does not explore the accuracy of the assertion as well as those of the top-scoring essays.

___-___2. Little attempt has been made to apply the aphorism or validate the assertion to modern society. The writer simply explains the author's (or article's) views or writes a wholly unrelated essay.

___-___3. The evidence is not well chosen, well used, or sufficient for the purpose.

___-___4. Superficial, confused or contradictory thinking are combined with an uninteresting or obvious thesis.

___-___5. The writer relies on illicit appeals or uses illogical thinking.

___-___6. Although adequate in number, the evidence in this essay is not as convincing as the top-scoring essay.

___-___7. A few lapses in diction or syntax may be present, but the message is clear.

___-___8. The organization of this essay is less appropriate than those of the top-scoring essays.

___-___9. The writer makes consistent errors in grammar and/ or other basic elements of composition.

RESULTS:

Grader 1: _____ - _____ = _____
              Step 1 Score   Step 2 Score

Grader 2: _____ - _____ = _____
              Step 1 Score   Step 2 Score

Grader 1 Score + Grader 2 Score = _____

Above sum
divided by 2 =

Score for essay

"Three Incidents"

from *The New Yorker*

Exercise Four: Part One

In this complete, unsigned essay, which appeared in *The New Yorker*, the writer is surprised by a conclusion reached inductively.   Read the selection carefully.   Then, to learn to read with more objective accurateness, practice paraphrasing by making a word-for-word rewriting of the article.

Here is the passage:

I am fully aware that anecdotal evidence is no longer, if it ever was, in good scientific repute. Nevertheless, in the course of the past few months I have been witness to three aberrations of nature that seem to me to be worth noting. They suggest, if nothing else, that, contrary to much received understanding, man is not the only form of life that is capable of making a fool of itself.

The first of these incidents occurred in the spring, just under the eaves on our front veranda. There is a fixture up there, a galvanized-iron box about the size and shape of a thick paperback book (it has something to do with the outdoor lights), that forms a kind of shelf. I came out on the veranda one morning in time to see a bird — a little red-breasted house finch — make a landing there on the top of the box and deposit a beakful of grass. I stood on tiptoe and craned my kneck, and saw the beginnings of a nest. It was in many ways an excellent nesting site — dry, airy, nicely sheltered. But it was also slippery as glass. And, as I watched, a gust of breeze came along and the nest slid off and blew away in pieces. Well, that, I thought, is that. The bird, however, thought differently. It went to work again, retrieving the scattered grasses, and started another nest. Another doomed nest, I should say. Because another little breeze came along and scattered that nest, too. But the finch was undismayed. I watched it start yet another nest, and I watched that nest blow away. That was enough for me. I went on with my own affairs. But every now and then through the rest of the day I went over to the door or the window and looked out. The finch was always there — sitting on the box, fluttering away, swooping back with a wisp of grass. And there still was nothing more than the pathetic beginnings of a nest.

The second incident occurred in the house, in the attic. I went up there a couple of weeks ago to look for something or other. I was feeling my way toward an old chest of drawers when something odd caught my eye. It was a strand of ivy espaliered on the wall above the little end window. It was two or three feet long, its leaves were sickly yellowy green, and it had forced itself, at God knows what exertion, through a tiny crack in the window frame from the life-giving sunlight into the deadly dusk of the attic.

And then just the other day, I was out weeding the garden and sat down on the bench to rest and noticed an anthill at my feet. There was much coming and going around the hole — a stream of foraging workers. I leaned down and watched a worker emerge from the hole, race away through the grass, pounce on a tiny something — a seed maybe, or an egg, or a miniscule creature — and head quickly back to the hole. Only, it headed in the wrong direction. It reaced this way and that, back and forth, farther and farther away from home. I had to get up from the bench to follow it. I finally lost it, in a weedy jungle, a good eight feet (the equivalent, perhaps, of a couple of miles) from where it wanted to be.I went back to the bench and sat down again and wondered. It might be possible, I thought, to somehow see the strivings of the finch as an example of determination, an iron procreative perserverance. And the ivy: its suicidal floundering, too, might be explained — as an evolutionary thrust, an urge (like that of some aquatic organism feeling its way up the beach) to try a new environment. But the ant! There was no way of rationalizing that: the phenomenon of a worker ant — an ant bred exclusively to forage for its queen — unable to find its way home. It shook and shattered the concept of a knowing and nurturing instinct, of a computerized infallibility, in nature. I felt a tug of something like sympathy for that errant ant. And also for the finch and the ivy. They gave me a new vision of nature: a nature unmechanized, a nature vulnerable, a nature appealingly natural.

Exercise Four: Part Two

After completing the paraphrase, answer the multiple choice questions that follow. The suggested time for each quiz is fifteen minutes.

1. The phrase "anecdotal evidence" in the context of the first sentence, "I am fully aware that anecdotal evidence is no longer, if it ever was, in good scientific repute," means all of the following EXCEPT:
  (A) based of personal experience
  (B) based on random observations
  (C) unverified by scientific evidence
  (D) based on systemized knowledge
  (E) based on little known facts

2. In the first paragraph, the writer suggests that a conclusion has been reached through inductive reasoning. That means that the writer has
  (A) added one piece of information to another until a
        conclusion was made
  (B) used earlier conclusion drawn to answer new
        questions about material
  (C) used a syllogism, composed of two statements,
        called premises, to reach a further conclusion
  (D) reaffirmed a previous conclusion by living an
        experience
  (E) established the authority of the person citing the
        facts and figures

3. Putting the phrase "it has something to do with the outdoor lights" in parentheses serves to
  (A) indicate a sharp shift in the thinking process
  (B) make the remark seem confidential
  (C) whisper an aside to the reader
  (D) announce items in a series
  (E) elaborate on the general subject with specifics

4. Using dashes to separate the phrase "a little red-breasted house finch" serves to
  (A) indicate a sharp shift in the thinking process
  (B) make the remark seem confidential
  (C) whisper an aside to the reader
  (D) announce items in a series
  (E) elaborate on the general subject with specifics

5. The sentence "The finch was always there — sitting on the box, fluttering away, swooping back with a wisp of grass" is a cumulative sentence because it begins with an independent clause and ends with a number of dependent phrases. Since these dependent phrases act as adjectives describing the finch, they are called

    (A) participle phrases

    (B) absolute phrases

    (C) noun phrases

    (D) verb fprms

    (E) descriptive phrases

6. The following sentence indicates the speaker of the passage is making an emotional observation:

    (A) "Another little breeze came along and scattered that nest, too."

    (B) "I watched it start yet another nest, and I watched that nest blow away."

    (C) "Every now and then through the rest of the day I went over to the door or the window and looked out. "

    (D) "The finch was always there — sitting on the box, fluttering away, swooping back with a wisp of grass."

    (E) "And there still was nothing more than the pathetic beginnings of a nest."

7. Which of the following phrases is an example of personification, giving human qualities to an inanimate thing?

    (A) "The second incident occurred in the house, in the attic."

    (B) "I went up there a couple of weeks ago to look for something or other."

    (C) "I was feeling my way toward an old chest of drawers when something odd caught my eye."

    (D) "It was a strand of ivy espaliered on the wall above the little end window. "

    (E) " Iit had forced itself, at God knows what exertion, through a tiny crack in the window frame"

8. The phrase "deadly dusk" is another example of a personification," but it is also an example of a(an)

    (A) simile

    (B) alliteration

    (C) anomaly

    (D) rhyme

    (E) haiku

9. The author of this article seems to use dashes to

    (A) whisper a witty aside to the reader

    (B) announce a series

    (C) elaborate on a previously stated general idea

    (D) rename a person, place, or thing

    (E) create a more active verb

10. Parallelism is created in the sentence, "I leaned down and
watched a worker emerge from the hole, race away through
the grass, pounce on a tiny something..." through the author's
repetitious use of the verbs "emerge... race" and "pounce"
followed by a

    (A) dependent clause

    (B) independent clause

    (C) participle phrase

    (D) prepositional phrase

    (E) cumulative phrase

Exercise Four: Part Four

After completing the multiple-choice exam, practice writing
with more objective accurateness by taking an essay exam.
Practice these in forty-minute segments or combine three questions to make a complete test.

Question One:
Evaluating an Argument
(Suggested Time: forty minutes)

In the following unsigned essay, which appeared in *The New
Yorker* in 1980, the writer is surprised by a conclusion reached
inductively. Read the article carefully. then write a carefully
reasoned, persuasive essay which analyzes the logical thinking used to reach the conclusion.

Remember:
Close Reading

Means Reading the
Passage Three Times

The Essay—Checklist
"Three Incidents" from
The New Yorker—
Evaluate the Argument

STEP 1:   Check each item listed below which accurately describes the positive aspects of the essay being graded. Add one point for each item checked from the list. This side describes the basic requirements for a well-written essay. (Grader one should check column one. Grader two should check column two):

___-___1. The writer clearly analyzes how the inductive method is used by the writer to reach the surprising conclusion made.

___-___2. The writer analyzes the fairness of the three examples used and the believabilty of the conclusion reached in this passage.

___-___3. The writer has reached valid, pertinent, and relevant conclusions about the effectiveness of the writer's argument.

___-___4. The writer has analyzed the validity of the assertion based on the passage's effective use of persuasive devices (arguments, assumptions, logos, ethos, and pathos, etc.).

___-___5. The thesis and topic sentences show a clear understanding of how the persuasive devices in the passage are used to sway the reader.

___-___6. The writer supports the discussion of each persuasive device with strong evidence (a minimum of three embedded bits of quotes per paragraph).

___-___7. The diction and sentence structure of this essay communicates a clear message.

___-___8. The organization of this essay aids in communicating a clear message.

___-___9. The grammar aids in communicating a clear message.

MAXIMUM SCORE RESULTS: Grader 1 _____
MAXIMUM SCORE RESULTS: Grader 2 _____

STEP 2:   Check each item below which accurately describes the negative aspects of the essay being graded. This side describes how the essay may not be as good as the higher-scoring essays. (Grader one should check column one. Grader two should check column two):

___-___1. The writer simply identifies the inductive method used with no discussion.

___-___2. The writer discusses the rhetorical and stylistic strategies with limited purpose or accuracy.

___-___3. The writer misinterprets the writer's conclusion.

___-___4. The writer simply catalogues the persuasive devices without relating them to the authors' use of those devices to convince the reader.

___-___5. The connection between the evidence and the author's assertion is less clear than those of the top-scoring essays.

___-___6. Although adequate in number, the evidence in this essay is not as convincing as the top-scoring essay.

___-___7. A few lapses in diction or syntax may be present, but the message is clear.

___-___8. The organization of this essay is less appropriate than those of the top-scoring essays.

___-___9. The writer makes consistent errors in grammar and/ or other basic elements of composition.

RESULTS:

Grader 1: _____ - _____ = _____
            Step 1 Score   Step 2 Score

Grader 2: _____ - _____ = _____
            Step 1 Score   Step 2 Score

Grader 1 Score + Grader 2 Score = _____

Above sum
divided by 2 =

Score for essay

CHAPTER Five:

The Classroom 40 Minute Essay

TONE, ATTITUDE, or View

The Classroom 40 Minute Essay - Part One: Analyzing Tone, Attitude, View

Any classroom essay that asks for an analysis is accompanied by an excerpt of a work of literature. You are expected to read the accompanying excerpt carefully — this usually means you have to read it three times — and refer to this passage directly or indirectly when answering the question. Learning to read the question and determine what the question is asking is the first step in reading the passage with an understanding that is necessary for clear writing.

Since all writing has an author's voice, a persona, it is natural that a lot of questions about literature would focus on the author's view, attitude, or tone. The key is to be able to recognize this as a focus in the prompt of the question. Here are some typical questions on tone, attitude, or view — although some may be disguised with slightly different wording. Study them so you can recognize their pattern when they appear on a test you have to write:

Question One:

The following paragraphs constitute the introduction of
E. M. Forster's essay "My Wood," written in 1936. In the
essay, Forster reflects on his reaction to owning the small
estate he bought with royalties from his novel A Passage to
India.

**Read the passage carefully. Then write a well-organized es-
say that defines Forster's attitude toward owning this property and analyze how he creates this attitude through such
rhetorical and stylistic devices as word choice, manipulation
of sentences, and Biblical allusions.**

The key phrase that describes the focus of the essay is the reference to Foster's "reaction to owning the small estate he
bought." Based on this key phrase, each topic sentence must
focus on "Forster's (shifting) attitude toward owning this property." Read the accompanying passage carefully to determine
Forster's true attitude toward owning property.

E. M. Foster "My Wood"

A few years ago I wrote a book which dealt in part
with the difficulties of the English in India. Feeling that they
would have no difficulties in India themselves, the Americans
read the book freely. The more they read it the better it made
them feel, and a cheque to the author was the result. I bought
a wood with the cheque. It is not a large wood — it contains
scarcely any trees, and it is intersected, blast it, by a public
footpath. Still, it is the first property that I have owned, so it is
right that other people should participate in my shame, and
should ask themselves, in accents that will vary in horror, this
very important question: What is the effect of the property
upon the character? Don't let's touch economics; the effect of
private ownership upon the community as a whole is another
question — a more important question perhaps, but another
one. Let's keep to psychology. If you own things, what's their
effect on you? What's the effect on me of my wood?
   In the first place, it makes me feel heavy. Property
does have this effect. Property produces men of weight, and it

was a man of weight who failed to get into the kingdom of heaven.* He was not wicked, that unfortunate millionaire in the parable, he was only stout; he stuck out in front, not to mention behind, and as he wedged himself this way and that in the crystalline trance and bruised his well-fed flanks, he saw beneath him a comparatively slim camel passing through the eye of a needle and being woven into the robe of God. The Gospels all through couple stoutness and slowness. They point out what is perfectly obvious, yet seldom realized: that if you have a lot of things you cannot move about a lot, that furniture requires dusting, dusters require servants, servants require insurance stamps, and the whole tangle of them makes you think twice before you accept an invitation to dinner or go for a bathe in Jordan.** Sometimes the Gospels proceed further and say with Tolstoy that property is sinful; they approach the difficult ground of asceticism here, where I cannot follow them. But as to the immediate effects of property on people, they just show straightforward logic. It produces men of weight. Men of weight cannot, by definition, move like the lightning from the East unto the West, and the ascent of a four-teen-stone*** bishop into a pulpit is thus the exact antithesis of the coming of the son of man. My wood makes me feel heavy.

* Matthew 19:24 "It is easier for a camel to go through the eye of a needle than for a rich man to enter the kingdom of heaven."
** The Jordan is the River in which John the Baptist christened repentant sinners.
*** A stone is a British unit of weight; 14 stones equal 196 pounds.

The Introduction

No points are given for making an inane general statement about owning property; no points are given for summarizing the question, complete with author and title. If you have marked up the passage, brainstorming for ten to fifteen minutes before writing, you should be able to make a fairly intelligent statement about your initial reaction to the reading, concluding with some sort of hypothesis about E. M. Foster's attitudes. Keep your introduction brief and connected to answering the question. The body and conclusion are the paragraphs that count in a timed essay.

Structure your body paragraphs around "CSI"

Claim: Your topic sentence is your claim, your analysis about what Foster's attitude is at the beginning of the passage. Change your paragraph when Foster's reaction to owning property changes.

Support: The middle of each paragraph should be your analysis of how Foster creates this attitude through such rhetorical and stylistic devices as word choice, manipulation of sentences, and Biblical allusions — whatever is appropriate for the particular part of the passage you are analyzing. Your support should refer to the text directly — using embedded quotes — or indirectly. The purpose of the support section of the paragraph is to show how E. M. Foster manipulates the language to help us experience his reaction to owning property.

Interpretation: Each paragraph should end with a personal interpretation — a judgment about the effectiveness of the author's language choices. Here, also, is where you can make insightful comments about the ambiguities of the subtle messages given in Foster's passage. Here's where you can get a nine by saying something about the passage beyond what is most easy to grasp.

The Conclusion

The conclusion should be the strongest part of your essay. This represents the culmination of your findings; this represents the original incites that you have discovered after the close reading you have done. If you find you are running out of time, start your conclusion. Finish strong! Your final sentence should be a personal judgement about the overall effectiveness of Forster's language choices.

Checklists

Use the specific checklist on the nest two pages to score the essay you wrote on Forster's "My Wood." Study the similar checklists on later pages so you can recognize their pattern of requirements and apply them to the next essay you have to write on attitude.

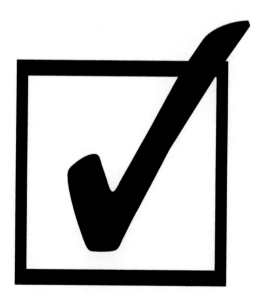

Checklist for E. M. Forster's **Attitude** in "My Wood"

STEP 1:   Check each item listed below which accurately describes the positive aspects of the essay being graded. Add one point for each item checked from the list. This side describes the basic requirements for a well-written essay. (Grader one should check column one. Grader two should check column two):

___-___1. The writer recognizes the playful seriousness of Forster's account of how his "wood" makes him feel heavy.

___-___2. The writer recognizes Forster's ultimate disapproval of material concerns.

___-___3. The writer analyzes how such rhetorical and stylistic devices such as word choice, manipulation of sentences, and Biblical allusions convey his complex stance.

___-___4. The writer's use of embedded quotes shows an appreciation of the Forster's style.

___-___5. The writer's explanations of the evidence are clear, concise and consistent with the meaning of the passage.

___-___6. This writer supports the discussion of each language device with apt and specific references to the text.

___-___7. The diction and sentence structure of this essay communicate a clear message.

___-___8. The implicit organization of this essay aids in communicating a clear message.

___-___9. The grammar aids in communicating a clear message.

MAXIMUM SCORE RESULTS: Grader 1 _____
MAXIMUM SCORE RESULTS: Grader 2 _____

STEP 2:   Check each item below which accurately describes the negative aspects of the essay being graded. This side describes how the essay may not be as good as the higher-scoring essays. (Grader one should check column one. Grader two should check column two):

___-___1. The writer's discussion of the Forster's attitude is less incisive than those of the top-scoring essays.

___-___2. The writer's interpretations of Forster's attitude is correct but misses how such things as Forster's account of his *Passage to India* royalties or his colloquial embroidering of Matthew 19:24 is done playfully.

___-___3. The writer discussion of the stylistic devices is limited or inconsistently pertinent.

___-___4. The writer's use of quotes is awkward, inappropriate, or uninteresting.

___-___5. The writer simply catalogues the rhetorical or stylistic devices without relating them to the creation of Forster's attitude.

___-___6. The writer's references to the text are simple paraphrase or summary, rather than the needed analysis.

___-___7. Distracting errors in diction or syntax make the message unclear.

___-___8. The organization of this essay is less appropriate than those of the top-scoring essays.

___-___9. The essay reveals consistent weakness in grammar and/or other basic elements of composition.

RESULTS:

Grader 1: _____ - _____ = _____
           Step 1 Score   Step 2 Score

Grader 2: _____ - _____ = _____
           Step 1 Score   Step 2 Score

Grader 1 Score + Grader 2 Score = _____

Above sum divided by 2 =

Score for essay

Question Two:

In the following paragraphs Lytton Strachey presents his conception of Florence Nightingale. Read the passage carefully. Then write a well-organized essay that defines Strachey's view and analyze how he conveys it. You might want to consider such elements as diction, imagery, syntax and tone.

The key phrase that describes the focus of the essay is the reference to "his conception of Florence Nightingale." Based on this key phrase, each topic sentence must focus on defining "Strachey's view." Read the accompanying passage carefully to define the different views portrayed by Stratchey.

Lytton Strachey

Everyone knows the popular conception of Florence Nightingale.* The saintly, self-sacrificing woman, the delicate maiden of high degree who threw aside the pleasures of a life of ease to succor the afflicted, the Lady with the Lamp, gliding through the horrors of the hospital at Scutari, and consecrating with the radiance of her goodness the dying soldier's couch — the vision is familiar to all. But the truth was different. The Miss Nightingale of fact was not as facile fancy painted her. She worked in another fashion, and towards another end; she moved under the stress of an impetus which finds no place in the popular imagination. A Demon possessed her. Now demons, whatever else they may be, are full of interest. And so it happens that in the real Miss Nightingale there was more that was interesting than in the legendary one . . . .

What was the secret voice in her ear, if it was not a call? Why had she felt, from her earliest years, those mysterious promptings towards . . . she hardly knew what but certainly towards something very different from anything around her? Why, as a child in the nursery, when her sister had shown a healthy pleasure in tearing her dolls to pieces, had *she* shown an almost morbid one in sewing them up again? Why was she driven now to minister to the poor in their cottages, to watch by sick-beds, to put her dog's wounded paw into elaborate splints as if it was a human being? Why had her head filled with queer imaginations of the country house at Embly turned, by some enchantment, into a hospital, with herself as matron moving about among the beds? Why was even her vision of heaven itself filled with suffering patients to whom she was being useful? So she dreamed and wondered, and, taking out her diary, she poured into it the agitation of her soul.. . .

A weaker spirit would have been overwhelmed by the load of such distresses — would have yielded or snapped. But this extraordinary young woman held firm, and fought her way to victory. With an amazing persistency, during the eight years that followed her rebuff over Salisbury Hospital, she struggled and worked and planned. While superficially she was carrying on the life of a brilliant girl in high society, while internally she was a prey to the tortures of regret and remorse, she yet possessed the energy to collect the knowledge and to undergo the experience which alone could enable her to do what she had determined she would do in the end. In secret she devoured the reports of medical commissions, the pamphlets of sanitary authorities, the histories of hospitals and homes. She spent the intervals of the London season in ragged schools and workhouses. When she went abroad with her family, she used her spare time so well that there was hardly a great hospital in Europe with which she was not acquainted, hardly a city whose slums she had not passed through.. . .

Three more years passed, and then at last the pressure of time told; her family seemed to realize that she was old enough and strong enough to have her way; and she became the superintendent of a charitable nursing home in Harley Street. She had gained her independence, though it was not in meager spirit enough; and her mother was still quite resigned: surely Florence might at least spend the summer in the country. At times, indeed, among other intimates, Mrs. Nightingale almost wept. "We are ducks, " she said with tears in her eyes, " who have hatched a wild swan." But the poor lady was wrong; it was not a swan that they had hatched; it was an eagle."
* English nurse and founder of modern nursing (1820-1910)

The Introduction

No points are given for making an inane general statement about nursing; no points are given for summarizing the question, complete with author and title. If you have marked up the passage, brainstorming for ten to fifteen minutes before writing, you should be able to make a fairly intelligent statement about your initial reaction to the reading, concluding with some sort of hypothesis about Lytton Strachey's attitudes. Keep your introduction brief and connected to answering the question. The body and conclusion are the paragraphs that count in a timed essay.

Structure your body paragraphs around "CSI"

Claim: Your topic sentence is your claim, your analysis about what conception of Florence Nightingale is initially introduced by Stratchey. Change your paragraph when Stratchey introduces a new view of Florence Nightingale.

Support: The middle of each paragraph should be your analysis of how Stratchey helps us see these different conceptions of Florence through his use of such rhetorical and stylistic devices as diction, imagery, syntax, tone — what- ever is appropriate for the particular part of the passage you are analyzing. Your support should refer to the text directly — using embedded quotes — or indirectly. The purpose of the support section of the paragraph is to show how Lytton Stratchey manipulates the language to contrast two views of Florence Nightingale: the mythological versus the real.

Interpretation: Each paragraph should end with a personal interpretation — a judgment about the effectiveness of the Stratchey's language choices. Here, also, is where you can make insightful comments about the ambiguities of the subtle messages given in Stratchey's passage. Here's where you can get a nine by saying something about the passage beyond what is most easy to grasp.

The Conclusion

The conclusion should be the strongest part of your essay. This represents the culmination of your findings; this represents the original incites that you have discovered after the close reading you have done.   If you find you are running out of time, start your conclusion. Finish strong!   Your final sentence should be a personal judgement about the overall effectiveness of Stratchey's language choices.

Checklists

Use the specific checklist on the next two pages to score the essay you wrote on Lytton Stratchey's essay. Study the similar checklists on later pages so you can recognize their pattern of requirements and apply them to the next essay you have to write on attitude.

Checklist for Lytton Stratchey's **Views** of Florence Nightingale

STEP 1:   Check each item listed below which accurately describes the positive aspects of the essay being graded. Add one point for each item checked from the list. This side describes the basic requirements for a well-written essay. (Grader one should check column one. Grader two should check column two):

___-___1. The writer clearly defines Stratchey's complex views of Florence Nightingale.

___-___2. The writer recognizes that Stratchey makes his case by contrasting the "real" Nightingale with the sentimental notion of her in the popular imagination defined at the beginning of the passage.

___-___3. The writer analyzes how such rhetorical and stylistic devices as diction, imagery, syntax and tone are used to convey his complex views of Florence Nightingale.

___-___4. The writer's use of embedded quotes shows an appreciation of the Stratchey's style.

___-___5. The writer's explanations of the evidence are clear, concise and consistent with the meaning of the passage.

___-___6. This writer supports the discussion of each language device with apt and specific references to the text.

___-___7. The diction and sentence structure of this essay communicate a clear message.

___-___8. The implicit organization of this essay aids in communicating a clear message.

___-___9. The grammar aids in communicating a clear message.

MAXIMUM SCORE RESULTS: Grader 1 _____
MAXIMUM SCORE RESULTS: Grader 2 _____

STEP 2: Check each item below which accurately describes the negative aspects of the essay being graded. This side describes how the essay may not be as good as the higher-scoring essays. (Grader one should check column one. Grader two should check column two):

___-___1. The writer's discussion of the Stratchey's views of Florence Nightingale is less incisive than those of the top-scoring essays.

___-___2. The writer recognizes the contrast employed by Stratchey but misses the unconventionality of Stratchey's view

___-___3. The writer's discussion of the stylistic devices is less effective, less developed, limited, inconsistently pertinent, meager, or unconvincing.

___-___4. The writer's use of quotes is awkward, inappropriate, or uninteresting.

___-___5. The writer simply catalogues the rhetorical or stylistic devices without relating them to the creation of Stratchey's view of Florence Nightingale.

___-___6. The writer's references to the text, although adequate, may be vague or too generalized, or they may be simple paraphrase or summary, rather than the needed analysis.

___-___7. Distracting errors in diction or syntax make the message unclear.

___-___8. The organization of this essay is less appropriate than those of the top-scoring essays.

___-___9. The essay reveals consistent weakness in grammar and/or other basic elements of composition.

RESULTS:

Grader 1: _____ - _____ = _____
             Step 1 Score   Step 2 Score
Grader 2: _____ - _____ = _____
             Step 1 Score   Step 2 Score
Grader 1 Score + Grader 2 Score = _____

Above sum divided by 2 =

Score for essay

Question Three:

Read the following poem carefully. Then write a well-organized essay in which you analyze how the speaker uses varied imagery to reveal his attitude toward the nature of love.

The key phrase that describes the focus of the essay is "how the speaker uses varied imagery to reveal his attitude toward the nature of love." Since Donne uses shifting images to convey one attitude toward love — its devastating nature — your topic sentence could focus on John Donne's shifting imagery about the nature of love. Note: Most of the time you cannot structure your essay around the manipulation of language. However, this essay id an exception to the rule. Remember to focus your essay of the particular shifts made by the author. In this case the shifts have to do with the imagery.

John Donne "The Broken Heart"

He is stark mad, who ever says,
    That he hath been in love an hour,
Yet not that love so soon decays,
    But that it can ten in less space devour;
5   Who will believe me if I swear
That I have had the plague a year?
    Who would not laugh at me, if I should say,
    I saw a flask of powder burn a day?

Ah, what a trifle is a heart,
10   If once into love's hands it come!
All other griefs allow a part
    To other griefs, and ask themselves but some;
They come to us, but us Love draws,
He swallows us, and never chaws:
15   By him, as by chain'd shot, whole ranks to die,
    He is the tyrant pike, our hearts the fry.

If 'twere not so, what did become
　　Of my heart, when I first saw thee?
I brought a heart into the room,
20　　But from the room, I carried none with me:

If I had gone to thee, I know
Mine would have taught thine heart to show
　　More pity unto me: but Love, alas,
　　At one first blow did shiver it as glass.

25　Yet nothing can to nothing fall,
　　Nor any place be empty quite,
Therefore I think my breast hath all
　　Those pieces still, though they be not unite;
And now as broken glasses show
30　A hundred lesser faces, so
　　My rags of heart can like, wish, and adore,
　　But after one such love, can love no more.

The Introduction

No points are given for making an inane general statement about the nature of love; no points are given for copying
the question, complete with author and title. If you have
marked up the passage, brainstorming for ten to fifteen minutes before writing, you should be able to make a fairly intelligent statement about your initial reaction to the reading, concluding with some sort of hypothesis about John Donne's use
of varied imagery to show the devastating nature of love. Keep
your introduction brief and connected to answering the question. The body and conclusion are the paragraphs that count
in a timed essay.

Structure your body paragraphs around "CSI"

Claim: Your topic sentence is your claim, your analysis about what specific image has been chosen by John Donne in the beginning to convey the speaker's attitude toward the devastating nature of love. Change your paragraph when Donne uses different imagery to show that same attitude toward the destructive nature of love.

Support: The middle of each paragraph should be your analysis of how Stratchey's choice of imagery helps us experience different aspects of the varied ways that love can be devastating.

Interpretation: Each paragraph should end with a personal interpretation — a judgment about the effectiveness of the Stratchey's choice of imagery. Here, also, is where you can make insightful comments about the ambiguities of the subtle messages given in Donne's passage. Here's where you can get a nine by saying something about the passage beyond what is most easy to grasp.

The Conclusion

The conclusion should be the strongest part of your essay. This represents the culmination of your findings; this represents the original incites that you have discovered after the close reading you have done.   If you find you are running out of time, start your conclusion. Finish strong!   Your final sentence should be a personal judgement about the overall effectiveness of Donne's choice of imagery.

Checklists

Use the specific checklist on the next two pages to score the essay you wrote on John Donne's essay.   Study the similar checklists on later pages so you can recognize their pattern of requirements and apply them to the next essay you have to write on attitude.

Checklist for Donne's **Attitude** toward love in "The Broken Heart"

STEP 1:   Check each item listed below which accurately describes the positive aspects of the essay being graded. Add one point for each item checked from the list. This side describes the basic requirements for a well-written essay. (Grader one should check column one. Grader two should check column two):

___-___1. The writer clearly demonstrates an understanding of how the speaker in "The Broken Heart" uses varied imagery to convey his attitude toward the devastating nature of love.

___-___2. The writer recognizes that John Donne describes a complex view of the devastating nature of love.

___-___3. The writer analyzes how each image chosen is used to convey his complex views of the devastation nature of love

___-___4. The writer's use of embedded quotes shows an appreciation of the John Donne's style.

___-___5. The writer's explanations of the evidence are clear, concise and consistent with the meaning of the passage.

___-___6. This writer supports the discussion of each language device with apt and specific references to the text.

___-___7. The diction and sentence structure of this essay communicate a clear message.

___-___8. The implicit organization of this essay aids in communicating a clear message.

___-___9. The grammar aids in communicating a clear message.

MAXIMUM SCORE RESULTS: Grader 1 _____
MAXIMUM SCORE RESULTS: Grader 2 _____

STEP 2: Check each item below which accurately describes the negative aspects of the essay being graded. This side describes how the essay may not be as good as the higher-scoring essays. (Grader one should check column one. Grader two should check column two):

___-___1. The writer demonstrates an understanding of John Donne's poem, but, compared to the best essays, this writer is less thorough or less precise in analyzing how the speaker uses imagery to convey attitude.

___-___2. The writer recognizes the negative view of love that is portrayed by Donne, but portray an oversimplified version of his attitude.

___-___3. The writer's discussion of the varied imagery used by John Donne is less effective, less developed, limited, inconsistently pertinent, meager, or unconvincing.

___-___4. The writer's use of quotes is awkward, inappropriate, or uninteresting.

___-___5. The writer simply catalogues the rhetorical or stylistic devices without relating them to the creation of Stratchey's view of Florence Nightengale.

___-___6. The writer's references to the text, although adequate, may be vague or too generalized, or they may be simple paraphrase or summary, rather than the needed analysis.

___-___7. Distracting errors in diction or syntax make the message unclear.

___-___8. The organization of this essay is less appropriate than those of the top-scoring essays.

___-___9. The essay reveals consistent weakness in grammar and/or other basic elements of composition.

RESULTS:

Grader 1: _____ - _____ = _____
          Step 1 Score   Step 2 Score

Grader 2: _____ - _____ = _____
          Step 1 Score   Step 2 Score

Grader 1 Score + Grader 2 Score = _____

Above sum divided by 2 =

Score for essay

Question Four:

In the passage below, composer Igor Stravinsky compares orchestra conductors to politicians and actors. In a well-organized essay, analyze the language and the rhetorical devices Stravinsky uses to convey his view.

The key phrase that describes the focus of the essay is how Stravinsky analyzes "the language and the rhetorical devices . . . to convey his view. Here again you have to read the passage to determine the shifts. Since Stravinsky uses shifting rhetorical devices to convey one attitude toward conductors — his dislike of contemporary conductors — your topic sentence should focus on Stravinsky's shifting rhetorical devices that are used to help us see why he dislikes contemporary conductors. Note: Most of the time you cannot structure your essay around the manipulation of language. However, for the second time in a row, this essay is an exception to the rule. Remember to focus your essay on the particular shifts made by the author. In this case the shifts have to do with the various techniques used to show a similar dislike for contemporary conductors.

Igor Stravinsky

Conducting, like politics, rarely attracts original minds, and the field is more for the making of careers and the exploitation of personalities — another resemblance to politics — than a profession for the application of exact and standardized disciplines. A conductor may be less equipped for his work than his players, but no one except the players need know it, and his career is not dependent on them in any case, but on the society women (including critics) to whom his musical qualities are of secondary importance. The successful conductor can be an incomplete musician, but he must be a compleat angler. His first skill has to be power politics.

In such people the incidence of ego disease is naturally high to begin with, and I hardly need add that the disease grows like a tropical weed under the sun of a pandering public. The results are that the conductor is encouraged to impose a purely egotistical, false, and arbitrary authority, and that he is accorded a position out of all proportion to his real value in the musical, as opposed to the music-business, community. He soon becomes a "great" conductor, in fact, or as the press agent of one of them recently wrote me, a "titan of the podium," and as such is very nearly the worst obstacle to genuine music-making. "Great" conductors, like "great" actors, are unable to play anything but themselves; being unable to adapt themselves to the work, they adapt the work to themselves, to their "style," their mannerisms. The cult of the "great" conductor also tends to substitute looking for listening, so that to conductor and audience alike (and to reviewers who habitually fall into the trap of describing a conductor's appearance rather than the way he makes music sound, and of mistaking the conductor's gestures for music's meanings), the important part of the performance becomes the gesture.

If you are incapable of listening, the conductor will show you what to feel. Thus the film-actor type of conductor will act out a life of Napolean in his *Eroica,* * wear an expression of noble suffering on the retreat from Moscow (TV having circumvented the comparatively merciful limitation to the dorsal view) and one of ultimate triumph in the last movement, during which he even dances the Victory Ball. If you are unable to listen to the music, you watch the corybantics, * and if you *are* able, you had better not go to the concert.

* Beethoven's Third Symphony, originally dedicated to Napolean

++Wild, frenzied dancing

Checklist for Igor Stavinsky's **Attitude** Toward Conductors

STEP 1:   Check each item listed below which accurately describes the positive aspects of the essay being graded. Add one point for each item checked from the list. This side describes the basic requirements for a well-written essay. (Grader one should check column one. Grader two should check column two):

___-___1. The writer clearly demonstrates an understanding of the passage as a whole.

___-___2. The writer recognizes that Igor Stravinsky describes a complexly negative view of conductors.

___-___3. The writer analyzes specifically the language and rhetorical devices Stravinsky uses, accurately defining or describing his point of view.

___-___4. The writer's use of embedded quotes shows an appreciation of the John Donne's style.

___-___5. The writer's explanations of the evidence are clear, concise and consistent with the meaning of the passage.

___-___6. This writer supports the discussion of each language device with apt and specific references to the text.

___-___7. The diction and sentence structure of this essay communicate a clear message.

___-___8. The implicit organization of this essay aids in communicating a clear message.

___-___9. The grammar aids in communicating a clear message.

MAXIMUM SCORE RESULTS: Grader 1 _____
MAXIMUM SCORE RESULTS: Grader 2 _____

STEP 2:   Check each item below which accurately describes the negative aspects of the essay being graded.

___-___1. The writer' understanding of Igor Stravinsky's passage is correct, but has less detail or fewer supporting examples than the best-scoring essays

___-___2. The writer recognizes the negative view of conductors that is portrayed by Stravinsky, but portray an oversimplified version of his attitude.

___-___3. The writer's discussion of the varied devices used by Stravinsky is less effective, less developed, limited, inconsistently pertinent, meager, or unconvincing.

___-___4. The writer's use of quotes is awkward, inappropriate, or uninteresting.

___-___5. The writer simply catalogues the rhetorical or stylistic devices without relating them to the creation of Stravinsky's view of conductors.

___-___6. The writer's references to the text, although adequate, may be a restatement or summary of the passage with little analysis; an argument consisting largely of assertions without persuasive supporting evidence, or imprecise or incomplete treatment of Stravinsky's point of view. (Responses that merely restate or paraphrase Stravinsky's point of view may earn no higher than a 3.)

___-___7. Distracting errors in diction or syntax make the message unclear.

___-___8. The organization of this essay is less appropriate than those of the top-scoring essays.

___-___9. The essay reveals consistent weakness in grammar and/or other basic elements of composition.

RESULTS:

Grader 1: _____ - _____ = _____
　　　　　Step 1 Score　　　　Step 2 Score

Grader 2: _____ - _____ = _____
　　　　　Step 1 Score　　　　Step 2 Score

Grader 1 Score + Grader 2 Score = _____

Above sum divided by 2 =

Score for essay

Question Five:

Read the following poem carefully. Then write a well-organized essay that discusses how Anne Bradstreet, a colonial
American poet, uses an extended metaphor to express the
complex attitude of the speaker.

The key phrase that describes the focus of the essay is how
Bradstreet expresses "the complex attitude of the speaker."
Because of this question's focus, each topic sentence should be
about Anne Bradstreet's attitude. Then your support, or evidence in the middle of each body paragraph must show how
the extended metaphor expresses her attitude.

Anne Bradstreet
"The Author to Her Book"

Thou ill-formed offspring of my brain,
Who after birth did'st by my side remain,
Till snatched from thence by friends, less wise than true,
(line) Who thee abroad exposed to public view;
5   Made thee in rags, halting, to the press to trudge,
Where errors were not lessened, all may judge.
At thy return my blushing was not small.
My rambling brat (in print) should mother call,
I cast thee by as one unfit for light,
10   Thy visage was so irksome in my sight;
Yet being mine own, at length affection would
Thy blemishes amend, if so I could.
I washed thy face, but more defects I saw,
And rubbing off a spot, still made a flaw.
15   I stretched thy joints to make thee even feet,
Yet still thou run'st more hobbling than is meet;
In better dress to trim the was my mind,
But nought save homespun cloth in the house I find.
In this array, 'mongst vulgars mat'st thou roam;
20   In critic's hands beware thou dost not come;
And take thy way where yet thou art not known.
If for thy father asked, say thou had'st none;
And for thy mother, she alas is poor,
Which caused her thus to send thee out the door.

The Introduction

No points are given for making an inane general statement about children or books; no points are given for copying the question, complete with author and title. If you have marked up the passage, brainstorming for ten to fifteen minutes before writing, you should be able to make a fairly intelligent statement about your initial reaction to the reading, concluding with some sort of hypothesis about Anne Bradstreet's attitude toward the complexities and uncertainties of writing as shown by her extended comparison of her book to an offspring.

Structure your body paragraphs around "CSI"

Claim: Your first topic sentence should be your claim about what specific attitude Anne Bradstreet conveys in the beginning through her descriptions of the controlling metaphor. Following Bradsteet's organization, you should change your paragraph when Bradstreet's attitude changes.

Support: The middle of each paragraph should be your analysis of how the descriptions of Bradstreet's offspring illustrate her attitude toward the complexities and uncertainties of writing

Interpretation: Each paragraph should end with a personal interpretation — a judgment about the effectiveness of the Bradstreet's language choices Here, also, is where you can say something about the passage beyond what is most easy to grasp.

The Conclusion

The conclusion should be the strongest part of your essay. This represents the culmination of your findings; this represents the original incites that you have discovered after the close reading you have done.   If you find you are running out of time, start your conclusion. Finish strong!   Your final sentence should be a personal judgement about the overall effectiveness or power of Bradstreet's message.

Checklists

Use the specific checklist on pages 136 and 137 to score the essay you wrote on Anne Bradstreet's poem. Study the similar checklists on later pages so you can recognize their pattern of requirements and apply them to the next essay you have to write on attitude.

Spend up to 15 minutes brainstorming.

Spend 25 minutes writing the essay.

Time's up!

Checklist for Anne Bradstreet's **Attitude** Toward Writing

STEP 1:   Check each item listed below which accurately describes the positive aspects of the essay being graded. Add one point for each item checked from the list. This side describes the basic requirements for a well-written essay. (Grader one should check column one. Grader two should check column two):

___-___1. The writer clearly demonstrates an understanding the complex attitude of the speaker.

___-___2. The writer recognizes that Bradstreet's view shifts as the poem continues.

___-___3. The writer analyzes how the controlling metaphor in Bradstreet's poem expresses that shifting attitude.

___-___4. The writer's use of embedded quotes shows an appreciation of Anne Bradstreet's style.

___-___5. The writer's explanations of the evidence are clear, concise and consistent with the meaning of the passage.

___-___6. This writer supports the discussion of each language device with apt and specific references to the text.

___-___7. The diction and sentence structure of this essay communicate a clear message.

___-___8. The implicit organization of this essay aids in communicating a clear message.

___-___9. The grammar aids in communicating a clear message.

MAXIMUM SCORE RESULTS: Grader 1 _____
MAXIMUM SCORE RESULTS: Grader 2 _____

STEP 2:   Check each item below which accurately describes the negative aspects of the essay being graded. This side describes how the essay may not be as good as the higher-scoring essays. (Grader one should check column one. Grader two should check column two):

___-___1. The writer' understanding of Anne Bradstreet's poem is correct, but the complexities may be insufficiently identified

___-___2. The writer's recognition of Bradstreet's shifting attitudes may not be as precise or insightful as the best papers.

___-___3. The writer's discussion of Anne Bradstreet's use of the controlling metaphor may be less effective, less developed, limited, inconsistently pertinent, meager, or unconvincing.

___-___4. The writer's use of quotes is awkward, inappropriate, or uninteresting.

___-___5. Although clear, the writer's explanations may only deal with what is most obvious and easy to grasp.

___-___6. The writer's references to the text, although adequate, may be a restatement or summary of the passage with little analysis, or an argument consisting largely of assertions without persuasive supporting evidence. (Responses that merely restate or paraphrase Bradstreet's point of view may earn no higher than a 3.)

___-___7. Distracting errors in diction or syntax make the message unclear.

___-___8. The organization of this essay is less appropriate than those of the top-scoring essays.

___-___9. The essay reveals consistent weakness in grammar and/or other basic elements of composition.

RESULTS:

Grader 1: _____ - _____ = _____
          Step 1 Score   Step 2 Score
Grader 2: _____ - _____ = _____
          Step 1 Score   Step 2 Score
Grader 1 Score + Grader 2 Score = _____

Above sum divided by 2 =

Score for essay

Question Six:

In the following letter, Charles Lamb writes to English Romantic poet, William Wordsworth, to decline Wordsworth's invitation to visit him at his country setting. Read the letter carefully. Then, paying careful attention to the tone of Lamb's letter, write a well-organized essay which analyzes the techniques Lamb uses to decline the invitation.

The key phrase that describes the focus of the essay is " **paying careful attention to the tone of Lamb's letter. . . .**" Because of this question's focus, each topic sentence should be about Charles Lamb's attitude toward Wordsworth, the country, and the city. Here is the passage

Charles Lamb
A Letter to William Wordsworth

I ought before this to have reply'd to your very kind invitation into Cumberland. With you and your Sister I could gang anywhere. But I am afraid whether I shall ever be able to afford so desperate a Journey. Separate from the pleasure of your company, I don't much care if I never see a mountain in my life. I have passed all my days in London, until I have formed as many and intense local attachments, as any of your *Mountaineers* can have done with dead nature. The Lighted shops of the Strand and Fleet Street, the innumerable trades, tradesmen, and customers, coaches, wagons, playhouses, all the bustle and wickedness round about Covent Gardens, the very women of the Town, the Watchmen, drunken scenes, rattles; — life awake, if you awake, at all hours of the night, the impossibility of being dull in Fleet Street, the crowds, the dirt & the mud, the Sun shining upon houses and pavements, the print shops, the old *Book* stalls, parsons cheap'ning books, coffee houses, steams of soup from kitchens, the pantomimes, London itself a pantomime and a masquerade, all these things work themselves into my mind and feed me without a power of satiating me. The wonder of these sights impels me into night walks about the crowded streets, and I often shed tears in the motley Strand from fullness of joy at so much *Life*. — All these emotions must be strange to you. So are your rural emotions to me. But consider, what must I have been doing all my life, not to have lent great portions of my heart with usury to such scenes — ?

My attachments are all local, purely local — . I have no passion (or have had none since I was in love, and then it was the spurious engendering of poetry & books) to groves and valleys. — The rooms where I was born, the furniture which has been before my eyes all my life, a book case which has followed me about (like a faithful dog, only exceeding him in knowledge) wherever I moved, old tables, streets, squares, when I have sunned myself, my old school, — these are my mistresses. Have I not enough, without your mountains?" I do not envy you, I should pity you, did I not know, that the Mind will make friends of anything. Your sun & your moon and skies and hills & lakes affect me no more, or scarcely come to me in more venerable characters, than as a gilded room with tapestry and tapers, where I might live with handsomer visible objects. —

The Introduction

Begin with some intelligent statement about your initial reaction to the reading, concluding with some sort of hypothesis about Lamb'ss use of various stylistic and rhetorical devices to convey his respect for Wordsworth but his dislike for country.

Structure your body paragraphs around "CSI"

Claim: Each topic sentence should be your claim about what specific view is portrayed by Lamb through his use of a particular language or rhetorical device.

Support: The middle of each paragraph should be your analysis of how Lamb's language or rhetoric helps us understand his views.

Interpretation: Each paragraph should end with a judgment about the effectiveness of Lamb's choices.

The Conclusion

The conclusion represents the original incites that you have discovered after the close reading you have done.

Checklist

Use the following checklists to grade your essay:

Checklist for Charles Lamb's **Attitude** Toward Wordsworth, the country, and the city

STEP 1: Check each item listed below which accurately describes the positive aspects of the essay being graded. Add one point for each item checked from the list. This side describes the basic requirements for a well-written essay. (Grader one should check column one. Grader two should check column two):

___-___1. The writer clearly demonstrates an understanding of Lamb's complex, shifting attitude.

___-___2. The writer analyzes how Lamb uses selection of detail, comparison and contrast, and other stylistic devices to defend his rejection of Wordsworth and the country.

___-___3. The writer analyzes the persuasive techniques used by Charles Lamb to decline the invitation.

___-___4. The writer's use of embedded quotes shows an appreciation of Charles Lamb's style.

___-___5. The writer's explanations of the evidence are clear, concise and consistent with the meaning of the passage.

___-___6. This writer supports the discussion of each language device with apt and specific references to the text.

___-___7. The diction and sentence structure of this essay communicate a clear message.

___-___8. The implicit organization of this essay aids in communicating a clear message.

___-___9. The grammar aids in communicating a clear message.

MAXIMUM SCORE RESULTS: Grader 1 _____
MAXIMUM SCORE RESULTS: Grader 2 _____

STEP 2:   Check each item below which accurately describes the negative aspects of the essay being graded.

___-___1. The writer' understanding of Charles Lamb's letter is correct, but the complexities and shifts may be insufficiently identified.

___-___2. The writer's discussion of Charles Lamb's use of selection of detail, comparison and contrast, and other stylistic devices may be less effective, less developed, limited, inconsistently pertinent, meager, or unconvincing.

___-___3. The writer's discussion of Charles Lamb's use of persuasive devices may be less effective, less developed, limited, inconsistently pertinent, meager, or unconvincing.

___-___4. The writer's use of quotes is awkward, inappropriate, or uninteresting.

___-___5. Although clear, the writer's explanations may only deal with what is most obvious and easy to grasp.

___-___6. The writer's references to the text, although adequate, may be a restatement or summary of the passage with little analysis, or an argument consisting largely of assertions without persuasive supporting evidence. (Responses that merely restate or paraphrase Charles Lamb's point of view may earn no higher than a 3.)

___-___7. Distracting errors in diction or syntax make the message unclear.

___-___8. The organization of this essay is less appropriate than those of the top-scoring essays.

___-___9. The essay reveals consistent weakness in grammar and/or other basic elements of composition.

RESULTS:

Grader 1: _____ - _____ = _____
                 Step 1 Score   Step 2 Score

Grader 2: _____ - _____ = _____
                 Step 1 Score   Step 2 Score

Grader 1 Score + Grader 2 Score = _____

Above sum divided by 2 =

Score for essay

The Classroom 40 Minute Essay - Part Two Analyzing Effect

The first type of essay (on tone, attitude, or view) asked you to analyze a passage from the author's perspective. This second type of essay (on effect) asks you to analyze a passage from the reader's perspective. How did you feel?

On the 1999 AP English literature exam, students were asked to show how the techniques used by Cormac McCarthy in the novel *The Crossing* are used to convey the impact of the dramatic experience on the main character.

Question One:

Read the following passage carefully. Then write an essay that analyzes the effect of the passage on the reader. Pay particular attention to how the writer uses diction, syntax, imagery, and tone to produce that effect.

Paret was a Cuban, a proud club fighter who had become welterweight champion because of his unusual ability to take a punch. His style of fighting was to take three punches to the head in order to give back two. At the end of ten rounds, he would still be bouncing, his opponent would have a headache. But in the last two years, over fifteen-round fights, he had started to take some bad maulings.

This fight had its turns, Griffin had most of the early rounds, but Paret knocked Griffin down in the sixth. Griffin had trouble getting up, but made it, came alive and was dominating Paret again before the round was over. Then Paret began to wilt. In the middle of the eighth round, after a clubbing punch had turned his back to Griffin, Paret walked three disgusted steps away, showing his hindquarters. For a champion, he took much too long to turn back around. It was the first hint of weakness that Paret had ever shown, and it must have inspired a particular shame, because he fought the rest of the fight as if he were seeking to demonstrate that he could take more punishment than any man alive. In the twelfth, Griffin caught him. Paret got caught in a corner. Trying to duck away, his left arm and his head became entangled on the wrong side of the top rope. Griffin was like a cat ready to rip the life out of a huge boxed rat. He hit him eighteen right hands in a row, an act which took perhaps three or four seconds. Griffin making a pent-up whimpering sound all the while he attacked, the right hand whipping like a piston rod which had broken through the crankcase, or like a baseball bat demolishing a pumpkin. I was sitting in the second row of that corner — they were not ten feet away from me, and like everybody else, I was hypnotized. I had never seen one man hit another so hard and so many times. Over the referee's face came a look of woe as if some spasm had passed its way through him, and then he leaped on Griffin to pull him away. It was the act of a brave man. Griffith was uncontrollable. His trainer leaped into the ring, his manager, his cut man, there were four people holding Griffith, but he was off on an orgy, he had left the Garden, he was back on a hoodlum's street. If he had been able to break loose from his handler's and the referee, he would have jumped Paret to the floor and whaled on him.

And Paret? Paret died on his feet. As he took those eighteen punches something happened to everyone who was in psychic range of the event. Some part of the death reached out to us. One felt it hover in the air. He was still standing in the ropes, trapped as he had been before, he gave some little half-smile of regret, as if he were saying, " didn't know I was going to die just yet," and then, his head leaning back but still erect, his death came to breathe about him. He began to pass away. As he passed, so his limbs descended beneath him, and he sank slowly to the floor. He went down more slowly than any fighter had ever gone down, he went down like a large ship which turns on end and slides second by second into its grave. As he went down, the sound of Griffith's punches echoed in the mind like a heavy ax in the distance chopping into a wet log.

The Introduction

Begin with some intelligent statement about the changing effects that this reading had on you.

Structure your body paragraphs around:

"CSI"

The body should be organized around the organization of the passage. What effect is produced in the beginning? Make this your opening body paraghraph. How and where does the effect change? Make a new paragraph every time the effect intensifies or changes.

Claim: Each topic sentence should be your claim about what specific effect is produced.
Support: The middle of each paragraph should be your analysis of how the diction, syntax, imagery, and/or tone of that section is used to produce that effect.
Interpretation: Each paragraph should end with a judgment about the effectiveness of the author's language.

The Conclusion

The conclusion represents the original incites that you have discovered after the close reading you have done.

Checklist

Use the checklists on pages 146-147 to grade your essay.

Practice writing under timed conditions. Each of these essays should be finished in one class period.

On the Advanced Placements English Language and English Literature Tests, three essays must be completed in two hours. The suggested time for each essay is forty minutes. If one of these essays is not finished, you will fail!

Time's Up!

Checklist for Effect
"Paret"

STEP 1: Check each item listed below which accurately describes the positive aspects of the essay being graded. Add one point for each item checked from the list. This side describes the basic requirements for a well-written essay. (Grader one should check column one. Grader two should check column two):

___-___1. The writer correctly defines the varying effects produced by the reading.

___-___2. The writer analyzes how the author uses diction, syntax, imagery, and tone to produce that effect.

___-___3. The writer analysis reveals a careful reading of the text.

___-___4. The writer's use of embedded quotes shows an appreciation of theauthor's style.

___-___5. The writer's explanations of the evidence are clear, concise and consistent with the meaning of the passage.

___-___6. This writer supports the discussion of each language device with apt and specific references to the text.

___-___7. The diction and sentence structure of this essay communicate a clear message.

___-___8. The implicit organization of this essay aids in communicating a clear message.

___-___9. The grammar aids in communicating a clear message.

MAXIMUM SCORE RESULTS: Grader 1 _____
MAXIMUM SCORE RESULTS: Grader 2 _____

STEP 2: Check each item below which accurately describes the negative aspects of the essay being graded.

___-___1. The writer' understanding of the overall effect may be correct but the complexities may be insufficiently identified.

___-___2. The writer's discussion of the author's use of literary devices may be less effective, less developed, limited, inconsistently pertinent, meager, or unconvincing.

___-___3. The writer's discussion lacks the details and original isights that come only after a close reading of the text.

___-___4. The writer's use of quotes is awkward, inappropriate, or uninteresting.

___-___5. Although clear, the writer's explanations may only deal with what is most obvious and easy to grasp.

___-___6. The writer's references to the text, although adequate, may be a restatement or summary of the passage with little analysis, or an argument consisting largely of assertions without persuasive supporting evidence. (Responses that merely restate or paraphrase the narrator's point of view may earn no higher than a 3.)

___-___7. Distracting errors in diction or syntax make the message unclear.

___-___8. The organization of this essay is less appropriate than those of the top-scoring essays.

___-___9. The essay reveals consistent weakness in grammar and/or other basic elements of composition.

RESULTS:

Grader 1: _____ - _____ = _____
           Step 1 Score   Step 2 Score

Grader 2: _____ - _____ = _____
           Step 1 Score   Step 2 Score

Grader 1 Score + Grader 2 Score = _____

Above sum divided by 2 =

Score for essay

Franklin D. Roosevelt

First Inaugural Address — March 4, 1933

Exercise:

Elected during the depression, Roosevelt's first inaugural speech had to give hope to a hopeless people. The speech he crafted with the help of Raymond Moley continues to have an important influence in today's political life. Read the speech carefully. Then write a well-organized essay in which you describe the effect the speech had on a deprived nation and analyze how he uses the resources of the language — such as parallel structure that invites a rhythm in delivery, phrasemaking that remains memorable today, metaphors that empower the speech with great images, tone and diction that fit the occasion, repetition that emphasizes the positive power of hope, and loaded words which make effect.

This is a day of national consecration.

I am certain that my fellow Americans expect that on my induction into the presidency I will address them with a candor and a decision which the present situation of our nation impels. This is preeminently the time to speak the truth, frankly and boldly. Nor need we shrink from honestly facing conditions in our country today. This great nation will endure as it has endured, will revive and will prosper. So, first of all, let me assert my firm belief that the only thing we have to fear is fear itself — nameless, unreasoning, unjustified terror which paralyzes needed efforts to convert retreat into advance. In every dark hour of our national life a leadership of frankness and vigor has met with that understanding and support of the people themselves which is essential to victory. I am convinced that you will again give that support to leadership in these critical days.

In such a spirit on my part and on yours we face our common difficulties. They concern, thank God, only material things. Values have shrunken to fantastic levels; taxes have risen; our ability to pay has fallen; government of all kinds is faced by serious curtailment of income; the means of exchange are frozen in the currents of trade; the withered leaves of industrial enterprise lie on every side; farmers find no markets for their produce; the savings of many years in thousands of families are gone.

More important, a host of unemployed citizens face the grim problem of existence, and an equally great number toil with little return. Only a foolish optimist can deny the dark realities of the moment.

Yet our distress comes from no failure of substance. We are stricken by no plague of locusts. Compared with the perils which our forefathers conquered because they believed and were not afraid, we have still have much to be thankful for. Nature still offers her bounty, and human efforts have multiplied it. Plenty is at our doorstep, but generous use of it languishes in the very sight of the supply. Primarily this is because rulers of the exchange of mankind's goods have failed through their own stubbornness and their own incompetence, have admitted their failure, and abdicated. Practices of the unscrupulous money changers stand indicted in the court of public opinion, rejected by the hearts and minds of men.

True they have tried, but their efforts have been cast

the pattern of an outworn tradition. Faced by failure of credit they have proposed only the lending of more money. Stripped by the lure of profit by which to induce our people to follow their false leadership, they have resorted to exhortations, pleading tearfully for restored confidence. They know only the rules of a generation of self-seekers. They have no vision, and when there is no vision the people perish.

The money changers have fled their high seats in the temple of our civilization. We may now restore that temple to the ancient truths. The measure of the restoration lies in the extent to which we apply social values more noble than mere monetary profit.

Happiness lies not in the mere possession of money; it lies in the joy of achievement, in the thrill of creative effort. The joy and moral stimulation of work no longer must be forgotten in the mad chase of evanescent profits. These dark days will be worth all they cost us if they teach us that our true destiny is not to be ministered unto but to minister to ourselves and to our fellow men.

Recognition of the falsity of material wealth as the standard of success goes hand in hand with the abandonment of the false belief that public office and high political position are to be valued only by the standards of pride of place and personal profit; and there must be an end to a conduct in banking and in business which too often has given to a sacred trust the likeness of callous and selfish wrongdoing. Small wonder that confidence languishes, for it thrives only on honesty, on honor, on the sacredness of obligations, on faithful protection, on unselfish performance; without them it cannot live.

Restoration calls, however, not for changes in ethics alone. This Nation asks for action, and action now.

Our greatest primary task is to put people to work. This is no unsolvable problem if we face it wisely and courageously. It can be accomplished in part by direct recruiting by the Government itself, treating the task as we would treat the emergency of a war, but at the same time, through this employment, accomplishing greatly needed projects to stimulate and reorganize the use of our natural resources.

Hand in hand with this we must frankly recognize the overbalance of population in our industrial centers and, by engaging on a national scale in a redistribution, endeavor to provide a better use of the land for those best fitted for the land. The task can be helped by definite efforts to raise the values of agricultural products and with this the power to purchase the output of our cities. It can be helped by preventing realistically the tragedy of the growing loss through foreclosure of our small homes and our farms. It can be helped by insistence that the Federal, State, and local governments act forthwith on the demand that their cost be drastically reduced. It can be helped by the unifying of relief activities which today are often scattered, uneconomical, and unequal. It can be helped by national planning for and supervision of all forms of transportation and of communication and other utilities which have a definitely public character. There are many ways in which it can be helped, but it can never be helped merely by talking about it. We must act and act quickly.

Finally, in our progression toward a resumption of work we require two safeguards against a return of the evils of the old order; there must be a strict supervision of all banking and credits and investments; there must be an end to speculation with other people's money, and there must be provision for adequate and sound currency.

There are lines of attack. I shall presently urge upon a new Congress in a special session detailed measures for their fulfillment, and I shall seek the immediate assistance of several states.

Through this program of action we address ourselves to putting our national house in order an making income balance outgo. Our international trade relations, though vastly important, are in point of time and necessity secondary to the establishment of a sound national economy. I favor as a practical policy the putting of first things first. I shall spare no effort to restore world trade by international economic readjustment, but the energy at home cannot wait on that accomplishment.

The basic thought that guides these specific means of natural recovery is not narrowly nationalistic. It is the insistence, as a first consideration, upon the interdependence of the various elements in all the parts of the Unites States — a recognition of the old and permanently important manifestation of the American spirit of the pioneer. It is the way to recovery. It is the immediate way. It is the strongest assurance that the recovery will endure.

In the field of world policy, I would dedicate this Na

tion to the policy of the good neighbor — the neighbor who resolutely respects himself and, because he does so, respects the rights of others — the neighbor who respects his obligations and respects the sanctity of his agreements in and with a world of neighbors.

If I read the temper of our people correctly, we now realize as we have never realized before our interdependence on each other; that we cannot merely take but we must give as well; that if we are to go forward, we must move as a trained and loyal army willing to sacrifice for the good of a common discipline, because without such discipline no progress is made, no leadership becomes effective. We are, I know, ready and willing to submit our lives and property to such discipline, because it makes possible a leadership which aims at a larger good. This I propose to offer, pledging that the larger purposes will bind upon us all as a sacred obligation with a unity of duty hitherto evoked only in time of armed strife.

With this pledge taken, I assume unhesitating the leadership of this great army of our people dedicated to a disciplined attack upon our common problems.

Action in this image and to this end is feasible under the form of government which we have inherited from our ancestors. Our Constitution is so simple and practical that it is possible always to meets extraordinary needs by changes in emphasis and arrangement without loss of essential form. This is why our constitutional system has proved itself the most superably enduring political mechanism the modern world has produced. It has met every stress of vast expansion of territory, of foreign wars, of bitter internal strife, of world relations.

It is hoped that the normal balance of executive and legislative authority may be wholly adequate to meet the unprecedented task before us. But it may be that an unprecedented demand and need for undelayed action may call for a temporary departure from the normal balance of public procedure.

I am prepared under my constitutional duty to recommend the measures that a stricken nation in the midst of a stricken world may require. These measures, or such other measures as the Congress may build out of its experience and wisdom, I shall seek, within my Constitutional authority, to bring a speedy adoption.

But in the event that Congress shall fail to take one of

these two courses, and in the event that the national emergency is still critical, I shall not evade the clear course of duty that will then confront me. I shall ask the Congress for the one remaining instrument to meet the crisis — broad Executive power to wage a war against the emergency, as great as the power that would be given to me in we were in fact invaded by a foreign foe.

For the trust reposed in me I will return the courage and the devotion that befit the time. I can do no less.

We face the arduous days that lie before us in the warm courage of the national unity; with the clear consciousness of seeking old and precious moral values; with the clean satisfaction that comes from the stem performance of duty by old and young alike. WE aim at the assurance of a rounded and permanent national life.

We do not distrust the future of essential democracy. The people of the United States have not failed. In their need they have registered a mandate that they want direct, vigorous action. They have asked for discipline and direction under leadership. They have made me the present instrument of their wishes. In the spirit of the gift I take it.

In this dedication of a Nation we humbly ask the blessing of God. May he protect each and every one of us. May He guide me in the days to come.

Checklist for Effect Roosevelt's First Inaugural Address — March 4, 1933

STEP 1: Check each item listed below which accurately describes the positive aspects of the essay being graded. Add one point for each item checked from the list. This side describes the basic requirements for a well-written essay. (Grader one should check column one. Grader two should check column two):

___-___1. The writer demonstrates an understanding of the hopelessness of America in 1933 as initially described.

___-___2. The writer demonstrates the intended effect of Roosevelt's speech — to give hope to the hopeless nation.

___-___3. The writer comments with psychological insight on the probable effect the speech had on a deprived nation.

___-___4. The writer analyzes how Roosevelt uses the resources of the language — such as parallel structure that invites a rhythm in delivery, phrasemaking that remains memorable today, metaphors that empower the speech with great images, tone and diction that fit the occasion, repetition that emphasizes the positive power of hope, and loaded words which make you feel good just to hear them spoken — to achieve this effect.

___-___5. The concluding thesis clearly addresses how the "direct, vigorous action" promised by Roosevelt's speech helped rededicate the Nation with hope.

___-___6. The writer persuasively substantiates the discussion of each language device with a minimum of three embedded quotes per paragraph.

___-___7. The diction and sentence structure of this essay communicate an understandable message.

___-___8. The ideas in this essay are expressed in an ordered or logical sequence.

___-___9. The grammar aids in communicating a clear message.

MAXIMUM SCORE RESULTS: Grader 1 _____
MAXIMUM SCORE RESULTS: Grader 2 _____

STEP 2:   Check each item below which accurately describes the negative aspects of the essay being graded. This side describes how the essay may not be as good as the higher-scoring essays. (Grader one should check column one. Grader two should check column two):

___-___1. The writer defines the hopelessness of America at the time but misses "the language of fear" associated with it.

___-___2. The writer fails to say anything beyond what is obvious and easy to grasp about the image of courage, trustworthiness and hope that President Roosevelt portrays.

___-___3. The writer addresses the powerful effect this speech must have had on a deprived nation, but misses the ambiguity of the problem — the diversity of American hopelessness.

___-___4. The writer simply catalogues the rhetorical or stylistic devices without relating them to his power to affect other people.

___-___5. The conclusions reached by this writer offer a correct interpretation of the effect of Roosevelt's speech, but may be too simplistic, too full of cliches, or too vague to be as meaningful as those of the highest-scoring essays.

___-___6. Although adequate in quantity, the evidence in this essay is not as convincing as the top-scoring essay.

___-___7. A few lapses in diction or syntax may be present, but the message is clear.

___-___8. The organization of this essay is less appropriate than those of the top-scoring essays.

___-___9. The essay reveals consistent weakness in grammar and/or other basic elements of composition.

RESULTS:

Grader 1: _____ - _____ = _____
           Step 1 Score   Step 2 Score

Grader 2: _____ - _____ = _____
           Step 1 Score   Step 2 Score

Grader 1 Score + Grader 2 Score = _____

Above sum divided by 2 =

Score for essay

CHAPTER Six:

Evaluating
an Argument

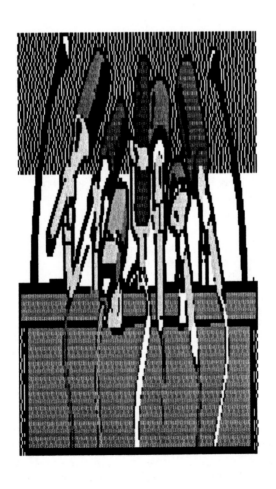

Chapter Six:

Evaluating
an Argument

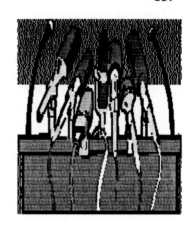

Ask the following questions of any excerpt with persuasive elements:

1. What is the assertion (proposition or claim) made by the author? State this in your own words.

2. What is your initial position on the issue? Do you have any prejudicial attitudes, sentiments, or stereotypes?

3. LOGOS - What arguments (logical reasoning) are made? Do they meet the USA AR test (unified, specific, adequate, accurate, and representative?)
> A. Does the author represent the important opposing arguments fairly. This is usually mentioned early, then refuted throughout the remainder of the essay by confirmation and amplification.
> B. Does the author use specific examples, detailed description, quotations from authorities, facts, statistics, etc. that meet the USA AR test?
> C. Does the author's use of amplification (widening of perspectives through analogies, comparisons or other aspects of experience) meet the USA AR test?
> D. Are there any omissions?

4. PATHOS - What emotional appeals are made?
> A. Does the author arouse desires useful to the persuader's purpose and demonstrate how these desires can be satisfied by acceptance of the persuader's assertion (proposition or proposal or claim)?

B. Does the author's summary include an arousal of indignation for the opponent's view, and an arousal of sympathy for the speaker/writer's view?

C. Be aware of illogical fallacies which are based on appeals to traditions, desires, hatreds, prejudices, etc. Does the writer (speaker or presenter) misuse the evidence or sabotage or distort the argument by relying on any of the following illogical fallacies:

(1.) **Hasty Generalization** - Be suspicious of any unsubstantiated conclusions. Also called "the Bare Assertion." Don't be swayed by a speaker who refuses to back up a disputed claim by simply saying or implying "That's just the way it is." Any sound generalization must be based on a great deal of evidence or on many personal observations.

(2.) **Stereotype** - Do not allow a writer (speaker or presenter) to convince you that allmembers of a certain group share certain characteristics just because they are a member of that group. People should be judged on their individual merits, not on their group identities.

(3.) **Cause-and-effect fallacy** - Avoid the mistake of assuming that just because on event preceded another, the first event caused the second event.

(4.) **Only cause fallacy** - Most situations are complex enough to have several causes. Be open-minded enough to be able to see that more than one cause is possible, and that, similarly, more than one solution exists. Almost no dispute among reasonably intelligent people can be boiled down to "It's as simple as that."

(5.) **False analogy** - Analogies are used to clarify a point. Because false analogies are weak or far-fetched examples, they usually confuse the message.

(6.) **Non sequitur** - Make sure the conclusion logically follows from the premise.

(7.) **Circular reasoning** - This common mistake occurs when no specific reasons are given to back up an opinion. Instead, the writer simply restates the and rephrases the same position.

(8.) **Begging the question** - This occurs when the writer expects the reader to accept a position just because everyone else accepts it.

D. Be aware of illogical fallacies which are based on appeals to traditions, desires, hatreds, prejudices, etc. Does the author (speaker or presenter) misuse the language by trying to persuade you emotionally through any of the following dishonest propaganda techniques:

(1.) **Loaded Words** - Be aware of the strong negative or positive connotations that certain words carry with them. Do not let the use of the words be the only factor involved in reaching a decision. This technique is also known as using "slanted words" because the speaker or writer will choose words because of their persuasive emotional charge. Bertrand Russell once illustrated how words have emotional bias when he chose three synonyms to define different emotional aspects of the word stubborn. "I am firm. You are obstinate. He is pigheaded."

(2.) **Glittering Generalities** - Do not be swayed by words that are so overly positive that you feel good just hearing them.

(3.) **BandWagon** - Do not come to a decision just because you do not want to be left out. These are also called "appeals to popular sentiment" because they are used to seduce the reader or listener into a smiling, mindless agreement.

(4.) **Plain-Folks Appeal** - When the speaker tries to acknowledge the opposition by pretending to be just like all common people, he is using this appeal.

(5.) **Snob Appeal** - When the speaker tries to associate himself/herself with beautiful, wealthy, or special people, he/she is using this appeal.

(6.) **Testimonial** - When a speaker uses an association with a famous person to sell an idea or product, he/she is using this propaganda technique.

E. Appeals to common sense, democratic principle, pride, hope or commitment may be done honestly or dishonestly.

5. ETHOS - What attempts are made to establish the writer's credentials?

A. Does the writer use a reasonable tone, treating the opponent with respect by avoiding such things as illogical statements or inflammatory language?

B. Does the writer have some relevant experience with the issue?

C. Does the writer seem to have any prejudicial attitudes, sentiments, or stereotypes?

D. Does the writer make an attempt to embody some evidence of personal knowledge of the subject, good will toward the reader/audience, good sense, perspective, taste in judgment, or disinterest in personal benefit?

E. Note the features of the writer's style: sentences or vocabulary which was effective, too simple, or too difficult . . . Where was the writing clear? Where was it difficult to track? Where was the language appropriate or inappropriate for the intended audience?

6. Did the article change or modify your initial position on the subject?

Thomas Huxley

"The Method of Scientific Investigation"

This famous nineteenth century lecture on the scientific method is placed in this chapter because of its well-written explanations of the logical processes of induction and deduction. Read the article carefully. Then summarize these logical processes in your own words. Apply Huxley's theories when evaluating the effectiveness of an argument's logic.

The method of scientific investigation is nothing but the expression of the necessary mode of working of the human mind. It is simply the mode at which all phenomena are reasoned about, rendered precise and exact. There is no more difference, but there is just the same kind of difference, between the mental operations of a man of science and those of an ordinary person, as there is between the operations and methods of a baker or of a butcher weighing out his goods in common sales, and the operations of a chemist in performing a difficult and complex analysis by means of his balance and finely graduated weights. It is not that the action of the scales in the one case, and the balance in the other, differ in the principle of their construction or manner of working; but the beam of one is set on an infinitely finer axis than the other, and of course turns by the addition of a much smaller weight.

You will understand this better, perhaps, if you give some familiar example. You have all heard it repeated, I dare say, that men of science work by means of induction and deduction, and that by the help of these operations, they, in a sort of sense, wring from Nature certain other things, which are called natural laws, and causes, and that out of these, by some cunning skill of their own, they build up hypotheses and theories. And it is imagined by many, that the operations of the common mind can be by no means compared with these processes, and that they have to be acquired by a sort of special apprenticeship to the craft. To hear all these large words, you would think that the mind of a man of science must be constituted differently from that of his fellow men; but if you will not be frightened by terms, you will discover that you are quite wrong, and that all these terrible apparatus are being used by yourselves every day and every hour of your lives.

There is a well-known incident in one of Moliere's plays, where the author makes the hero express unbounded delight on being told that he had been talking prose during the whole of his life. In the same way, I trust that you will take comfort and be delighted with yourselves, on the discovery that you have been acting on the principles of inductive and deductive philosophy during the same period. Probably there is not one here who has not in the course of the day had occasion to set in motion a complex train of reasoning, of the very same kind though differing of course in degree, as that which a scientific man goes through in tracing the causes of natural phenomena.

A very trivial example will serve to exemplify this. Suppose you go into a fruiterer's shop, wanting an apple — you take up one, and, on biting it, you find it is sour; you look at it, and see that it is hard and green. You take up another one, and that too is hard, green, and sour. The shopman offers you a third; but, before biting it, you examine it, and find that it is hard and green, and you immediately say that you will not have it, as it must be sour, like those that you have already tried.

Nothing can be more simple than that, you think; but, if you will take the trouble to analyze and trace out into its logical elements what has been done by the mind, you will be greatly surprised. In the first place, you have performed the operation of induction. You found that, in two experiences, hardness and greenness in apples went together with sourness. It was so in the first case, and it was confirmed in the second. True, it is a very small basis, but still it is enough to make an induction from; you generalize the facts, and you expect to find sourness in apples where you get hardness and greenness. You have found upon that a general law, that all hard and green apples are sour; and that, so far as it goes, is a perfect induction. Well, having got your natural law in this way, when you are offered another apple which you find is hard and green, you say, "All hard and green apples are sour; this apple is hard and green, therefore this apple is sour." That train of reasoning is what logicians call a syllogism, and has all its various parts and terms — its major premise, its minor premise, and its conclusion. And, by the help of further reasoning, which, if drawn out, would have to be exhibited in two or three other syllogisms, you arrive at your final determination, "I will not have that apple." So that, you see, you have, in the first place, established a law of induction, and upon that you have founded a deduction, and reasoned out the special conclusion of the particular case. Well now, suppose, having got your law, that at some time afterwards, you are discussing the qualities of apples with a friend: you will say to him, "It is a very curious thing — but I find that all hard and green apples are sour!" Your friend says to you, "But how do you know that?" You at once reply, "Oh, because I have tried them over and over again, and have always found them to be so." Well, if we were talking science instead of common sense, we should call that experimental verification. And, if still opposed, you could go further, and say, "I have heard from people in Somerset shire and Devonshire, where a large number of apples are grown, that they have heard the same thing. It is also found to be the case in Normandy, and in North America. In short, I find it to be the universal experience of mankind wherever attention has been directed to the subject." Whereupon, your friend, unless he is a very unreasonable man, agrees with you, and is convinced that you are quite right in the conclusion you have drawn. He believes, although perhaps he does not know he believes, that the more extensive verifications are — that the more frequently experiments have been made, and the results of the same arrived at — that the more varied the conditions under which the same results are attained, the more certain is the ultimate conclusion, and he disputes the question no further. He sees that the experiment has been tried under all sorts of conditions, as to time, place, and people, with the same result; and he says with you, therefore, that the lay you have laid down must be a good one, and he must believe it.

In science we do the same thing; the philosopher exercises precisely the same faculties, though in a much more delicate manner. In scientific inquiry it becomes a matter of duty to expose a supposed law to every possible kind of verification, and to take care, moreover, that this is done intentionally, and not left to a mere accident, as in the case of the apples. And in science, as in common life, our confidence in a law is in exact proportion to the absence of variation in the result of our experimental verifications. For instance, if you let go your grasp of an article you may have in your hand, it will immediately fall to the ground. That is a very common verification of one of the best established laws of nature — that of gravitation. The method by which men of science established the existence of that law is exactly the same as that by which we have established the trivial proposition about the sourness of hard and green apples. But we believe it in such an extensive, thorough, and unhesitating manner because the universal experience of mankind verifies it, and we can verify it with ourselves at any time; and that is the strongest possible foundation on which any natural law can rest.

So much, then, by way of proof that the method of establishing laws in science is exactly the same as that pursued in common life. Let us now turn to another matter (though really it is but another phase of the same question), and that is, the method by which, from the relations of certain phenomena, we prove that some stand in the position of causes toward others.

I want to put the case clearly before you, and I will therefore show you what I mean by another familiar example. I will suppose that one of you, on coming down in the morning to the parlor of your house, finds that a teapot and some spoons which had been left in the room on the previous evening are gone — the window is open, and you observe the mark of a dirty hand on the window frame, and perhaps, in addition to that, you notice the impress of a hobnailed shoe on the gravel outside. All these phenomena have struck your attention instantly, and before two seconds have passed you say, "Oh, somebody has broken open the window, entered the room, and run off with the spoons and teapot!" That speech is out of your mouth in a moment. And you will probably add, "I know there has; I am sure of it!" You mean to say exactly what you know; but in reality you are giving expression to what is, in all essential particulars, an hypothesis. You do not know it all; it is nothing but an hypothesis rapidly framed in your own mind. And it is an hypothesis founded on a long train of inductions and deductions.

What are those inductions and deductions, and how have you got at this hypothesis? You have observed in the first place, that the window is open; but by a train of reasoning involving many inductions and deductions, you have **prob**

ably arrived long before at the general law — and a very good one it is — that windows do not open of themselves; and you therefore conclude that something has opened the window. A second general law that you have arrived at in the same way is that teapots and spoons do not go out of a window spontaneously, and you are satisfied that, as they are not now where you left them, they have been removed. In the third place, you look at the marks on the windowsill, and the shoe marks outside, and you say that in all previous experience the former kind of mark has never been produced by anything else but the hand of a human being; and the same experience shows that no other animal but man at present wears shoes with hobnails in them such as would produce the marks in the gravel. I do not know, even if we could discover any of those "missing links" that are talked about, that would help us to any other conclusion! At any rate the law which states our present experience is strong enough for my present purpose. You next reach the conclusion, that as these kinds of marks have not been left by any other animals than men, or are liable to be formed in any other way that by man's hand and shoe, the marks in question have been formed by a man in that way. You have, further, a general law, founded on observation and experience, and that, too, is, I am sorry to say, a very universal and unimpeachable one — that some men are thieves; and you assume at once from all these premises — and that is what constitutes your hypothesis — that the man who made the marks outside and on the windowsill, opened the window, got into the room, and stole your teapot and spoons. You have arrived at a vera casa — you have assumed a cause which, it is plain, is competent to produce all the phenomena you have observed. You can explain all the phenomena only by the hypothesis of a thief. But it is a hypothetical conclusion, of the justice of which you have no absolute proof at all; it is only rendered highly probable by a series of inductive and deductive reasonings.

I support your first action, assuming that you are a man of ordinary common sense, and that you have established this hypothesis to your own satisfaction, will very likely be to go off for the police, and set them on the track of the burglar, with the view to the recovery of your property. But just as you are string with this object, some person comes in, and on learning what you are about, says, "My good friend, you are going on a great deal too fast. How do you know that the man who really made the marks took the spoons? It might have been a monkey that took them, and the man may have merely looked in afterwards." You would probably reply, "Well, that is all very well, butyou see it is contrary to all experience of the way treapots and spoons are abstracted; so that, at any rate, your hypothesis is less probable than mine." While you are talking the thing over in this way, another friend arrives, one of that good kind of people that I was talking of a while ago. And he might say, "Oh, my dear sir, you are certainly going on a great deal too fast. You are most presumptuous. You admit that all these occurences took place when you were fast asleep, at a time when you could not have possibly known anything about what was taking place. How do you know that the laws of Nature are not suspended during the night? It may be that there has been some kind of supernatural interference in this case." In point of fact, he declares that your hypothesis is one of which you cannot at all demonstrate the truth, and that you are by no means sure that the laws of Nature are the same when you are asleep as when you are awake.

Well, now, you cannot at the moment answer that kind of reasoning. You feel that your worthy friend has you somewhat at a disadvantage. You will feel perfectly convinced in your own mind, however, that you are quite right, and you say to him, "My good friend, I can only be guided by the natural probabilities of the case, and if you will be kind enough to stand aside and permit me to pass, I will go fetch the police." Well, we will suppose that your journey is successful, and that by good luck you meet with a policemen; that eventually the burgular is found with your property on his person, and the marks correspond to his hand and to his boots. Probably any jury would consider those facts a very good experimental verification of your hypothesis, touching the cause of the abnormal phenomena observed in your parlor, and would act accordingly.

Now, in this supposititious case, I have taken phenomena of a very common kind, in order that you might see what are the different steps in an ordinary process of reasoning, if you will only take the trouble to analyze it carefully. All of the operations I have described, you will see, are involved in the mind of any man of sense in leading him to a conclusion as to the course he should take in order to make good a robbery and punish the offender. I say that you are led, in this case, to your conclusion by exactly the same train of reasoning as that which a man of science pursues when he is endeavoring to discover the origin and laws of the most occult phenomena. The process is, and always must be, the same; and precisely the same mode of reasoning was employed by Newton and Laplace in their endeavors to discover and define the causes of the movements of the heavenly bodies, as you, with your own common sense, would employ to detect a burglar. The only difference is that, the nature of the inquiry being more abstruse, every step has to be more carefully watched, so that there may not be a single crack or flaw in your hypothesis. A flaw or crack in many of the hypotheses of daily life may be of little or no moment as affecting the general correctness of the conclusions at which we arrive; but, in a scientific inquiry, a fallacy, great or small, is always of importance, and is sure to be in the long run constantly productive of mischievous, if not fatal, results.

Do not allow yourself to be misled by the common notion that an hypothesis is untrustworthy simply because it is an hypothesis. It is often urged, in respect to some scientific conclusion, that, after all, it is only an hypothesis. But what more have we to guide us in nine-tenths of the most important affairs of daily life than hypotheses, and often very ill-based ones?

Mark Twain

"The Art of Lying"

Mark Twain wrote the following essay, then read it at the Historical and Antiquarian Club of Hartford as an entrant for a thirty dollar prize. He did not win the prize.

Read the essay. Then write a carefully reasoned essay evaluating Mark Twain's arguments about the "decay of the art of writing." You might consider Twain's unusual use of both logical and emotional appeals, his conscious creation of irony and humor, as well as his conscious use of some of the illogical fallacies defined in this chapter.

Observe, I do not mean to suggest that the custom of lying has suffered any decay or interruption, — no, for the

Lie, as a Virtue, a Principle, is eternal; the Lie, as a recreation, a solace, a refuge in the time of need, the Fourth Grace, the Tenth Muse, man's best and surest friend, is immortal, and cannot perish from the earth while this Club remains. My complaint simply concerns the decay of the art of lying. No high-minded man, no man of right feeling, can contemplate the lumbering and slovenly lying of the present day without grieving to see a noble art so prostituted. In this veteran presence I naturally enter upon this theme with diffidence; it is like an old maid trying to teach nursery matters to the mothers in Israel. It would not become me to criticize you, gentlemen, who are nearly all my elders — and my superiors, in this thing — and so, if I should here and there seem to do it, I trust it will in most cases be more in a spirit of admiration than of fault-finding; indeed if this finest of the fine arts had everywhere received the attention, encouragement, and conscientious practice and development which this Club had devoted to it, I should not need to utter this lament, or shed a single tear. I do not say this to flatter: I say it in a spirit of just and appreciative recognition. (It had been my intention, at this point, to mention names and give illustrative specimens, but indications observable about me admonished me to beware of particulars and confine myself to generalities.

No fact is more firmly established than that lying is a necessity of our circumstances, — the deduction that it is then a Virtue goes without saying. No virtue can reach its highest usefulness without careful and diligent cultivation, — therefore, it goes without saying, that this one ought to be taught in the public schools — at the fireside — even in the newspapers. What chance has the ignorant, uncultivated liar against the educated expert? What chance have I against Mr Per — against a lawyer? Judicious lying is what the world needs. I sometimes think it were even better and safer not to lie at all than to lie injudiciously. An awkward, unscientific lie is often as ineffectual as the truth.

Now let us see what the philosophers say. Note that venerable proverb: Children and fools always speak the truth. The deduction is plain, — adults and wise persons never speak it. Parkman, the historian, says, "The principle of truth may itself be carried into absurdity." In another place in the same chapter he says, "The saying is old that truth should not be spoken at all times; and those whom a sick conscience worries into habitual violation of the maxim are imbeciles and nuisances." It is strong language, but true. None of us could live with an habitual truth-teller; but thank goodness none of us has to. An habitual truth-teller is simply an impossible creature; he does not exist; he never has existed. Of course there are people who think they never lie, but it is not so, — and this ignorance is one of the very things that shame our so-called civilization. Everybody lies — every day; every hour; awake; asleep; in his dreams; in his joy; in his mourning; if he keeps his tongue still, his hands, his feet, his eyes, his attitude, will convey deception — and purposely. Even in sermons — but that is a platitude.

In a far country where I once lived the ladies used to go around paying calls, under the humane and kindly pretense of wanting to see each other; and when they returned home, they would cry out with a glad voice saying, "We made sixteen calls and found fourteen of the out," — not meaning that they found out anything against the fourteen, — no, that was only a colloquial phrase to signify that they were not at home, — and their manner of saying it expressed their lively satisfaction in that fact. Now their pretence of wanting to see the fourteen — and the other two whom they had been less lucky with — was that commonest and mildest form of lying which is sufficiently described as a deflection from the truth. Is it justifiable? Most certainly. It is beautiful, it is noble; for its object is, not to reap profit, but to convey a pleasure to the sixteen. The iron-souled truth-monger would plainly manifest, or even utter the fact that he didn't want to see those people, — and he would be an ass, and inflict a totally unnecessary pain. And next, those ladies in that far country — but never mind, they had a thousand pleasant ways of lying, that grew out of gentle impulses, and were a credit to their intelligence and an honor to their hearts. Let the particulars go.

The men in that far country were liars, every one. Their mere howdy-do was a lie, because they didn't care how you did, except they were undertakers. To the ordinary inquirer you lied in return; for you made no conscientious diagnosis of your case, but answered at random, and usually missed it considerably. You lied to the undertaker, and said your health was failing — a wholly commendable lie, since it cost you nothing and pleased the other man. If a stranger called and interrupted you, you said with your hearty tongue, "I'm glad to see you," and said with your heartier soul, "I wish you were with the cannibals and it was dinner time." When he went, you said regretfully, "Must you go?" and followed it with a "Call again;" but you did no harm, for you did not deceive anybody nor inflict any hurt, whereas the truth would have made you both unhappy.

I think that this courteous lying is a sweet and loving art, and should be cultivated. The highest perfection of politeness is only a beautiful edifice, built, from the base to the dome, of graceful and gilded forms of charitable and unselfish lying.

What I bemoan is the growing prevalence of the brutal truth. Let us do what we can to eradicate it. An injurious truth had no merit over an injurious lie. Neither should ever be uttered. The man who speaks an injurious truth lest his soul be not saved if he do otherwise, should reflect that that sort of soul is not strictly worth saving. The man who tells a lie to help a poor devil out of trouble, is one of whom the angels doubtless say, "Lo, here is an heroic soul who casts his own welfare into jeopardy to succor his neighbor's; let us exalt this magnanimous liar."

An injurious lie is an uncommendable thing; an so, also, and in the same degree, is an injurious truth, — a fact which is recognized by the law of libel.

Among other common lies, we have the silent lie, — the deception which one conveys by simply keeping still and concealing the truth. Many obstinate truth-mongers indulge in this dissipation, imagining that if they speak no lie, they lie not at all. In that far country where I once lived, there was a lovely spirit, a lady whose impulses were always high and pure, and whose character answered to them. One day I was there at dinner, and remarked, in a general way, that we are all liars. She was amazed, and said, "Not all ?" It was before Pinafore's time, so I did not make the response which would naturally follow in our day, but frankly said, "Yes, all — we are all liars; there are no exceptions." She looked almost offended and said, "Why, do you include me ?" "Certainly," I said, "I think you even rank as an expert." She said, "Sh — sh! The children!" So the subject was changed in deference to the children's presence, and we went on talking about other things. But as soon as the young people were out of the way, the lady came warmly back to the matter and said, "I have made it the rule of my life to never tell a lie; and I have never departed from it in a single instance." I said, "I don't mean the least harm or disrespect, but really you have been lying like smoke ever since I have been sitting here. It has caused me a good deal of pain, because I am not used to it." She required of me an instance — just a single instance. So I said, —

"Well, here is the unfilled duplicate of the blank which the Oakland hospitable sent to you by the hand of the sick-nurse when she comes here to nurse your little nephew through his dangerous illness. This blank asks all manner of questions as to the conduct of that sick-nurse: 'Did she ever sleep on her watch? Did she ever forget to give the medicine? ' and so forth and so on. You are warned to be very careful and explicit in your answers, for the welfare of the service requires that the nurses be promptly fined or otherwise punished for derelictions. You told me you were perfectly delighted with that nurse — that she had a thousand perfections and only one fault: you found you could never depend on her wrapping Johnny up half sufficiently while he waited in a chilly chair for her to re-arrange the warm bed. You filled up the duplicate of this paper, and sent it back to the hospital by the hand of the nurse. How do you answer this question, — 'Was the nurse at any time guilty of negligence which was likely to result in the patient's taking cold?' Come — everything is decided by a bet here in California: ten dollars to ten cents you lied when you answered that question." She said, "I didn't. I left it blank!" Just so — you have told a silent lie; you have left it to be inferred that you had no fault to find in that matter." She said, "Oh, was that a lie? And how could I mention her one single fault, and she so good? — it would have been cruel." I said, "One ought always to lie, when one can do good by it; your impulse was right, but your judgment was crude; this comes of unintelligent practice. Now observe the result of this inexpert deflection of yours. You know Mrs. Jones's Willie is lying very low with scarlet fever; well, your recommendation was so enthusiastic that the girl is there nursing him, and the worn-out family have all been trustingly sound asleep for the last fourteen hours, leaving their darling with full confidence in those fatal hands, because you, like George Washington, have a reputation — However, if you are not going to have anything to do, I will come around to-morrow and we'll attend the funeral together, for of course you'll naturally feel a peculiar interest in Willie's case, — as personal a one, in fact, as the undertaker.

But all that was lost. Before I was half-way through she was in a carriage and making thirty miles an hour toward the Jones mansion to save what was left of Willie and tell all she knew about the deadly nurse. All of which was unnecessary, as Willie wasn't sick; I had been lying myself. But that same day, all the same, she sent a line to the hospital which filled up the neglected blank, and stated the facts, too, in the squarest possible manner.

Now, you see, this lady's fault was not in lying, but only in lying injudiciously. She should have told the truth, there, and made it up to the nurse with a fraudulent compliment further along in the paper. She could have said, "In one respect this sick-nurse is perfection, — when she is on watch, she never snores." Almost any little pleasant lie would have taken the sting out of that troublesome but necessary expression of the truth.

Lying is universal — we all do it; we all must do it. Therefore, the wise thing is for us to diligently train ourselves to lie thoughtfully, judiciously; to lie with a good object, and not an evil one; to lie for others' advantage, and not our own; to lie healingly, charitably, humanely, not cruelly, hurtfully, maliciously; to lie gracefully and graciously, not awkwardly and clumsily; to lie firmly, frankly, squarely, with head erect, not haltingly, tortuously, with pusillanimous mien, as being ashamed of our high calling. Then shall we be rid of the rank and pestilent truth that is rotting the land; then shall we be great and good and beautiful, and worthy dwellers in a world where even benign Nature habitually lies, except when she promises execrable weather. Then — But I am but a new and feeble student in this gracious art; I cannot instruct this club.

Joking aside, I think there is much need of wise examination into what sorts of lies are best and wholesomest to be indulged, seeing we must all lie and do all lie, and what sorts it may be best to avoid, — and this is a thing which I feel I can confidently put into the hands of the experienced Club, — a ripe body, who may be termed, in this regard, and without undue flattery, Old Masters.

1882

Evaluating an Argument

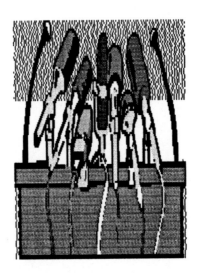

Use the checklists on the following pages to grade your essay.

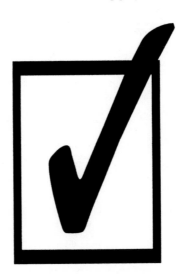

Checklist for Evaluating Mark Twain's "Art of Lying" Argument

STEP 1: Check each item listed below which accurately describes the positive aspects of the essay being graded. Add one point for each item checked from the list. This side describes the basic requirements for a well-written essay.

___-___1. The writer clearly identifies Mark Twain's stance on the art of lying.

___-___2. The writer evaluates Mark Twain's use of illogical fallacies to create humor.

___-___3. The write addressing how Mark Twain biases the letter by shaping the information to match his position.

___-___4. The writer analyzes Mark Twain's's unusual use of logical and emotional appeals, his conscious creation of irony and humor, as well as his conscious use of illogical fallacies.

___-___5. The thesis and topic sentences show a clear understanding of how the persuasive devices in the passage are used to sway the reader.

___-___6. The writer supports the discussion of each persuasive device with strong evidence (a minimum of three embedded bits of quotes per paragraph).

___-___7. The diction and sentence structure of this essay communicates a clear message.

___-___8. The organization of this essay aids in communicating a clear message.

___-___9. The grammar aids in communicating a clear message.

MAXIMUM SCORE RESULTS: Grader 1 _____
MAXIMUM SCORE RESULTS: Grader 2 _____

STEP 2: Check each item below which accurately describes the negative aspects of the essay being graded. This side describes how the essay may not be as good as the higher-scoring essays. (Grader one should check column one. Grader two should check column two):

___-___1. The writer's identification of Mark Twain's argument is less incisive than those of the highest-scoring essays.

___-___2. The writer fails to adequately address Twain's obvious choice of illogical fallacies.

___-___3. The writer discusses Mark Twain's biases with limited purpose or accuracy.

___-___4. The writer simply catalogues some of the illogical fallacies defined in this chapter without relating them to the authors' use of those devices to convince the reader.

___-___5. The connection between the evidence and the author's assertion is less clear than those of the top-scoring essays.

___-___6. Although adequate in number, the evidence in this essay is not as convincing as the top-scoring essay.

___-___7. A few lapses in diction or syntax may be present, but the message is clear.

___-___8. The organization of this essay is less appropriate than those of the top-scoring essays.

___-___9. The writer makes consistent errors in grammar and/or other basic elements of composition.

RESULTS:

Grader 1: _____ - _____ = _____
      Step 1 Score   Step 2 Score

Grader 2: _____ - _____ = _____
      Step 1 Score   Step 2 Score

Grader 1 Score + Grader 2 Score = _____

Above sum divided by 2 =

Score for essay

Editorial

from *The Iowa City Press-Citizen*

This anonymous editorial was published in December 1985 after Dale Burr, a 63 year old farmer, faced with the loss of his farm because he could no longer repay his loans, shot the bank president, his wife, and himself. Read the editorial carefully. Then write a carefully reasoned essay evaluating the argument for reaching out to suffering farmers. Analyze the logical and emotional appeals made as well as the manipulation of syntax, repetition, and other stylistic devices used. Here is the editorial:

Imagine for a minute that tomorrow, your boss tells you that for the next twelve months, you're going to earn only two-thirds of your salary. You can't quit your job.

What would you do? Quick.

The mortgage payment is already a week overdue. The kids ned boots, and it's snowing. Quick.

The last two checks you wrote bounced, and the bank wouldn't pay them. The pediatrician's bill is overdue. The corner grocery store won't let you put anything on your charge account. Quick.

Your spouse is angry; you're not holding up your end of the deal. What are you going to do. Quick.

Your father and grandfather have done the same job as you're doing now. They went through the Depression. They lived on pork and potatoes, and they made it. You are the third generation. You're blowing it. Think fast. You don't have much time. Weeks, maybe months.

The pressure builds, the stress is stronger. You keep going to work, hanging on. It doesn't matter. Nothing you do matters. You are powerless.

This is the kind of thing Dale Burr probably felt. And it is the kind of thing many other Iowa farmers feel every day.

There are accounts of bank transactions and economic explanations and other hypotheses as the murder and suicide story unravels. But that's not what it's really about. It's about people — alone, desperate and powerless with nowhere to turn.

Once the Burr's were one of the wealthier families in the county. They were well-thought-of people. Salt of the earth. Churchgoers. A family of farmers carrying on a tradition. That was a year or two ago. That's how fast things crumble.

Target prices, price supports, ceilings, sealing crops. The terminology doesn't matter. It's welfare. Farmers know it. And farmers are proud people. Nobody really wants to live that way. But for now, there is no choice.

Many Iowa farmers already have deep pay cuts. They've scaled down operations. They've swallowed their pride — gone to stress clinics, sought therapy, stood in line at the market with food stamps in their pockets.

Some of it was bad judgment. Some of it was bad luck. The mid-1970's was a boom time for Iowa agriculture, but everyone else caught on. Physician's fees rose, hospital costs rose, the cost of cars and homes and tractors and loans and mortgages and a college education rose. Then the bottom fell out — for farmers. Now things are so out of kilter that people who once were pillars of the communities are falling into poverty, depression and disrepute.

This is the farm crisis — the people who are alive and hanging on, and those who have died at the hands of anger, frustration, humiliation. And they are here.

Politicians tell us it is only a matter of balancing the books, that if we can reduce the deficit, deflate the value of the dollar, increase exports and give the free market reign — then everything will be all right.

But if there's only thing that is clear from Monday's tragic series of murders and suicide, it is that the farm crisis is *not* numbers and deficits and bushels of corn. It is people and pride and tears and blood.

The time has come for the state and the country to reach out to farmers who are suffering — not because they are failed business men and women, but because they are human beings who are fsalling apart — fast.

Checklist for Evaluating the Argument of the Editorial

STEP 1: Check each item listed below which accurately describes the positive aspects of the essay being graded. Add one point for each item checked from the list. This side describes the basic requirements for a well-written essay.

___-___1. The writer clearly identifies the stance taken in the editorial.

___-___2. The writer analyzes the logical appeals made.

___-___3. The writer analyzes the emotional appeals made.

___-___4. The writer analyzes how the author's manipulation of syntax, use of repetition, and other stylistic devices add to the effectiveness of the argument.

___-___5. The thesis and topic sentences show a clear understanding of how the persuasive devices in the passage are used to sway the reader.

___-___6. The writer supports the discussion of each persuasive device with strong evidence (a minimum of three embedded bits of quotes per paragraph).

___-___7. The diction and sentence structure of this essay communicates a clear message.

___-___8. The organization of this essay aids in communicating a clear message.

___-___9. The grammar aids in communicating a clear message.

MAXIMUM SCORE RESULTS: Grader 1 _____
MAXIMUM SCORE RESULTS: Grader 2 _____

STEP 2:   Check each item below which accurately describes the negative aspects of the essay being graded. This side describes how the essay may not be as good as the higher-scoring essays. (Grader one should check column one. Grader two should check column two):

___-___1. The writer's summary of the editorial's stance is more simplistic than those of the better essays.

___-___2. The writer names the logical appeals but adds no more discussion.

___-___3. The writer names the emotionl appeals but adds no mor discussion.

___-___4. The writer simply catalogues some examples of the author's manipulation of syntax, use of repetition, and other stylistic devices without relating them to the authors' use of those devices to convince the reader.

___-___5. The connection between the evidence and the author's assertion is less clear than those of the top-scoring essays.

___-___6. Although adequate in number, the evidence in this essay is not as convincing as the top-scoring essay.

___-___7. A few lapses in diction or syntax may be present, but the message is clear.

___-___8. The organization of this essay is less appropriate than those of the top-scoring essays.

___-___9. The writer makes consistent errors in grammar and/ or other basic elements of composition.

RESULTS:

Grader 1: _____ - _____ = _____
                 Step 1 Score   Step 2 Score

Grader 2: _____ - _____ = _____
                 Step 1 Score   Step 2 Score

Grader 1 Score + Grader 2 Score = _____

Above sum divided by 2 =

Score for essay

Speech

Dan Rather

"Leadership in the Nineties"

This speech was delivered in the J. W. Marriott Hotel in Washington, D. C., on April 6, 1990, at a luncheon meeting during a three-day convention for the highly influential American Society of Newspaper Editors. The ASNE is influential because its members determine editorial and news policy on daily newspapers and four wire services throughout the United States and Canada. Here is Dan Rather's speech:

Thank you, ladies and gentleman, Jack and I especially appreciate that overly generous introduction. Ladies and gentleman, you know what Abe Lincoln said about introductions such as that: "Never take time to deny them, the audience will find out the truth soon enough for themselves."

I'm also reminded of one of Winston Churchill's trips to the United States, on one of his speaking tours, when he was waiting in the wings to come before a group not too dissimilar from this one. And one of his aides said, "Sir, you should feel terrific. Look at all these people who've come to hear you speak. You must feel a great sense of satisfaction." And Churchill said, "no, not really, because I know three times this many people would pay to see me hanged."

It may be widely believed in this room and beyond that I'm a follower of Colonel McCormick's maxim: "It's our job to print the news and raise hell." I never really think of myself that way; I certainly didn't start out to do that.

I was taught that one of the fundamentals of being a good journalist was to play no favorites, pull no punches and, insofar as is humanly possible, not to operate from a baseline of fear. I was taught that by a man who is in the room this morning, the new editor of the Ankorage Alaska Times , my old Journalism teacher, the only one I had at Sam Houston State Teacher's College, Hugh Cunningham. I hope you'll indulge me ,when I ask you to recognize Hugh, as I recognize the debt that I owe him.

Hugh Cunningham.

Having said to you that, Hugh did not   teach: as a journalist your job is to print the news and raise hell. I do have ringing in my ears of all those times that then-professor Cunningham did   teach: especially that a public journal, whether it be a newspaper or a magazine, a radio station or a television station, a public journal is a public trust.

Having said all that, I'm pretty sure that, when I'm sitting in my rocker on the porch in the old folk's home, that among my regrets will be that I didn't raise enough hell, not that I raised too much.

I do like the fact that the diminishing few good reporters left who believe in asking tough questions are asking some pretty tough questions these days about leadership. Time magazine put it most bluntly last fall with this cover: "Is Government Dead? UNWILLING To Lead, Politicians Are Letting The Country Drift Into Paralysis."

Davis Broder expanded the discussion a few weeks ago in the Washington Post. The headline read: "Nation's Capital In Eclipse As Pride And Power Slip Away."

Broder lays the blame at the feet of the politicians who are too weak to exert American influence in a time of global change. There's a lot of talk around Washington about a pussy-footing Congress and a President who refuses to lead from the front. Mark well, I'm quoting.

Most recently the New York Times did a series on leadership in government being replaced by an obsession with public opinion polls. Michael Orestes came up with some pithy quotes.

From Congressman David Obey, quote: "Is American politics so brain dead that we're reduced to having political shysters manipulate symbols?"

From Lee Atwater: "Bull permeates everything."

That level of frustration and cynicism from government officials is disturbing, and it's news. It's good honest reporting, the kind of tough questioning we're supposed to do to bring it to the public's attention.

And I don't think we should go around apologizing to those who point out, correctly, that we in journalism are long on questions and short on answers. For whatever it's worth, I think people should be suspicious any time reporters start seeing themselves as some kind of shadow government.

I also think people should be suspicious of reporters who are trying too hard to please the people they are covering.

Most importantly, I don't think we should apologize when our questions become too disturbing. We're suppose to be honest brokers of information and our job isn't always to make America feel good about itself. One of the things this country can feel good about is our history, our tradition of being a nation, a society of people who keep facing up to the tough questions and don't duck them.

But as we in journalism ask these tough questions, good honest reporting demands that we also face some facts about newspaper and broadcast news.

One of those facts is when it comes to leadership, we aren't in a very good position to be casting stones. There's the cartoon showing the politician on a stump saying "If it is demonstrated to me that the American want leadership, I will by God, give them leadership." Journalists denounce government by public opinion poll. Good! But we ought to acknowledge that our coverage is more and more driven by what's called market research and public opinion polls.

You and I both know the phone banks are humming. "What kind of news are you most interested in hearing? Are you more interested in medicine, consumer affairs, the Trumps, or Tiananmen Square? Some networks long ago started screening some news programs for what are called focus groups, trying to find out which stories are most popular, not which are most important, which stories are most popular. And you know that focus groups have long been used by a lot of newspapers.

Market research purports to tell us that the public isn't clamoring for more news about government. Stories about the national debt and trade deficits, we're told, don't sell newspapers or broadcasts, and way too many of us use that to avoid covering issues that will shape our lives and those of our children.

Market research and the polls also tell us that international news isn't at the top of the public's interest. So sure enough the trend in coverage is away from, not toward foreign stories.

Last fall one of those fancy thinker tanks in New York that seem to specialize in bashing television news published a study titled "The International Newshole, an Endangered Species." This study was about newspapers. It documents how deeply ten of our most acclaimed newspapers have slashed foreign news coverage in the past two decades. In 1971, over 10 percent of their editorial space was devoted to foreign news. In 1988 foreign coverage dropped to a quarter of that, 2.6 percent, and this is in our best newspapers. Two point six per cent foreign news coverage at the very time when it became indisputably clear that America's future depends on having a better understanding of the world beyond the oceans. Foreign news coverage was slashed by our best newspapers at the very time when we watched our economy falter in the face of foreign competition. I mean this in no self-serving way, because we make a lot of mistakes and in some important ways the evening news is not as good as your average newspaper.

In television, too, there are powerful forces arguing against foreign news. Consultants tell local station news directors that foreign news is a turnoff and you don't see much foreign news on local station newscasts. At the networks now accountants mill and swarm, damning what they see as the comparatively high price tag of foreign coverage. Too often the question now comes up: "Why do you need all those foreign bureaus and foreign correspondents? Why not just buy pictures from somebody else and narrate them from New York?"

For years, newspapers asked one of the right questions, which was, "Isn't it dangerous to have all those anchormen and managing editors making decisions, setting the nation's priorities on the evening news, while cooped-up in windowless rooms on the west side of Manhattan?" Now our accountants' basic question is, "Come on, Dan, do you really ever have to leave New York?"

As our profession, our craft — journalism — becomes more and more competitive, all of us are falling back on tried and true local news formulas. We have by and large accepted the proposition that people don't care about foreign news, don't really care much about hard news, that feel-good news, entertainment and features, and gossip sell better than anything too serious, and certainly sell better than anything very disturbing.

I believe that kind of talk is wrong. I believe that kind

of talk is dangerous. And I know that kind of talk has nothing to do with leadership and public service.

Using public opinion polls as a limited tool is one thing. Using them as an excuse is another. And being slaves to them is yet another and even worse.

Harry Truman once said, "If Moses had taken an opinion poll, he would never have left Egypt.

Partly because of public opinion polls and fear of them, leadership in government has become so rare that the Kennedy library at Harvard will this year bestow its first annual Profile in Courage Award on a public official who follows his conscience instead of the polls.

And sad as that is — and it's pretty sad — I'm afraid we may have to start thinking about a new Pulitzer Prize category, an award for journalistic leadership.

Where are the publishers, editors, and reporters of grit, gumption, and guts? Where are the ones who will follow their consciences, or even a nose for news, instead of public opinion polls? Leadership is of course a problem for us who like to report the news that others make. We are trained to set our opinions aside insofar as that's humanly possible, to try to keep open minds. By and large we aren't joiners, and we know we don't have any secret formulas to answer important questions. So we ask, who are we to lead?

But leadership is a problem for everyone. The members of Broder's pussyfooting Congress have excuses that are just as good as ours, and so do those around the White House. I do think politicians are ducking leadership, and so are we.

George Bernard Shaw once said, "Newspapers are unable to discriminate between a bicycle accident and the collapse of civilization." Today we might say we are unable to discriminate between the breakup of the Trump marriage and the breakup of the Communist world. Leadership is a willingness to distinguish between what's just interesting and what's important.

Now, when someone says that some stories are more important than others, he or she is apt to be labeled an elitist, someone who doesn't understand what quote "real people" care about. That is the defense for trash TV and for trash tabloids, and it's one of the defenses for reducing foreign coverage.

There are a lot of people in my end of the business and

yours who say "real people" won't care unless it bleeds or burns. There are a lot of news doctors out there who say "real people" care only about entertainment , sex, and cats.

They say "real people" want the words American and United States plastered on news like flags on a campaign platform.

I don't buy it. I'm from a family of people who worked their backs and hands. Sam Houston State Teacher's College has about as much Ivy on it as your average McDonald's.

I didn't grow up with, and I didn't go to school with, any of the "real people" these news consultants talk about. I travel a lot and talk to a lot of people, but none fits that description of real people.

The people I meet are concerned about their jobs and their families and their country. They want their lives to have meaning and they worry that their children's lives may not be better than theirs. They are struggling to understand the change they know is happening all around them. I think they would be offended to hear what some editors and reporters say they care about.

Those who say the "real people" only care about trash TV and tabloid front pages are the ones who are out of touch. They are the elitists.

In Search of Excellence became a runaway best-seller because it talked to the real concerns of real people. America's real people want a country of excellence and quality and principle.

Let me relate a story a friend told me. He's rebuilding a house in upstate New York.

One day not too long ago my friend paid a visit to his contractor. After the usual chatter about the weather, the contractor asked, "What about Mandela?" For the next half hour, he says, the discussion with the contractor, the plumber, and the plumber's helper was about South Africa, Mikhail Gorbechev, and how long Fidel Castro can hold out.

Television has become much more than a means of entertainment and information. It is that, but it's become much more. We have become, like it or not, part of a kind of worldwide electronic democracy.

We saw the English-language barriers in Tiananmen Square and heard "We Shall Overcome" in front of the Berlin Wall. Television has become a two-way visual telephone. We talk to the world, and the world talks back to us.

But if we keep shutting down one end of the telephone because it "doesn't sell newspapers" or because "the ratings go down when we're overseas," forget leadership. We may make money. Ratings and circulation may go up. But we won't lead, and we will have prostituted a public trust.

Okay, you say, so what are your answers? What's your idea?

Well, for one, simple as it may sound — and I hope it sounds simple because we can accomplish it — we need a re-dedication to original reporting and original analysis, by first rate writers, reporters, and thinkers. Sometimes that'll mean paying money for more reporters and better minds and giving them a chance to do what they do best and what they want to do.

Television news and newspapers are in danger of sink-ing into a miasma of mediocrity, with a whole new generation of hacks turning out cliched images which match their cliched writing in formats that are degenerating into formulas.

Responsible, honest reporting — play no favorites, pull no punches reporting — says we are losing our appeal to the best and brightest of the next generation. We're now attract-ing in journalism more than our fair share of lightweights and careerists instead of writers, reporters, and dreamers. Too many of us are giving up our reputations as organizations that will pay any price, go any distance to get an important story. Too many of us are becoming known as news packagers, not news gatherers.

We in print and broadcast can dish it out and we should dish it out. Many politicians are not doing their jobs at either end of Pennsylvania Avenue, not around most state capitals, not around most city halls or courthouses.

The Time cover is right: unwilling to lead, politicians are letting America slip into paralysis. But we in journalism must not stop with the politicians. There is such a thing as journalistic leadership and it has nothing to do with arrogance and self-righteousness. It has nothing to do with ratings or circulation or bigger profits. It has to do with public service and caring and patriotism.

The Time article talks about a "frightening inability to define and debate American's emerging problems," "a now-nowism, our collective shortsightedness," and it concludes: the list of missed opportunities and challenges is already much too long. The sooner government sets about doing its job again, the better." To which I say, "Amen."

But I add, the sooner we in the press set about doing our job again, the better.

And now I am glad to take your tough questions. Thank you.

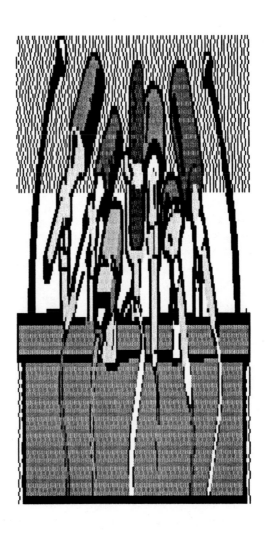

Checklist for Evaluating the Argument of Dan Rather's Speech

STEP 1:   Check each item listed below which accurately describes the positive aspects of the essay being graded. Add one point for each item checked from the list. This side describes the basic requirements for a well-written essay.

___-___1. The writer clearly identifies the stance taken in the by Dan Rather about leadership in the nineties.

___-___2. The writer analyzes how the logical appeals make the argument more effective.

___-___3. The writer analyzes how the emotional appeals make the argument more effective.

___-___4. The writer analyzes how the author's manipulation of diction and syntax, selection of detail, and other stylistic devices helps to convince the audience of journalists and broadcasters to want to start doing their job again.

___-___5. The writer discusses the creditability of the speaker based on the standards of ethos explained in this chapter.

___-___6. The writer supports the discussion of each persuasive device with strong evidence (a minimum of three embedded bits of quotes per paragraph).

___-___7. The diction and sentence structure of this essay communicates a clear message.

___-___8. The organization of this essay aids in communicating a clear message.

___-___9. The grammar aids in communicating a clear message.

MAXIMUM SCORE RESULTS: Grader 1 _____
MAXIMUM SCORE RESULTS: Grader 2 _____

STEP 2: Check each item below which accurately describes the negative aspects of the essay being graded. This side describes how the essay may not be as good as the higher-scoring essays. (Grader one should check column one. Grader two should check column two):

___-___1. The writer's summary of Dan Rather's stance is more simplistic than those of the better essays.

___-___2. The writer names the logical appeals but adds no more discussion.

___-___3. The writer names the emotionl appeals but adds no mor discussion.

___-___4. The writer simply catalogues some examples of the author's manipulation of diction and syntax, selection of detail, and other stylistic devices without relating them to the authors' use of those devices to convince the reader.

___-___5. The discussion of the ethos of the speaker is more limited than those of the highest-scoring essays.

___-___6. Although adequate in number, the evidence in this essay is not as convincing as those of the top-scoring essays.

___-___7. A few lapses in diction or syntax may be present, but the message is clear.

___-___8. The organization of this essay is less appropriate than those of the top-scoring essays.

___-___9. The writer makes consistent errors in grammar and/ or other basic elements of composition.

RESULTS:

Grader 1: _____ - _____ = _____
           Step 1 Score   Step 2 Score

Grader 2: _____ - _____ = _____
           Step 1 Score   Step 2 Score

Grader 1 Score + Grader 2 Score = _____

Above sum
divided by 2 =

Score for essay

Editorial

Joseph Addison

"The Purpose of the Spectator Papers"

The Spectator, a popular periodical which appeared betwen 1711 and 1712, increased its circulation from three thousand to as many as twenty thousand copies of certain issues. The periodical was like a newspaper in that it was issued daily and contained advertisements and classified ads. It was different from our modern day newspapers in that the ads were of Wanted, Lost or Stolen, Amusements, and Merchandise; the writing was of a more polished form; and each issue had only one article. *The Spectator* also was different from today in that its various issues were dedicated to any one of the following Club members: a lawyer, a merchant, an ex-army captain, an elderly gallant, and a country baronet.

The Spectator lasted through five hundred and fifty-five numbers.

The following editorial appeared in *The Spectsator,* No. 10. Rather than defining the purpose of his publication, he is really trying to convince more people in London and Westminster to order this paper daily "for their own good . . . to be punctually served . . . as a part of their tea equipage." Read the selection carefully. Then write a carefully reasoned essay that evaluates the effectiveness of Joseph Addison's persuasion. Here is the editorial:

It is with much satisfaction that I hear this great city inquiring day by day after these papers, and receiving my morning lectures with a becoming seriousness and attention. My publisher tells me that there are already three thousand of them distributed every day: so if I allow twenty readers to every paper, which I look upon as a modest computation, I may reckon about threescore thousand disciples in London and Westminster, who I hope will take care to distinguish them selves from the thoughtless herd of their ignorant and unattentive brethren. Since I have raised to myself so great an audience, I shall spare no pains to make their instruction agreeable, and their diversion useful. For which reasons I will endeavor to enliven morality with wit, and to temper wit with morality, that my readers may, if possible, both ways find their account in the speculation of the day. And to the end that their virtue and discretion may not be short, transient, intermitting starts of thought, I have resolved to refresh their memories from day to day, till I have recovered them out of that desperate state of vice and folly into which the age has fallen. The mind that lies fallow but a single day sprouts up in follies that are only to be killed by a constant and assiduous culture. It was said of Socrates, that he brought philosophy down from heaven, to inhabit among men; and I shall be ambitious to have it said of me that I have brought philosophy out of the closets and libraries, schools and colleges, to dwell in clubs and assemblies, at tea-tables and in coffee-houses.

I would, therefore, in a very particular manner recommend these my speculations to all well-regulated families, that set apart an hour in every morning for tea and bread and butter; and would earnestly advise them for their good to order this paper to be punctually served up, and to be looked upon as a part of the tea equipage.

Sir Francis Bacon observes that a well-written book, compared with its rivals and antagonists, is like Moses' serpent, that immediately swallowed up and devoured those of the Egyptians. I shall not be so vain as to think that where *The Spectator* appears the other public prints will vanish; but shall leave it to my reader's consideration, whether it is not much better to be let in the knowledge of one's self, than to hear what passes in Muscovy or Poland; and to amuse ourselves with such writings as tend to the wearing out of ignorance, passion, and prejudice than such as naturally conduce to inflame hatreds and make enmities irreconcilable?

In the next place, I would recommend this paper to the daily perusal of those gentlemen whom I cannot but consider as my good brothers and allies; I mean the fraternity of spectators who live in the world without having anything to do in it, and either by the affluence of the fortunes or the laziness of their dispositions have no other business with the rest of mankind but to look upon them. Under this class of men are comprehended all contemplative tradesmen, titulat physicians, fellows of the Royal Society, Templars that are nor given to be contentious, and statesmen who are out of business; in short, everyone that considers the world as a theater, and desires to form a right judgment of those who are the actors on it.

There is another set of men that I must likewise lay a claim to, whom I have lately called the blanks of society, as being altogether unfurnished with ideas till the business and conversation of the day has supplied them. I have often considered these poor souls with an eye of commiseration, when I have heard them asking the first man they have met with, whether there was any news stirring? and by that means gathering together materials for thinking. These needy persons do not know what to talk of till about twelve o'clock in the morning; for by that time they are pretty good judges of the weather, know which way the wind sits, and whether the Dutch mail be come in. As they lie at the mercy of the first man they meet, and are grave or impertinent all the day long, according to the notions which they have imbibed in the morning, I would earnestly entreat them not to stir out of their chambers till they have read this paper, and do promise them that will daily instill into them such sound and wholesome sentiments, as shall have a good effect on their conversation for the ensuing twelve hours.

But there are none to whom this paper will be more useful than to the female world. I have often thought there has not been sufficient pains taken in finding out proper employments and diversions for the fair ones. Their amusements seem contrived for them, rather as they are women, than as they are reasonable creatures; and are more adapted to the sex than to the species. The toilet is thier great scene of business, and the right adjusting of their hair the principal employment of their lives. The sorting of a suit of ribbons is reckoned a very good morning's work; and if they make an excursion to a mercer's, or a toy-shop, so great a fatigue makes them unfit for anything else all the day after. Their more serious operations are sewing and embroidery, and their greatest drudgery the preparation of jellies and sweet-meats. This, I say is, the state of ordinary women; though I know there are multitudes of those of a more elevated life and conversation, that move in a exalted sphere of knowledge and virtue, that join all the beauties of the mind to the ornament of the dress, and inspire a kind of awe and respect, as well as love, into their male be holders. I hope to increase the number of these by publishing this daily paper, which I shall always endeavor to make an innocent, if not improving, entertainment, and by that means at least divert the minds of my female readers from greater trifles. At the same time, I would fain give some finishing touches to those which are already the most beautiful pieces in human nature, I shall endeavor to point out all those imperfections that are the blemishes, as well as those virtues which which are the embellishments, of the sex. In the meanwhile I hope these my gentle readers, who have so much time on their hands, will not grudge throwing away a quarter of an hour in a day on this paper, since they may do it without any hindrance to business.

I know several of my friends and well-wishers are in great pain for me, lest I should not be able to keep up the spirit of a paper which I oblige myself to furnish every day; but to make them easy in this particular, I will promise them faithfully to give it over as soon as I grow dull. This I know will be matter of great raillery to the small wits; who will frequently put me in mind of my promise, desire me to keep my word, assure me that it is high time to give over, with many other little pleasantries of the like nature, which men of a little smart genius cannot forbear throwing out against their best friends, when they have such a handle given them of being witty. But let them remember that I do hereby enter my caveat against theis piece of raillery.

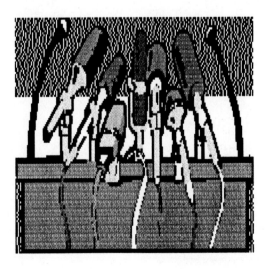

Checklist for Evaluating the Argument of Joseph Addison's Editorial

STEP 1:   Check each item listed below which accurately describes the positive aspects of the essay being graded. Add one point for each item checked from the list. This side describes the basic requirements for a well-written essay.

___-___1. The writer clearly identifies the stance taken by Joseph Addison about the importance of *The Spectator*.

___-___2. The writer analyzes how the logical appeals make the argument more effective.

___-___3. The writer analyzes how the emotional appeals make the argument more effective.

___-___4. The writer analyzes how the author's manipulation of diction and syntax, allusion, or other stylistic devices helps to convince the audience to buy *The Spectator*.

___-___5. The writer discusses the creditability of the speaker based on the standards of ethos explained in this chapter.

___-___6. The writer supports the discussion of each persuasive device with strong evidence (a minimum of three embedded bits of quotes per paragraph).

___-___7. The diction and sentence structure of this essay communicates a clear message.

___-___8. The organization of this essay aids in communicating a clear message.

___-___9. The grammar aids in communicating a clear message.

MAXIMUM SCORE RESULTS: Grader 1 _____
MAXIMUM SCORE RESULTS: Grader 2 _____

STEP 2:   Check each item below which accurately describes the negative aspects of the essay being graded. This side describes how the essay may not be as good as the higher-scoring essays. (Grader one should check column one. Grader two should check column two):

___-___1. The writer's summary of Joseph Addison's stance is more simplistic than those of the better essays.

___-___2. The writer names the logical appeals but adds no more discussion.

___-___3. The writer names the emotionl appeals but adds no mor discussion.

___-___4. The writer simply catalogues some examples of the author's manipulation of diction and syntax, allusion, or other stylistic devices without relating them to the authors' use of those devices to convince the reader.

___-___5. The discussion of the ethos of the speaker is more limited than those of the highest-scoring essays.

___-___6. Although adequate in number, the evidence in this essay is not as convincing as those of the top-scoring essays.

___-___7. A few lapses in diction or syntax may be present, but the message is clear.

___-___8. The organization of this essay is less appropriate than those of the top-scoring essays.

___-___9. The writer makes consistent errors in grammar and/ or other basic elements of composition.

RESULTS:

Grader 1: _____ - _____ = _____
                 Step 1 Score   Step 2 Score
Grader 2: _____ - _____ = _____
                 Step 1 Score   Step 2 Score
Grader 1 Score + Grader 2 Score = _____

Above sum divided by 2 =

Score for essay

Essay

Daniel Defoe

"The Education of Women" from *An Essay Upon Projects*

Daniel Defoe wrote what is considered to be the first novel written in English — *Robinson Crusoe* (1719). He also wrote several other novels including *Moll Flanders* (1722). This excerpt comes from *An Essay Upon Projects* — a book of essays dealing with subjects such as the education of women, roads, banks, jails, asylums, insurance, income tax — subjects which created controversy in Defoe's life. He seemed to always be in trouble because of his opinions. Read the following excerpt on the education of women. Then write a well-organized essay which evaluates the effectiveness of Daniel Defoe's championship of the education of women with his 18th Century, male audience. Here is the essay:

I have often thought of it as one of the most barbarous customs in the world, considering us a civilized and a Christian country, that we deny the advantages of learning to women. We reproach the sex every day with folly and impertinence, while I am confident, had they the advantages of education equal to us, they would be gui;lty of less than ourselves.

One would wonder, indeed, how it should happen that women are conversible at all, since they are only beholding to natural parts for all their knowledge. Their youth is spent to teach them to stitch and sew or make baubles. They are taught to read, indeed, and perhaps to write their names or so, and that is the height of a woman's education. And I would but ask any who slight the sex for their understanding, what is a man (a gentleman, I mean) good for that is taught no more?

I need not give instances, or examione the character of a gentleman with a good estate, and of a good family, and with tolerable parts, and examine what figure he makes for want of an education?

The soul is placed in the body like a rougfh diamond, and must be polished, or the luster of it will never appear: and 'tis manifest that as the rational soul distinguishes us from brutes, so education carries on the distinction and makes some less brutish than others. This is too evident to need any demonstration. But why then should women be denied the benefit of instruction? If knowledge and understanding had been useless additions to the sex, God Almighty would never have given them capacities, for He made nothing needless. Besides, I would ask such what they can see in ignorance that they should think it a necessary ornament to a woman? or how much worse is a wise woman than a fool? or what has the woman done to forfeit the priviledge of being taught? Does she plague us with her pride and importance? Why did we not let her learn, that she might have had more wit? Shall we upbraid women with folly, when 'tis only the error of this inhuman custom that hindered them being made wiser?

The capacities of women are supposed to be greater and their senses quicker than those of the men; and what they may be capable of being bred to is plain from some instances of female wit, which this age is not without; which upbraids us with injustice, and looks as if we denied women the advantages of education for fear they should vie with the men in their improvements.

To remove this objection, and that women might have at least a needful opportunity of education in all sorts of useful learning, I propose the draught of an Academy for that purpose. . . .

The academy I propose should differ little from public schools, wherein such ladies as were willing to study should have all the advantages of learning suitable to their genius. . .

To such whose genius would lead them to it, I would deny no sort of learning; but the chief thing, in general, is to cultivate the understandings of the sex, that they may be capable of all sorts of conversation; that, their parts and their judgments being improved, they may be as profitable in the conversation as they are pleasant. . . .

A woman well bred and well taught, furnished with the additional accomplishments of knowledge and behavior, is a creature without comparison; her society is the emblem of sublimer enjoyments; her person id angelic and her conversation heavenly; she is all softness and sweetness, peace, love, wit, and delight. She is every way suitable to the sublimest wish, and the man that has such a one to his portion has nothing to do but rejoice in her and be thankful.

On the other hand, suppose her to be the very same woman, and rob her of the benefit of education, and it follows thus:

If her temper be good, want of education makes her soft and easy. Her wit, for want of teaching, makes her impertent and talkative. Her knowledge, for want of judgment and experience, makes her fanciful and whimsical. If her temper be bad, want of breeding makes her worse, and she grows haughty, insolent, termagant and a scold, which is much at one with lunatic. If she be proud, want od discretion (which still is breeding) makes her conceited, fantastic, and ridiculous. And from these she degenerates to be turbulent, clangorous, noisy, nasty, and the devil . . . .

I believe it might be defended if I should say that I do suppose God has given to all amnking equal gifts and capacities in that he has given them all souls equally capable, and that the whole difference in mankind proceeds either from accidental difference in the make of their bodies or from the foolish difference of education . . . .

And herein it is that that I take upon me to make such a bold assertion that all the world are mistaken in their practice about women; for I cannot think that God Almighty ever made them so delicate, so glorious creatures, and furnished them with such charms, so agreeable and so delightful to mankind, with souls capable of the same accomplishments, and all to be only stewards of our houses, cooks, and slaves.

Not that I am exalting the female government in the least; but, in short, I would have men take women for companions, and educate them to be fit for it. A woman of sense and breeding will scorn as much as encroah upon the prerogative of the man as a man of sense will scorn to oppress the weakness of the women. But if the women's souls were refined and improved by teaching, that word would be lost; to say, the *weakness of the sex* as to judgment, would be nonsense, for ignorance and folly would be no more found among women than men. I remember a passage which I heard from a very fine woman; she had wit and capacity enough, an extraordinary shape and face, and a great fortune, but had been cloistered up all her time, and, for fear of being stolen, had not had the liberty of being taught the commen necessary knowledge of women's affairs; and when she came to converse in the world, her natural wit made her sensible of the want of education that she gave this short reflection upon herself — "I am ashamed to talk to my very maids," says she, "for I don't know when they do right and when they do wrong. I had more need to go to school than to be married."

I need not enlarge on the loss the defect of education is to the sex, nor argue the benefit of the contrary practice; 'tis a thing will be more esasily granted than remedied. This chapter is but an essay at the thing, and I prefer the practice to those happy days, if ever they shall be, which men shall be wise enough to mens it.

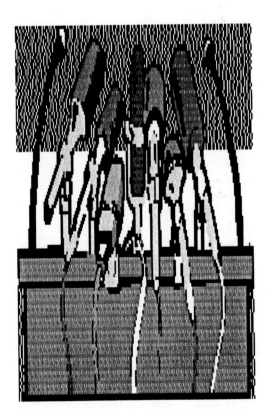

Checklist for Evaluating the Argument of Daniel Defoe's Essay

STEP 1:   Check each item listed below which accurately describes the positive aspects of the essay being graded. Add one point for each item checked from the list. This side describes the basic requirements for a well-written essay.

___-___1. The writer clearly identifies the stance taken by Daniel Defoe about the importance of education for women.

___-___2. The writer analyzes how the logical appeals make the argument more effective.

___-___3. The writer analyzes how the emotional appeals make the argument more effective.

___-___4. The writer analyzes how the author's manipulation of diction and syntax, or other stylistic devices helps to convince the audience to support an Academy for Women.

___-___5. The writer discusses the creditability of the speaker based on the standards of ethos explained in this chapter.

___-___6. The writer supports the discussion of each persuasive device with strong evidence (a minimum of three embedded bits of quotes per paragraph).

___-___7. The diction and sentence structure of this essay communicates a clear message.

___-___8. The organization of this essay aids in communicating a clear message.

___-___9. The grammar aids in communicating a clear message.

MAXIMUM SCORE RESULTS: Grader 1 _____

MAXIMUM SCORE RESULTS: Grader 2 _____

STEP 2:   Check each item below which accurately describes the negative aspects of the essay being graded. This side describes how the essay may not be as good as the higher-scoring essays. (Grader one should check column one. Grader two should check column two):

___-___1. The writer's summary ofDaniel Defoe's stance is more simplistic than those of the better essays.

___-___2. The writer names the logical appeals but adds no more discussion.

___-___3. The writer names the emotionl appeals but adds no mor discussion.

___-___4. The writer simply catalogues some examples of the author's manipulation of diction and syntax, or other stylistic devices without relating them to the authors' use of those devices to convince the reader.

___-___5. The discussion of the ethos of the speaker is more limited than those of the highest-scoring essays.

___-___6. Although adequate in number, the evidence in this essay is not as convincing as those of the top-scoring essays.

___-___7. A few lapses in diction or syntax may be present, but the message is clear.

___-___8. The organization of this essay is less appropriate than those of the top-scoring essays.

___-___9. The writer makes consistent errors in grammar and/ or other basic elements of composition.

RESULTS:

Grader 1: _____ - _____ = _____
          Step 1 Score   Step 2 Score

Grader 2: _____ - _____ = _____
          Step 1 Score   Step 2 Score

Grader 1 Score + Grader 2 Score = _____

Above sum
divided by 2 =

Score for essay

CHAPTER Seven: Writing an Argument

Defend, Challenge, or Qualify?

Agree or Disgaree?

Chapter Six: Writing an Argument:

Suggestions for Answering the Free Response Questions on the AP Examination.

One of the three essay questions asked on the English Language and Composition Essay Examination will always be some form of AGREE OR DISAGREE — DEFEND, CHALLENGE, OR QUALIFY question. With this type of question the student needs to persuasively agree or disagree OR defend, challenge, or qualify a stated aphorism through a well-reasoned presentation of evidence developed from observation, experience, or reading. These papers should display carefully nuanced thought and detailed development of evidence. This type of question needs to display the student's ability to write sound argument with persuasive force. Practicing this type of writing will also be beneficial for the English Literature and Composition student since the required literary writing also needs to demonstrate sound argument and persuasive force.

Use the following strategy suggestions for writing successful argumentation:

1. BRAINSTORM FOR FIFTEEN MINUTE BEFORE WRITING ANYTHING IN THE ESSAY BOOKLET! To insure a thoughtful reaction and a correct and meaningful interpretation, read the question three times, marking key words. Make sure you understand the task. Read the assertion three times, making personal observations about the different levels of meaning that are implied and the types of specific evidence you could use to develop your stance. State the meaning of

the assertion in your own words. Be aware that most of the time this meaning will be complex and can not be explained in one simple statement. Take a stand concerning the author's ideas on the subject. What is your initial position on the issue? Be aware of any prejudicial attitudes, sentiments, or stereotypes you may have. DO NOT BEGIN WRITING IN THE PINK ESSAY BOOKLET UNTIL YOU HAVE WRITTEN A THESIS SENTENCE ON THE GREEN ESSAY BOOKLET; THIS IS YOUR PLAN FOR WRITING!

2. BEGIN WRITING IN THE PINK ESSAY BOOKLET AFTER YOU HAVE A PLAN FOR WRITING.

Begin by writing a meaningful opening sentence or two which makes a personal observation about the focus of the question that reveals your thinking. Don't write flowery, general beginnings. Get right to the point. End with the thesis you wrote while brainstorming. (Note: Weak openings are forgiven if the paper ends strongly. If running out of time, skip part of the body to make your conclusion.)

Rather than force the same five paragraph model into every passage, simply write naturally, developing your stance on the topic in question. If the question requires an agree or disagree stance, be sure to demonstrate an understanding of argumentation by acknowledging both sides of the argument. This is usually done by writing a con-pro paragraph immediately after the introduction and the remainder of the essay becomes different paragraphs which confirm or amplify your agreement or disagreement with the assertion.

If the question requires a "defend, challenge, or qualify" stance on a political or philosophical assertion be sure to address all the issues raised by the assertion. A highly scored method of organizing this essay is to write a separate paragraph devoted to each level of meaning discovered about the assertion while brainstorming. Your topic sentence in this type of organization would be a generalized statement of one level of meaning discovered. Your evidence would be specifically named examples that support the claim you make in your topic sentence. If you can find examples in two unrelated areas or more (from your personal experience, observations, and reading) that make the same conclusion, your claim will be more valid. Each paragraph then would end with an interpretation of the similar conclusion that can be reached after ex amining differing types of evidence.

The well-written argument must transcend supporting narrative or emotional focus by making the experience
pertain to the argument. Avoid centering the essay on a typical teenage trauma or writing a simple agree or disagree di-
chotomy without sustaining support, argument, or persuasion.
Sustain support, argument, or persuasion by combining logos,
pathos and ethos.See chapter six for a specific listing od illogical fallicies.

Read the rubric graph to determine the requirements of an argument paper.

Then select questions from the following pages to practice writing the argument essay. Be sure to apply the three-step approach previously explained in some way appropriate to the
question.

Use the check list at the end of the section of questions to grade
the essays.

Defend, Challenge, or Qualify

Agree or Disagree?

Generic Rubric For Any Personal Essay:
Defend, Challenge or Qualify

Combines Logos, Pathos, and Ethos	9 8	Evidence from personal experiences, reading, or observations is unified, specific, adequate accurate and representative Thoughtful, articulate thesis Mature Command of Language and Style
Makes Immediate Sense: Does Not Repeat the Question	7 6	Less competent than 8 or 9 Sufficient detail to support thesis Does not explore complexity Clear ideas. Some sentence variety
Understands Aphorism or Assertion	5	Simplistic thinking Ideas hastily made - Intros and conclusions empty or repetitive
Unsub- stantiated Thesis	4 3	Writer needs help but has potential Weak sentence patterns Rambling Usage Errors Spelling Errors
Misreads Aphroism or Assertion Does Not Address the Question	2 1	Serious writing problems in usage Serious writing problems in spelling Serious writing problems in diction No support Little sense of what a paragraph is

Question One:

In an article written for the Baltimore Sun, H. L. Mencken defines the artist as one who has "an extraordinary capacity for irritation, a pathological sensitiveness to environmental pricks and stings." As a result, the artist is "actively hostile to his environment, and thus an indifferent patriot."

Write a carefully reasoned essay which defends, challenges, or qualifies Mencken's views on the artists relation to society. Be sure to support your argument with specific references to particular writers, composers, or other artists.

Question Two:

In the following excerpt from Henry James's novel The Portrait of a Lady , Madame Merle and Isabel Archer have conflicting views about what constitutes self. Read the passage carefully to determine each character's assertion about self. Then write a carefully reasoned, persuasive essay that demonstrates which of these two concepts of self is more valid. Be sure to use specific evidence from your observations, experiences, and reading to develop your position.

"When you've lived as long as I you'll see that every human being has his shell and that you must take the shell into account. By the shell I mean the whole envelope of circumstances. There's no such thing as an isolated man or woman; we're each of us made up of some cluster of appurtenances. What shall we call our 'self?' Where does it begin? Where does it end? It overflows into everything that belongs to us — and then it flows back again. I know a large part of myself is in the clothes I choose to wear. I've a great respect for things! One's self — for other people — is one's expression of one's self; and one's house, one's furniture, one's garments, the books one reads, the company one keeps — these things are all expressive.

This was very metaphysical; not more so, however, than several observations Madam Merle had already made. Isabel was fond of metaphysics, but was unable to accompany her friend into this bold analysis of the human personality. "I don't agree with you. I think just the other way. I don't know whether I succeed in expressing myself, but I know that nothing else expresses me. Nothing that belongs to me is any measure of me; everything's on the contrary a limit, a barrier, and a perfectly arbitrary one. Certainly the clothes which, as you say, I choose to wear, don't express me; and heaven forbid they should!"

"You dress very well," Madam Merle lightly imposed.

"Possibly; but I don't care to be judged by that. My clothes may express the dressmaker, but they don't express me. To begin with it's not my own choice that I wear them; they're imposed upon me by society."

"Should you prefer to go without them?" Madame Merle enquired in a tone which virtually terminated the discussion.

Question Three:

The following passage, "The Corner of the Eye" from *Late Night Thoughts on Listening to Mahler's Ninth Symphony,* is written by Lewis Thomas. Read the passage carefully. Then write a carefully reasoned, persuasive essay which defends, challenges, or qualifies Thomas's views on Artificial versus Human Intelligence. Use evidence from your observation, experience, or reading to develop your position.

I used to worry that computers would become so powerful and sophisticated as to take the place of human minds. The notion of Artificial Intelligence used to scare me half to death. Already, a large enough machine can do all sorts on intelligent things beyond our capacities: calculate in a split second the answer to mathematical problems requiring years for a human brain, draw accurate pictures from memory, even manufacture successions of sounds with a disarming resemblance to real music. Computers can translate textbooks, write dissertations of their own for doctorates, even speak in machine-tooled, inhuman phonemes any words read off from a printed page. They can communicate with one another, holding consultations and committee meetings of their own in networks around the earth.

Computers can make errors, of course, and do so all the time in small, irritating ways, but the mistakes can be fixed and nearly always are. In this respect they are fundamentally inhuman, and here is the relaxing thought: computers will not take over the world, they cannot replace us, because they are not designed, as we are, for ambiguity.

Write a carefully reasoned, persuasive essay that defends, challenges, or qualifies his assertion that computers cannot replace computers "because they are not designed, as we are, for ambiguity." Use evidence from your observation, experience, or reading to develop your position.

Question Six:

"The most dangerous enemy to truth and freedom amongst us is the compact majority."
from Henrik Ibsen's An Enemy of the People

Write a carefully reasoned, persuasive essay which defends, challenges, or qualifies this assertion. Use evidence from your observation, experience, or reading to develop your position.

Question Seven:

"Freedom is not something that anybody can be given; freedom is something people take and people are as free as they can be."
James Baldwin

Write a carefully reasoned, persuasive essay which defends, challenges, or qualifies this assertion. Use evidence from your observation, experience, or reading to develop your position.

Question Eight:

"There never was a good war or a bad peace."

Benjamin Franklin

Write a carefully reasoned, persuasive essay which defends, challenges, or qualifies this assertion. Use evidence from your observation, experience, or reading to develop your position.

Question Nine:

"All enemies, except for those fighting for the strictly limited food supply of a given territory, may be described as artificial enemies."

Aldous Huxley

Write a carefully reasoned, persuasive essay which defends, challenges, or qualifies this assertion. Use evidence from your observation, experience, or reading to develop your position.

Question Ten:

"The only reward of virtue is virtue; the only way to have a friend is to be one."

Ralph Waldo Emerson

Write a carefully reasoned, persuasive essay which defends, challenges, or qualifies this assertion. Use evidence from your observation, experience, or reading to develop your position.

Question Eleven:

"The real hero is always a hero by mistake; he dreams of being an honest coward like everybody else."

Umberto Eco

Write a carefully reasoned, persuasive essay which defends, challenges, or qualifies this assertion. Use evidence from your observation, experience, or reading to develop your position.

Question Twelve:

"Every time a friend succeeds I die a little."

Gore Vidal

Write a carefully reasoned, persuasive essay which defends, challenges, or qualifies this assertion. Use evidence from your observation, experience, or reading to develop your position.

Question Thirteen:

"Though I have looked everywhere, I can find nothing lowly in the universe."

A. R. Ammons

Write a carefully reasoned, persuasive essay which defends, challenges, or qualifies this assertion. Use evidence from your observation, experience, or reading to develop your position.

Question Fourteen:

"All a man can betray is his conscience."

Joseph Conrad

Write a carefully reasoned, persuasive essay which defends, challenges, or qualifies this assertion. Use evidence from your observation, experience, or reading to develop your position.

Question Fifteen:

"Revolutions are never peaceful."

Malcolm X

Write a carefully reasoned, persuasive essay which defends, challenges, or qualifies this assertion. Use evidence from your observation, experience, or reading to develop your position.

Question Sixteen:

"War is a poor chisel to carve out tomorrows."

Martin Luther King

Write a carefully reasoned, persuasive essay which defends, challenges, or qualifies this assertion. Use evidence from your observation, experience, or reading to develop your position.

Question Sixteen:

"Poverty is the mother of crime."

Marcus Aurelius
121 - 180

Write a carefully reasoned, persuasive essay which defends, challenges, or qualifies this assertion. Use evidence from your observation, experience, or reading to develop your position.

Question Seventeen:

"Extreme justice is extreme injustice."

Cicero
106 - 43 B. C.

Write a carefully reasoned, persuasive essay which defends, challenges, or qualifies this assertion. Use evidence from your observation, experience, or reading to develop your position.

Question Eighteen:

"To defend oneself against fear is simply to insure that one will, one day, be conquered by it; fears must be faced."

`James Baldwin

Write a carefully reasoned, persuasive essay which defends, challenges, or qualifies this assertion. Use evidence from your observation, experience, or reading to develop your position.

Question Nineteen:

"Justice canot be for one side alone, but musy be for both."
Elanor Roosevelt

Write a carefully reasoned, persuasive essay which defends, challenges, or qualifies this assertion. Use evidence from your observation, experience, or reading to develop your position.

Question Twenty:

"Someone who only reads newspapers and at best books of contemporary authors looks to me like an extremely near-sighted person who scorns eyeglasses. He is completely dependent on the prejudices and fashions of his times, since he never gets to see anything else."

Albert Einstein

Write a carefully reasoned, persuasive essay which defends, challenges, or qualifies this assertion. Use evidence from your observation, experience, or reading to develop your position.

Question Twenty-one:

"They say that man is born to the belief that he is superior to the lower animals, and that critical intelligence comes when he realizes that he is more similar than dissimilar."
James Thurber

Write a carefully reasoned, persuasive essay which defends, challenges, or qualifies this assertion. Use evidence from your observation, experience, or reading to develop your position.

Question Twenty-two:

"Our scientific power has outrun our spiritual power. We have guided missiles and misguided men."

Martin Luther King

Write a carefully reasoned, persuasive essay which defends, challenges, or qualifies this assertion. Use evidence from your observation, experience, or reading to develop your position.

Question Twenty-three:

"A friend in power is a friend lost."

Henry Brooks Adams

Write a carefully reasoned, persuasive essay which defends, challenges, or qualifies this assertion. Use evidence from your observation, experience, or reading to develop your position.

Question Twenty-four:

"High School is closer to the core of the American experience than anything else I can think of."

Kurt Vonnegut

Write a carefully reasoned, persuasive essay which defends, challenges, or qualifies this assertion. Use evidence from your observation, experience, or reading to develop your position.

Question Twenty-five:

"Violence is the instinctive response to fear."

Margaret Miller

Write a carefully reasoned, persuasive essay which defends, challenges, or qualifies this assertion. Use evidence from your observation, experience, or reading to develop your position.

Question Twenty-six:

"There's so much comedy on television. Does that cause comedy in the streets?
>   Dick Cavett

Write a carefully reasoned, persuasive essay which defends, challenges, or qualifies this assertion. Use evidence from your observation, experience, or reading to develop your position.

Question Twenty-seven:

"New opinions are always suspected and usually opposed, without any other reason but because they are not already common.
>   John Locke

Write a carefully reasoned, persuasive essay which defends, challenges, or qualifies this assertion. Use evidence from your observation, experience, or reading to develop your position.

Question Twenty-eight:

"I happen to believe we Americans are becoming a nation of liars. It is the lying at the top level of our society that concerns me the most, because morality, like water and unlike money, really does trickle down."
>   MacNeil Lehrer

Write a carefully reasoned, persuasive essay which defends, challenges, or qualifies this assertion. Use evidence from your observation, experience, or reading to develop your position.

The Essay—Checklist
Defend, Challenge, Qualify

STEP 1: Check each item listed below which accurately describes the positive aspects of the essay being graded. Add one point for each item checked from the list. This side describes the basic requirements for a well-written essay. (Grader one should check column one. Grader two should check column two):

___-___1. The writer defines the author's (or article's) aphorism or assertion.

___-___2. The writer has reached some conclusions about the assertion.

___-___3. The writer substantiates its points with evidence from personal observations, experiences, and/or reading.

___-___4. The writer has connected the evidence to the thesis with some insights about human nature.

___-___5. The writer has convinced the reader of the validity of his/her assertion based on an effective use of persuasive devices (arguments, assumptions, logos, ethos, and pathos, etc.).

___-___6. The writer supports the discussion of each personal observation, experience, or reading with strong evidence (unified, specific, accurate, adequate, and representative).

___-___7. The diction and sentence structure of this essay communicates a clear message.

___-___8. The organization of this essay aids in communicating a clear message.

___-___9. The grammar aids in communicating a clear message.

MAXIMUM SCORE RESULTS: Grader 1 _____
MAXIMUM SCORE RESULTS: Grader 2 _____

STEP 2: Check each item below which accurately describes the negative aspects of the essay being graded. This side describes how the essay may not be as good as the higher-scoring essays. (Grader one should check column one. Grader two should check column two):

___-___1. The writer does not explore the accuracy of the assertion as well as those of the top-scoring essays.

___-___2. Little attempt has been made to apply the aphorism or validate the assertion to modern society. The writer simply explains the author's (or article's) views or writes a wholly unrelated essay.

___-___3. The evidence is not well chosen, well used, or sufficient for the purpose.

___-___4. Superficial, confused or contradictory thinking are combined with an uninteresting or obvious thesis.

___-___5. The writer relies on illicit appeals or uses illogical thinking.

___-___6. Although adequate in number, the evidence in this essay is not as convincing as the top-scoring essay.

___-___7. A few lapses in diction or syntax may be present, but the message is clear.

___-___8. The organization of this essay is less appropriate than those of the top-scoring essays.

___-___9. The writer makes consistent errors in grammar and/or other basic elements of composition.

RESULTS:

Grader 1: _____ - _____ = _____
          Step 1 Score   Step 2 Score

Grader 2: _____ - _____ = _____
          Step 1 Score   Step 2 Score

Grader 1 Score + Grader 2 Score = _____

Above sum divided by 2 =

Score for essay

CHAPTER Eight:

The Classroom Essay

Comparison and Contrast

Chapter Eight: Comparison and Contrast

Many times when we need to make sense of something we compare and contrast to make a more informed choice or reach a more sound conclusion. This important skill is taught, explicitly or implicitly, in all English classrooms. You may be asked to compare any one of the following things (or more): similar passages written by different authors, similar actions undertaken by different characters, different drafts by the same writer, or even different stylistic or rhetorical techniques in the same passage by the same author. Many of the previous classroom essays used in this *Writer* require some sort of comparison and contrast. In most term papers you are required to examine various view points on a similar subject. In every case you are trying to make sense of something or make a more informed choice by reaching logical conclusions about discovered differences among similar things. Finding the similarities is the beginning of a comparison and contrast task. Reaching conclusions about discovered differences then becomes the goal.

This type of writing can be structured in one of two ways: the **"block method"** — or the **"point-by-point method."** In the block method of comparison and contrast — a passage by passage analysis sometimes called the "divided" or "subject-by-subject pattern" — you would write everything about one aspect of the subject in one paragraph, everything about another aspect of the subject in another paragraph. It is best to match the order of the details presented in the first paragraph with the order of details presented in the second paragraph.. For in stance, in the essay by Mark Twain called "Two Views of the River," which uses the block method, Twain's first point of comparison in the first paragraph is his romantic view of the sunset. In the second paragraph he matches this order by first mentioning his pragmatic view of the sunset. A comparison and contrast essay should end with some sort of conclusion about which is better. This a good method to use with a fairly uncomplicated question that requires a fairly brief essay.

Question One:

Read carefully the following passage by Mark Twain. Then write a well organized essay which analyzes how he uses the block method of comparison and contrast to reach a conclusion about his two views of the river.

Note: In this question you are asked to demonstrate your understanding of one option for structure in writing a comparison and contrast essay. Each topic sentence, then, should focus on one aspect of the definition of the block method. However, your organization should match the organization chosen by Mark Twain. What does he do first? Analyze that. What does he do second, etc. Reach some conclusion about the effectiveness of this type of organization in your conclusion.

Mark Twain
from *Life on the Mississippi*
Two Views of the River

Now when I had mastered the language of the water, and had come to know every trifling feature that bordered the great river as familiarly as I knew the letters of the alphabet, I had made a valuable acquisition. But I had lost something, too. I had lost something which could never be restored to me while I lived. All the grace, the beauty, the poetry, had gone out of the majestic river! I still keep in mind a certain wonderful sunset which I witnessed when steamboating was new to me. A broad expanse of the river was turned to blood; in the middle distance the red hue brightened into gold, through which a solitary log came floating black and conspicuous; in one place a long, slanting mark lay sparkling upon the water; in another the surface was broken by boiling, tumbling, rings that were as many-tinted as an opal; where the ruddy flush was faintest, was a smooth spot that was covered with graceful circles and radiating lines, ever so delicately traced; the shore on our left was densely wooded, and the sombre shadow that fell from this forest was broken in one place by a long, ruffled trail that shone like silver; and high above the forest wall a clean-stemmed dead tree waved a leafy bough that glowed like a flame in the unobstructed splendor that was flowing from the sun. There were graceful curves, reflected images, woody heights, soft distances; and over the whole scene, far and near, the dissolving lights drifted steadily, enriching it every passing moment with new marvels of coloring.

I stood like one bewitched. I drank it in, in a speechless rapture. The world was new to me, and I had never seen anything like this at home. But as I have said, a day came when I began to cease from noting the glories and the charms which the moon and the sun and the twilight wrought upon the river's face; another came when I ceased altogether to note them. Then, if that sunset scene had been repeated, I should have looked upon it without rapture, and should have commented on it, inwardly, after this fashion: "This sun means that we are going to have wind tomorrow; that floating log means that the river is rising, small thanks to it; that slanting mark on the water refers to a bluff reef which is going to kill somebody's steamboat one of these nights, if it keeps on stretching out like that; those tumbling 'boils' show a dissolving bar and a changing channel there; the lines and circles in the slick water over yonder are a warning that that troublesome place is shoaling up dangerously; that silver streak in the shadow of the forest is the 'break' from a new snag, and he has located himself in the very best place he could have found to fish for steamboats; that tall dead tree, with a single living branch, is not going to last long, and then how is a body ever going to get through this blind place at night without a friendly old landmark?

No, the romance and the beauty were all gone from the river. All the value any feature of it had for me now was the amount of usefulness it could furnish toward compassing the safe piloting of a steamboat. Since those days, I have pitied doctors from my heart. What does the lovely flush in a beauty's cheek mean to a doctor but a "break" that ripples above some deadly disease? Are not all her visible charms sown thick with what are to him the signs and symbols of hidden decay? Does he ever see her beauty at all, or doesn't he simply view her professionally, and comment upon her wholesome condition all to himself? And doesn't he sometimes wonder whether he has gained most or lost most by learning his trade?

Checklist for Comparison and Contrast Essay — Mark Twain's "Two Views of the River

STEP 1: Check each item listed below which accurately describes the positive aspects of the essay being graded. Add one point for each item checked from the list. This side describes the basic requirements for a well-written essay. (Grader one should check column one. Grader two should check column two):

___-___1. The writer demonstrates an understanding of the block method of organization by analyzing how Twain uses it.

___-___2. The writer shows how the organization of the paragraph dealing with Twain's romantic reaction to the river is matched by Twain's description of his practical reaction to the river.

___-___3. This writer has reached valid, pertinent, and relevant conclusions about the comparison.

___-___4. This writer has shown an appreciation of the contextual relationship between the two views of the river.

___-___5. The thesis clearly shows the connection between the author's choice of organization and the impact of the author's message.

___-___6. This writer supports the discussion of the author's choice of the block method with good and persuasive substantiation of both paragraphs (a minimum of three embedded quotes per paragraph).

___-___7. The diction and sentence structure of this essay communicate a clear message.

___-___8. The organization of this essay aids in communicating a clear message.

___-___9. The grammar aids in communicating a clear message.

MAXIMUM SCORE RESULTS: Grader 1 _____
MAXIMUM SCORE RESULTS: Grader 2 _____

STEP 2: Check each item below which accurately describes the negative aspects of the essay being graded. This side describes how the essay may not be as good as the higher-scoring essays. (Grader one should check column one. Grader two should check column two):

___-___1. The writer's understanding of the block method is adequate, although not as insightful as those of the top-scoring essays.

___-___2. The writer discusses the organization of Twain's use of the block method with limited purpose or accuracy.

___-___3. The writer simply paraphrases each paragraph.

___-___4. The writer simply catalogues the strategies of the block method without relating them to the impact of the authors' probable or intended message.

___-___5. The connection between the organizational strategy chosen and the impact of authors' message is less clear than those of the top-scoring essays.

___-___6. Although adequate in number, the evidence in this essay is not as convincing as the top-scoring essay.

___-___7. A few lapses in grammar, diction, or syntax may be present, but the message is clear.

___-___8. The organization of this essay is less appropriate than those of the top-scoring essays.

___-___9. The writer has consistent weakness in grammar and/or other basic elements of composition.

RESULTS:

Grader 1: _____ - _____ = _____
          Step 1 Score   Step 2 Score

Grader 2: _____ - _____ = _____
          Step 1 Score   Step 2 Score

Grader 1 Score + Grader 2 Score = _____

Above sum divided by 2 =

Score for essay

Question Two:

The second type of organization in a comparison and contrast essay is know as the **"point-by-point method"** — also known as the "alternating pattern" because the essay is organized around different points shared by each subject with evidence about that one point alternating between both subjects.

Read carefully the following passage from "My Brother's House" by Naomi Shihab Nye. Then write a well-organized essay which analyzes how the point-by-point method of comparison has been used by Naomi Shihab Nye to explain how she and her brother, though raised in the same houses, have become different people.

Note: In this question you are asked to demonstrate your understanding of one option for structure in writing a comparison and contrast essay. Each topic sentence, then, should focus on one aspect of the definition of the point-by-point method. However, your organization should match the organization chosen by Naomi Shihab Nye. What does she do first? Analyze that. What does he do second? Analyze that. What do you do in the third paragraph? Analyze that, etc. Reach some conclusion about the effectiveness of this type of organization in your conclusion.

Naomi Shihab Nye
"My Brother's House"

In the guest bedroom at my brother's brand-new house in the north Dallas suburbs are four sets of electrical sockets with no cords coming out of them. The possibilities feel overwhelming. My brother could plug in appliances I haven't even heard of yet.

Our ninety-year-old house in inner-city San Antonio sports intricate ugly tangles of extension cords and multiple power outlets. I am always stuffing them back under the skirt of the bed. I have heard it is not good for one's electromagnetic field to have electrical cords crisscrossing under your sleeping place, but have not yet learned how to activate my reading lamp, and alarm clock without them.

My brother's house smells of fresh paint and packaging — those foam bubbles and peanuts that come in big boxes.

It smells like carpet no one has ever stepped on. I cannot imagine the bravado of white carpet. My brother prefers if you remove your shoes at his front door. So do I, but no one ever does it in our house.

We have dusty wooden floors and raggedy little rugs from Turkey and Libya. We have throw rugs hand-knotted in Appalachia in 1968. We have a worn Oriental carpet that once belonged to my friend's reclusive father, a famous science fiction writer. He lived on an island all by himself. Our hour smells of incense and grandmother's attics in Illinois in the 1950s and vaguely sweetened shelf paper pressed into drawers.

My brother and his family are the first people to live in their house, which is part of a generically named and very expensive subdivision — something like Fair Oaks (but there aren't any oaks so it couldn't be) or Placid Plains or Rampant Meadows. They made some decisions about finishing details, deciding which wallpaper would go in the bathrooms and the shape of the pool and the color of its tiles. They chose a lion's head to be spitting water into the pool from beneath the flower bed. Even the curb beside their front sidewalk is sleek.

Our house with its high ceilings and columned wrap-around front porch was built in 1905 a block from the San Antonio River by a French family that started a "Steamship and Travel Company" downtown. Their agency still exists, mailing out travel tickets in blue envelopes imprinted with elegant, floating steamships. I visit their offices, scribbling checks under the watchful portrait of the man who built our house. His eyes say, "Can't you ever stay *home*?" . . . .

My brothers's house is made of pink recycled bricks. Recycled bricks are more expensive than new red bricks. Someone told me that. They make the house look organically weather-beaten, but only slightly. The other houses on the street, very similar in design to my brother's, with high-pitched roofs and enormous windows and exalted dormers, are made of redder bricks. Most of the families have planted beds of petunias and hibiscus as borders.

These are words that could apply to my brother's neighborhood: manicured, impeccable, formal, aloof. There are others: cookie-cutter, master plan. Words that could apply to ours: offbeat, down-at-the-heels.

Our house used to be made of wooden boards, but a few years ago we had our carpenter take the old boards off, stuff the thickest insulation he could find inside the walls (try facing west through a blazing Texas summer), and apply new boards. Then he painted them white so the house looked just like it used to look, but felt substantially cooler. Our neighbors thought we were crazy, wasting our money. Why didn't we put the old boards back on? . . . .

My brother has six fancy bathrooms in his house. One offers two toilets in separate closets and two gigantic gleaming sinks. I think I would dream about Dutch cleanser if I lived there. His bathrooms have five fan vents and special mirror lights for putting on makeup. I opened a sleek drawer under his sink and found 1,000 miniature bottles of hotel shampoo.

We have one old-fashioned bathroom downstairs tiled with blue flying birds from Mexico. We hauled those tiles home in our car after visiting the hand-painted tile factory in Delores Hidalgo. I was drinking Coca-Cola from a squatty Mexican bottle when we spotted them. Of course, we hadn't measured the bathroom back home, so we had to guess how many to buy which is why a plain navy blue border lines the bottom and top. We filled in. Our bathroom wall still features an ancient, ornately scrolled gas heater that we are afraid to turn on, but like to look at.

We have another bathroom upstairs with a claw foot bathtub. I found the tub on the front porch of an elderly lady's house on Maverick Street. I knocked on her door. "This is very brazen, but the fact that your bathtub is filled with — leaves — makes me wonder if it essential to your life anymore or if you might consider selling it." She took twenty dollars on the spot. . . .

When I spend the night in my brother's well-organized house, I wake up thinking, but there are no one else's legends lodged in these walls.

He likes it that way. His wife likes it that way. They are the main characters. . . .

I think the roots of old houses go deep down into our ground before we were born and the roots of new houses go out into the atmosphere, into our disembodied visions of developers and the crisp edges of dollar bills rolled up at the bank. . . .

My bother and I grew up in the same houses together, in St. Louis, Jerusalem, and San Antonio, three cities as dissimilar as pretzels, *hummos,* and salsa. So how did we become such different people? . . . .

Am I holding myself above my brother? Do I judge him by his house? He has told me what his monthly mortgage payment is — it is so large whole parts of our house could fit inside it. He could be eighty and still paying. Something like that.

He told me once, with a note of sadness in his voice, "It's like a carnival ride — if you're on, you can't just jump off."

We have no monthly mortgage payment. Our modest house was paid for long ago. The mortgage company stamped the receipt in red — PAID IN FULL. We used it as a centerpiece with flowers for a while.

What surprises me is this: my brother sometimes says he imagines a slow going, rural-tinted existence. He mentions stepping down, leafing out, taking the chance. Anyone who has worked more than a decade for a major corporation must carry these little bubbles inside. He delights his family with a weekend at a rugged bed-and-breakfast ranch in the Texas hill country. His son collects fresh eggs and his daughter washes a horse. He imagines having less and being happy.

I sit on the steps of our front porch in the evenings. Our son scrawls a picture on the sidewalk — blue chalk man with a runny nose vast as a volcano's eruption. For him this feels like spectacular, nasty fun.

Across the street, woman and men walk arm-in-arm around the quiet park, under the yellow lamp light, as they do in Mexico. What are they thinking of? I imagine they carry the days when their own sons and daughters were small tucked deep down inside them. When other children shout at dusk, swinging wooden bats or skidding onto the gravel jogging path on their bikes, something in them still shouts, Come back, come back! It's time for bed. It's time to go home!

My brother and I used to answer to a call like that. His skins smelled like pennies, the faint coppery twist of pockets and salt inside a fist. He kept his little cars all lined up in shoe boxes and would flip the doors of the milk truck and the fire truck open now and then before going to bed, just to make sure everything worked.

Checklist for Comparison and Contrast Essay — Naomi Shihab Nye's "My Brother's House"

STEP 1:   Check each item listed below which accurately describes the positive aspects of the essay being graded. Add one point for each item checked from the list. This side describes the basic requirements for a well-written essay. (Grader one should check column one. Grader two should check column two):

___-___1. The writer demonstrates an understanding of the point-by-point method of organization by analyzing how Nye uses it to explain how she and her brother, though raised in the same houses, have become different people.

___-___2. The writer shows how the first paragraph, organized around the electrical setup of both homes, shows a specified difference between she and her brother.

___-___3. This writer continues to show how the two house's differences — on such similar topics such as flooring, smells, history, looks, and bathrooms — help the author to make final conclusions on how she and her brother are different.

___-___4. This writer has defined the author's message about life-styles and happiness with psychological insight.

___-___5. The thesis clearly shows the connection between the authors' choice of organization and the impact of the author's message.

___-___6. This writer supports the discussion of the author's choice of the point-by-point method with good and persuasive substantiation.

___-___7. The diction and sentence structure of this essay communicate a clear message.

___-___8. The organization of this essay aids in communicating a clear message.

___-___9. The grammar aids in communicating a clear message.

MAXIMUM SCORE RESULTS: Grader 1 _____

MAXIMUM SCORE RESULTS: Grader 2 _____

STEP 2:   Check each item below which accurately describes the negative aspects of the essay being graded. This side describes how the essay may not be as good as the higher-scoring essays. (Grader one should check column one. Grader two should check column two):

___-___1. The writer's understanding of the point-by-point method is less clearly stated than those of the top-scoring essays.

___-___2. The writer's definition of the specified difference between the siblings is less insightful than those of the highest scoring essays.

___-___3. The writer's analysis of how Nye's organization helps the reader understand how she and her brother are different lacks the depth of those of the highest scoring essays.

___-___4. The writer oversimplifies or even partially misreads the author's message.

___-___5. The connection between the organizational strategy chosen and the impact of authors' message is less clear than those of the top-scoring essays.

___-___6. Although adequate in number, the evidence in this essay is not as convincing as the top-scoring essay.

___-___7. A few lapses in grammar, diction, or syntax may be present, but the message is clear.

___-___8. The organization of this essay is less appropriate than those of the top-scoring essays.

___-___9. The writer has consistent weakness in grammar and/or other basic elements of composition.

RESULTS:

Grader 1: _____ - _____ = _____
           Step 1 Score   Step 2 Score

Grader 2: _____ - _____ = _____
           Step 1 Score   Step 2 Score

Grader 1 Score + Grader 2 Score = _____

Above sum
divided by 2 =

Score for essay

Close Reading

The following question is a review of the type of question that is usually asked on the English Advanced Placement Language and Composition Examination. Experiment with each type of organization (block method or point-by-point method) to answer the question that follows.

Question Three:

In the two excerpts below, Nathaniel Hawthorne and Mark Twain have written caricatures that distort the victim's personality, exaggerating certain features and mannerisms for a satiric effect. Read the two passages carefully. Then write a well-organized essay that analyzes the rhetorical and stylistic chosen by each author to create differing probable and intended effects.

Nathaniel Hawthorne

From "The Customs House"

The Inspector, when I first knew him, was a man of fourscore years, or thereabouts, and certainly one of the most wonderful specimens of wintergreen that you would be likely to discover in a lifetime's search. With his florrid cheek, his compact figure, smartly arrayed in a bright-buttoned blue coat, his brisk and vigorous step and his hale and hearty aspect, altogether he seemed — not young, indeed — but a kind of new contrivance of Mother Nature in the shape of man, whom age and infirmity had no business to touch. His voice and laugh, which perpetually reechoed through the Custom House, had nothing of the tremulous quaver and cackle of an old man's utterance; they came strutting out of his lungs like the crow of a cock or the blast of a clarion. Looking at him merely as an animal — and there was very little else to look at — he was a most satisfactory object, from the thorough healthfulness and wholesomeness of his system, and his capacity, at that extreme age, to enjoy all, or nearly all, the delights which he had ever aimed at, or conceived of. The careless security of his life in the Custom House, on a regular income, and with but slight and infrequent apprehensions of removal, had no doubt contributed to make time pass lightly over him. The original and more potent causes, however, lay in the rare perfection of his animal nature, the moderate proportion of intellect, and the very trifling admixture of moral and spiritual ingredients; these latter qualities, indeed, being in barely enough measure to keep the old gentleman from walking on all fours. He possessed no power of thought, no depth of feeling, no troublesome sensibilities; nothing, in short, but a few commonplace instincts, which, aided by the cheerful temper that grew inevitably out of his physical well-being, did duty very respectably, and to general acceptance, in lieu of a heart. He had been the husband of three wives, all long since dead; the father of twenty children, most of whom, at every age of childhood or maturity, had likewise returned to dust. Here, one would suppose, might have been sorrow enough to imbue the sunniest disposition, through and through, with a sable ringe. Not so with our old Inspector! One brief sigh sufficed to carry off the entire burden of these dismal reminiscences. The next moment, he was ready for sport as any unbreeched infant; far readier than the Collector's junior clerk, who, at nineteen years, was much the elder and graver man of the two.

I used to watch and study this patriarchal personage with, I think, livelier curiosity, than any other form of humanity there presented to my notice. He was, in truth, a rare phenomenon; so perfect, in one point of view; so shallow, so delusive, so impalpable, such an absolute nonentity, in every other. My conclusion was that he had no soul, no heart, no mind; nothing, as I have already said, but instincts; and yet, withal, so cunningly had the few pieces of his character been put together, that there was no painful perception of deficiency, but, on my part, an entire contentment with what I found in him. It might be difficult — and it was so — to conceive how he should exist hereafter, so earthy and sensuous did he seem; but surely his existence here, admitting that it was to terminate with his last breath, had not been unkindly given; with no higher moral responsibilities than the beasts of the field, but with a larger scope of enjoyment than theirs, and with all their blessed immunity from the dreariness and duskiness of age.

One point, in which he had vastly the advantage over

his four-footed brethren, was his ability to recollect the good dinners which it had made no small portion of the happiness of his life to eat. His gourmandism was a highly agreeable trait; and to hear him talk of roast meat was as appetizing as a pickle or an oyster. As he possessed no higher attribute, and neither sacrificed nor vitiated any spiritual endowment by devoting all his energies and ingenuities to subserve the delight and profit of his maw, it always pleased and satisfied me to hear him expatiate on fish, poultry, and butcher's meat, and the most eligible methods of preparing them for the table. His reminiscences of good cheer, however ancient the date of the actual banquet, seemed to bring the savor of pig or turkey under one's nostrils. There were flavors on his palate, that had lingered there not less than sixty or seventy years, and were still apparently as fresh as that of the mutton chop which he had just devoured for breakfast. I have heard him smack his lips over dinners, every guest at which, except himself, had long been food for worms. It was marvelous to observe how the ghosts of by-gone meals were continually rising up before him; not in anger or retribution, but as if grateful for his former appreciation, and seeking to reduplicate an endless series of enjoyment, at once shadowy and sensual. A tenderloin of beef, a hind-quarter of veal, a sparerib of pork, a particular chicken, or a remarkably praiseworthy turkey which had perhaps adorned his board in the days of the elder Adams, would be remembered; while all the subsequent experience of our race, and all the events that brightened or darkened his individual career, had gone over him with as little permanent effect as the passing breeze. The chief tragic event of the old man's life, so far as I could judge, was his mishap with a certain goose, which lived and died some twenty or forty years ago; a goose of most promising figure, but which, at table, proved so inveterately tough that the carving knife would make no impression on its carcass, and it could only be divided with an axe and handsaw.

But it is time to quit this sketch; on which, however, I should be glad to dwell at considerable more length, because, of all men I have ever known, this individual was the fittest to be a Customs House officer. Most persons, owing to causes which I may not have space to hint at, suffer moral detriment from this peculiar mode of life. The old Inspector was incapable of it; and, were he to continue in office to the end of time, would be as good as he was then, and sit down to dinner with just as good an appetite.

Mark Twain

From "The Late Benjamin Franklin"

(Never put off till to-morrow what you can do day
after to-morrow as well." — B. F.)

This party was one of those persons whom they call
Philosophers. . . . (He) was of a vicious disposition, and early
prostituted his talents to the invention of maxims and aphorisms calculated to inflict suffering upon the rising generation
of all subsequent ages. His simplest acts, also, were contrived
with a view to their being held up for the emulation of boys
forever — boys who might have otherwise been happy . . . .
With a malevolence which is without parallel in history, he
would work all day, and then sit up nights, and let on to be
studying algebra by the light of a smoldering fire, so that all
other boys might have to do that also, or else have Benjamin
Franklin thrown up to them. Not satisfied with these proceed-
ings, ha had a fashion of living wholly on bread and water,
and studying astronomy at meal time — a thing which has
brought affliction to millions of boys since, whose father's had
read Franklin's pernicious biography.

His maxims were full of animosity toward boys.
Nowadays a boy cannot follow a single natural instinct without tumbling over some of those everlasting aphorisms and
hearing from Franklin on the spot. If he buys two cents' worth
of peanuts, his father says, "Remember what Franklin has said,
my son — 'A groat a day's a penny a year' "; and the comfort is
all gone out of those peanuts. If he wants to spin his top when
he has done work, his father quotes, "Procrastination is the
thief of time." If he does a virtuous action, he never gets anything for it, because "Virtue is its own reward." And that boy
is hounded to death and robbed of his natural rest, because
Franklin once said, in one of his inspired flights of malignity:

> Early to bed and early to rise
> Makes a man healthy, wealthy, and wise.

As if it were any object to a boy to be healthy and

wealthy and wise on such terms. The sorrow that that maxim has cost me, through my parents, experimenting on me with it, tongue cannot tell. The legitimate result is my present state of general debility, indigence, and mental aberration. My parents used to have me up before nine o'clock in the morning sometimes when I was a boy. If they had let me take my natural rest where would I have been now? Keeping store, no doubt, and respected by all.

And what an adroit old adventurer the subject of this memoir was! In order to get a chance to fly his kite on Sunday he used a hang key on the string and let on to be fishing for lightning. And a guileless public would go home chirping about the "wisdom" and "genius" of the hoary Sabbath-breaker. If anybody caught him playing "mumble-peg" by himself, after the age of sixty, he would immediately appear to be ciphering out how the grass grew — as if it was any of his business. My grandfather knew him well, and he says Franklin was always fixed — always ready. If a body, during his old age, happened on him unexpectedly when he was catching flies, or making mud-pies, or sliding on a cellar door, he would immediately look wise and rip out a maxim, and walk off with his nose in the air and his cap turned wrong side before, trying to appear absent-minded and eccentric. He was a hard lot.

He invented a stove that would smoke your head off in four hours by the clock. One can see the almost devilish satisfaction he took in it by his giving it his name.

He was always proud of telling how he entered Philadelphia for the first time, with nothing in the world but two shillings in his pocket and four rolls of bread under his arm. But really, when you come to examine it critically, it was nothing. Anybody could have done it . . . .

Benjamin Franklin did a great many notable things for his country, and made her young name to be honored in many lands as the mother of such a son. It is not the idea of such a memoir to ignore that or cover it up. No; the simple idea of it is to snub those pretentious maxims of his, which he worked up with a great show of originality out of truisms that had become wearisome platitudes as early as the dispersion of babel; and also to sub his stove, and his military inspirations, his unseemly endeavor to make himself conspicuous when he entered Philadelphia, and his flying his kite and fooling away his time in sorts of such ways when he ought to have been foraging for soap-fat, or constructing candles. I merely desired to do away with somewhat of the prevalent calamitous idea among heads of families that Franklin *acquired* his great genius by working for nothing, studying by moonlight, and getting up in the night instead of waiting until morning like a Christian; and that this program, rigidly inflicted, will make a Franklin of every father's fool. It is time these gentlemen were finding out that these execrable eccentricities of instinct and conduct are only *evidences* of genius, not the *creators* of it. I wish I had been the father of my parents long enough to make them comprehend this truth, and thus prepare them to let their son have an easier time of it. When I was a child I had to boil soap, notwithstanding my father was wealthy, and I had to get up early and study geometry at breakfast, and peddle my own poetry, and do everything just as Franklin did, in the solemn hope that I would be a Franklin some day. And here I am.

1870

Checklist for Comparison and Contrast Essay — Twain's and Hawthorne's Caricatures

STEP 1: Check each item listed below which accurately describes the positive aspects of the essay being graded. Add one point for each item checked from the list. This side describes the basic requirements for a well-written essay. (Grader one should check column one. Grader two should check column two):

___-___1. The writer demonstrates an understanding of the differing satiric effects created by each caricature.

___-___2. The writer analyzes how each author uses irony, hyperbole and other stylistic devices to create that satiric effect.

___-___3. This writer shows an appreciation of the contextual relationship between the two excerpts

___-___4. This writer has reached valid, pertinent, and relevant conclusions about the comparison.

___-___5. The thesis clearly shows the connection between the contrasting caricatures and the effect created.

___-___6. This writer supports the discussion of each excerpt with good and persuasive substantiation (a minimum of three embedded quotes per paragraph).

___-___7. The diction and sentence structure of this essay communicate a clear message.

___-___8. The organization chosen by the writer aids in communicating a clear message.

___-___9. The grammar aids in communicating a clear message.

MAXIMUM SCORE RESULTS: Grader 1 _____
MAXIMUM SCORE RESULTS: Grader 2 _____

STEP 2:   Check each item below which accurately describes the negative aspects of the essay being graded. This side describes how the essay may not be as good as the higher-scoring essays. (Grader one should check column one. Grader two should check column two):

___-___1. The writer definition of the differences, although accurate, illustrate only what is most easy to grasp.

___-___2. The writer discusses the stylistic devices with limited purpose or accuracy.

___-___3. The writer's discussion of the authors' language choices may be vague or inaccurate.

___-___4. The writer simply catalogues the use of contrast in general without relating them to the creation of the authors' meaning .

___-___5. The connection between the evidence and the authors' intended and probable effect is less clear than those of the top-scoring essays.

___-___6. Although adequate in number, the evidence in this essay is not as convincing as the top-scoring essay.

___-___7. A few lapses in grammar, diction, or syntax may be present, but the message is clear.

___-___8. The organization of this essay is less appropriate than those of the top-scoring essays.

___-___9. The writer has consistent weakness in grammar and/ or other basic elements of composition.

RESULTS:

Grader 1: _____ - _____ = _____
            Step 1 Score   Step 2 Score

Grader 2: _____ - _____ = _____
            Step 1 Score   Step 2 Score

Grader 1 Score + Grader 2 Score = _____

Above sum
divided by 2 =

Score for essay

Question Four:

Mark Twain

From *The Adventures of Huckleberry Finn*

In the two excerpts below, Mark Twain contrasts life on the river with life of the shore. Read the two passages carefully. Then write a well-organized essay that compares and contrasts Twain's use of these different settings to represent opposing forces or ideas.

Passage One:
Huck's Life on The River

Sometimes we'd have that whole river all to ourselves for the longest time. Yonder was the banks and the islands, across the water; and maybe a spark — which was a candle in a cabin window; and sometimes on the water you could see a spark or two — on a raft or a scow, you know; and maybe you could hear a fiddle or a song coming over from one of them crafts. It's lovely to live on a raft. We had the sky up there, all speckled with stars, and we used to lay on our backs and look up at them, and discuss whether they was made or only just happened. Jim he allowed they was just made, but I allowed they happened; I judged it would have took too long to make so many. Jim said the moon could 'a' laid them; well, that looked kind of reasonable, so I didn't say nothing against it, because I'd seen a frog lay most as many, so of course it could be done. We used to watch the stars that fell, too, and see them streak down. Jim allowed they got spoiled and was hove out of the nest.

Once or twice of a night we would see a steamboat slipping along in the dark, and now and then she would belch a whole world of sparks out of her chimbleys, and they would rain down in the river and look awful pretty; then she would turn a corner and her lights would wink out and her powwow shut off and leave the river still again; and by and by her waves would get to us, a long time after she was gone, and joggle the raft a bit, and after you wouldn't hear nothing for you couldn't tell, how long, except maybe frogs or something.

After midnight, the people on shore went to bed, and then for two or three hours the shores was black — no more sparks in the cabin windows. These sparks was our clock — that first one that showed again meant morning was coming, so we hunted a place to hide and tie up right away.

Passage Two:
Huck's Life on The Shore

I took up the river road as hard as I could put. By and by I began to hear guns a good ways off. When I came in sight of the log store and the woodpile where the steamboat lands I worked along under the trees and brush till I got to a good place, and then I clumb up into the forks of a cottonwood that was out of reach, and watched. There was a wood-rank four foot high a little ways in front of the tree, and first I was going to hide behind that; but maybe it was luckier I didn't.

There was four or five men cavorting around on their horses in the open place before the log store, cussing and yelling, and trying to get a couple of young chaps that was behind the wood-rank alongside of the steamboat landing; but they couldn't come it. Every time one if them showed himself on the river side of the wood pile he got shot at. The two boys were squatting back to back behind the pile, so they could watch both ways.

By and by the men stopped cavorting around and yelling. They started riding towards the store; then up gets one of the boys, draws a steady bead over the wood-rank, and drops one of them out of his saddle. All of the men jumped off of their horses and grabbed the hurt one and started to carry him to the store; and that minute the two boys started on the run. They got half-way to the tree I was in before the men noticed. Then the men see them, and jumped on their horses and took out after them. They gained on the boys, but it didn't do no good, the boys had too good a start; they got to the woodpile that was in front of my tree, and slipped in behind it, and so they had the bulge on the men again. One of the boys was Buck, and the other was a slim young chap about nineteen years old.

The men ripped around a while, and then rode away. As soon as they was out of sight I sung out to Buck and told him. He didn't know what to make of my voice coming out of the tree at first. He was awful surprised. He told me to watch out sharp and let him know when the men come in sight again; said they was up to some devilment or other — wouldn't be gone long. I wished I was out of that tree, but I dasn't come down. Buck began to cry and rip, and 'lowed that him and his cousin Joe (that was the other young chap) would make up for this day yet. He said his father and his two brothers was killed, and two or three of the enemy. Said the Shepardsons laid for them in ambush. Buck said his father and brothers ought to have waited for their relations — the Shepardsons was too strong for them. I asked him what was become of young Harney and Miss Sophia. He said they'd got across the river and was safe. I was glad of that; but the way Buck did take on because he didn't manage to kill Harney that day he shot at him — I hain't ever heard anything like it.

All of a sudden, bang! bang! bang! goes three or four guns — the men had slipped around through the woods and came in from behind without their horses! The boys jumped for the river — both of them hurt — and as they swum down the current the men run along the bank shooting at them and singing out, "Kill them, kill them!" It made me so sick I most fell out of the tree. I ain't a-going to tell all that happened — it would make me sick again if I was to do that. I wished I hadn't ever come ashore that night to see such things. I ain't ever going to get shut of them — lots of times I dream about them.

I stayed in that tree till it begun to get dark, afraid to come down. Sometimes I heard guns away off in the woods; and twice I seen little gangs of men gallop past the log store with guns; so I reckoned the trouble was still a-going on. I was mighty downhearted; so I made up my mind I wouldn't ever go anear that house again, because I reckoned I was to blame, somehow. I judged that that piece of paper meant that Miss Sophia was to meet Harney somewheres at half past two and run off; and I judged I ought to told her father about that paper and the curious way she acted, and then maybe he would 'a' locked her up, and this awful mess wouldn't ever happened.

When I got down out of the tree I crept along down the riverbank a piece, and found the two bodies laying in the edge of the water, and tugged at them till I got them ashore;

then I covered up their faces, and got away as quick as I could. I cried a little when I was covering up Buck's face, for he was mighty good to me.

Checklist for Comparison and Contrast Essay — Mark Twain's *The Adventures of Huckleberry Finn*

STEP 1: Check each item listed below which accurately describes the positive aspects of the essay being graded. Add one point for each item checked from the list. This side describes the basic requirements for a well-written essay. (Grader one should check column one. Grader two should check column two):

___-___1. The writer demonstrates an understanding of how each setting differs.

___-___2. The writer demonstrates an understanding of what each setting represents.

___-___3. This writer demonstrates an understanding of how this contrast contributes to an overall meaning.

___-___4. This writer has reached valid, pertinent, and relevant conclusions about the comparison.

___-___5. The thesis clearly shows the connection between the contrasting settings and the message conveyed.

___-___6. This writer supports the discussion of each setting with good and persuasive substantiation (a minimum of three embedded quotes per paragraph).

___-___7. The diction and sentence structure of this essay communicate a clear message.

___-___8. The organization of this essay aids in communicating a clear message.

___-___9. The grammar aids in communicating a clear message.

MAXIMUM SCORE RESULTS: Grader 1 _____
MAXIMUM SCORE RESULTS: Grader 2 _____

STEP 2:   Check each item below which accurately describes the negative aspects of the essay being graded. This side describes how the essay may not be as good as the higher-scoring essays. (Grader one should check column one. Grader two should check column two):

___-___1. The writer definition of the differences, although accurate, illustrate only what is most easy to grasp.

___-___2. The writer understanding of what each setting represents is less accurate, less specific, or less insightful than those of the highest-scoring essays.

___-___3. The writer's references to the overall meaning may be vague, inaccurate, or leave an indication that the writer did not read the entire work.

___-___4. The writer simply catalogues the use of contrast in general without relating them to the creation of the authors' meaning .

___-___5. The connection between the evidence and the authors' meaning is less clear than those of the top-scoring essays.

___-___6. Although adequate in number, the evidence in this essay is not as convincing as the top-scoring essay.

___-___7. A few lapses in grammar, diction, or syntax may be present, but the message is clear.

___-___8. The organization of this essay is less appropriate than those of the top-scoring essays.

___-___9. The writer has consistent weakness in grammar and/ or other basic elements of composition.

RESULTS:

Grader 1: _____ - _____ = _____
                Step 1 Score   Step 2 Score
Grader 2: _____ - _____ = _____
                Step 1 Score   Step 2 Score
Grader 1 Score + Grader 2 Score = _____

Above sum
divided by 2 =

Score for essay

Question Five:

In each of the following excerpts, one from *The Adventures of Huckleberry Finn* and the other from *The Scarlet Letter*, each writer has highlighted that society's values by creating a situation that alienates the major character. Read each passage carefully. Then write a well-organized essay which compares and contrasts the role that Huck and Hester play and how each character's alienation says something about the surrounding society's assumptions and moral values.

Mark Twain

From *The Adventures of Huckleberry Finn*

(Huck's alienation is caused by the fact that he is a runaway and he is harboring the runaway slave, Jim. The following narration occurs when Huck is confronted by a boatload of men with guns who are searching for five runaway slaves and think Huck may be harboring them. To protect Jim, Huck pretends that the man in the tent is his dad who is sick with smallpox. Here is his reaction to his action:)

They went off and I got aboard the raft, feeling bad and low, because I knowed very well I had done wrong, and I see it warn't no use for me to try to learn to do right; a body that don't get started right when he's little ain't got no show — when the pinch comes there ain't nothing to back him up and keep him to his work, and so he gets beat. Then I thought a minute, and says to myself, hold on; s'pose you'd 'a' done right and give Jim up, would you felt better than what you do now? No, says I, I'd feel bad — I'd feel just the same way I do now. Well, then, says I, what's the use you learning to do right when it's troublesome to do right and ain't no trouble to do wrong, and the wages is just the same? I was stuck. I couldn't answer that. So I reckoned I wouldn't bother no more about it, but after this always do whichever comes handiest at the time.

(However, this conflict comes to a climax about 200 pages later in the story when Huck finally makes a more permanent decision. He writes a letter to Miss Watson, confessing that he has been with Jim all this time. Here is his reaction to that action and Huck's final decision:)

I felt good and all washed clean of sin for the first time I had ever felt so in my life, and I knowed I could pray now. But I didn't do it straight off, but laid the paper down and set there thinking — thinking how good it was all this happened so, and how near I had come to being lost and going to hell. And went on thinking. And got to thinking about our trip down the river; and I see Jim before me all the time: in the day and in the nighttime, sometimes moonlight, sometimes storms, and we a-floating along, talking and singing and laughing. But somehow I couldn't seem to strike no places to harden me against him, but only the other kind. I'd see him standing my watch on top of his'n, 'stead of calling me, so I could go on sleeping; and see him how glad he was when I come back out of the fog; and when I come to see him again in the swamp, up there where the feud was; and such-like times; and would always call me honey, and pet me, and do everything he could think of for me, and how good he always was; and at last I struck the time I saved him by telling the men we had small-pox aboard, and he was so grateful, and said I was the best friend old Jim had ever had in the world, and the only one he's got now; and then I happened to look around and see that paper.

It was a close place. I took it up, and held it in my hand. I was a'trembling, because I'd got to decide, forever, betwixt two things, and I knowed it. I studied a minute, sort of holding my breath, and then says to myself:

"All right, then, I'll go to hell" — and tore it up.

It was awful thoughts and awful words, but they was said. And I let them stay said; and never thought no more about reforming. I shoved the whole thing out of my head, and said I would take up wickedness again, which was in my line, being brung up to it, and the other warn't. And for a starter I would go to work and steal Jim out of slavery again; and if I could think up anything worse, I would do that, too; because as long as I was in, and in for good, I might as well go the whole hog.

Nathaniel Hawthorne

From *The Scarlet Letter*

(Hester's alienation is caused by the fact that she had a baby
out of wedlock and lived in a Puritan society in early America
who thought it was their responsibility to punish such offenses.
The following narration occurs when Hester is put on the platform of the pillory, "a portion" of this Puritan society's "penal
machine," to accept the first stage of her imposed punishment.
Here is Hawthorne's description of the situation:)

A lane was forthwith opened through the crowd of
spectators. Preceded by the beadle, and attended by an ir-
regular procession of stern-browed men and unkindly visaged
women, Hester Prynne set forth towards the place appointed
for her punishment. A crowd of eager and curious school-
boys, understanding little of the matter in hand, except that it
gave them a half-holiday, ran before her progress, turning their
heads continually to stare into her face, and at the winking
baby in her arms, and at the ignominious letter on her breast.
It was no great distance, in those days, from the prison-door to
the market-place. Measured by the prisoner's experience, however, it might be reckoned a journey of some length; for,
haughty as her demeanor was, she perchance underwent an
agony from every footstep of those that thronged to see her, as
if her heart had been flung into the street for them all to spurn
and trample upon. In our nature, however, there is a provision, alike marvelous and merciful, that the sufferer should
never know the intensity of what he endures by its present
torture, but chiefly by the pang that rankles after it. With almost a serene deportment, therefore, Hester Prynne passed
through this portion of her ordeal, and came to a sort of scaffold, at the western extremity of the market-place. It stood
nearly beneath the eaves of Boston's earliest church, and appeared to be a fixture there.

In fact, this scaffold constituted a portion of a penal
machine, which now, for two or three generations past, had
been merely historical and traditionary among us, but was held,
in the old time, to be as effectual an agent, in the promotion of

good citizenship, as ever was the guillotine among the terrorists of France. It was, in short, the platform of the pillory; and above it rose the framework of that instrument of discipline, so fashioned as to confine the human head in its tight grasp, and thus holding it up to public gaze. The very ideal of ignominy was embodied and made manifest in this contrivance of wood and iron. There can be no outrage, methinks, against our common nature, — whatever be the delinquencies of the individual, — no outrage more flagrant than to forbid the culprit to hide his face for shame; as it was the essence of this punishment to do. In Hester Prynne's instance, however, as not unfrequently in other cases, her sentence bore, that she should stand a certain time upon the platform, but without undergoing that gripe about the neck and confinement of the head, the proneness to which was the most devilish characteristic of this ugly engine. Knowing well her part, she ascended a flight of wooden steps, and was thus displayed to the surrounding multitude, at about the height of a man's shoulder above the street.

Had there been a Papist among the crowd of Puritans, he might have seen in this beautiful woman, so picturesque in her attire and mien, and with the infant at her bosom, an object to remind him of the image of Divine Maternity, which so many illustrious painters have vied with one another to represent; something which should remind him, indeed, but only by contrast, of that sacred image of sinless motherhood, whose infant was to redeem the world. Here, there was the taint of deepest sin in the most sacred quality of human life, working such effect, that the world was only the darker for this woman's beauty, and the more lost for the infant she had borne.

The scene was not without a mixture of awe, such as must always invest the spectacle of guilt and shame in a fellow-creature, before society shall have grown corrupt enough to smile, instead of shuddering, at it. The witness of Hester Prynne's disgrace had not yet passed beyond their simplicity. They were stern enough to look beyond her death, had that been the sentence, without a murmur at its severity, but had none of the heartlessness of another social state, which would find only a theme for jest in an exhibition like the present.

Checklist for Comparison and Contrast Essay — Mark Twain and Nathaniel Hawthorne's Views on Alienation

STEP 1: Check each item listed below which accurately describes the positive aspects of the essay being graded. Add one point for each item checked from the list. This side describes the basic requirements for a well-written essay. (Grader one should check column one. Grader two should check column two):

___-___1. The writer demonstrates a perceptive understanding of the role that Huck and Hester play in each of the passages.

___-___2. The writer demonstrates an understanding of how the alienation of the major character in each passage highlights that society's values.

___-___3. This writer demonstrates an understanding of how this affects the development of theme, action, or other characters.

___-___4. This writer has reached valid, pertinent, and relevant conclusions about the comparison.

___-___5. The thesis clearly shows the connection between each character's role and the message conveyed.

___-___6. This writer supports the discussion of each setting with good and persuasive substantiation (a minimum of three embedded quotes per paragraph).

___-___7. The diction and sentence structure of this essay communicate a clear message.

___-___8. The organization of this essay aids in communicating a clear message.

___-___9. The grammar aids in communicating a clear message.

MAXIMUM SCORE RESULTS: Grader 1 _____
MAXIMUM SCORE RESULTS: Grader 2 _____

STEP 2:   Check each item below which accurately describes the negative aspects of the essay being graded. This side describes how the essay may not be as good as the higher-scoring essays. (Grader one should check column one. Grader two should check column two):

___-___1. The writer's definition of the role each character plays, although accurate, illustrates only what is most easy to grasp.

___-___2. The writer's understanding of how the alienation of the major character in each passage highlights that society's values is less accurate, less specific, or less insightful than those of the highest-scoring essays.

___-___3. The writer's references to the overall meaning of the work may be vague, inaccurate, or just plot summary.

___-___4. The writer simply catalogues the use of contrast in general without relating them to the creation of the authors' meaning .

___-___5. The connection between the evidence and the authors' meaning is less clear than those of the top-scoring essays.

___-___6. Although adequate in number, the evidence in this essay is not as convincing as the top-scoring essay.

___-___7. A few lapses in grammar, diction, or syntax may be present, but the message is clear.

___-___8. The organization of this essay is less appropriate than those of the top-scoring essays.

___-___9. The writer has consistent weakness in grammar and/ or other basic elements of composition.

RESULTS:

Grader 1: _____ - _____ = _____
         Step 1 Score   Step 2 Score

Grader 2: _____ - _____ = _____
         Step 1 Score   Step 2 Score

Grader 1 Score + Grader 2 Score = _____

Above sum
divided by 2 =

Score for essay

CHAPTER Nine:

Contests
of Knowledge

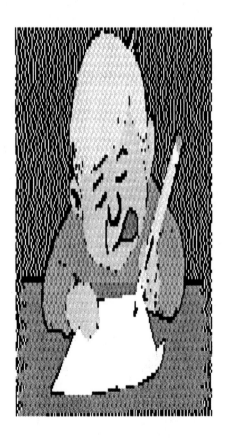

Chapter Nine:

Contests of Knowledge

Throughout the school year, I require that my students make presentations to the class. These presentations are designed by them to help improve reading comprehension, writing skills, and vocabulary retention. Exercises in persuasive, expository, descriptive, and narrative writing; fun journal entry suggestions; and art options can be found in the *Practical Guide to the Advanced Placement (AP) English Language and Composition Examination.* Fun exercises which test general knowledge, encourage internet use, and suggested more creative ways of responding to literature can be found in the *Practical Guide to the Advanced Placement (AP) English Literature and Composition Examination.* These can be ordered at "Amazon.com" or you may use the order form at the end of this *Writer* to purchase these books directly from *School House Books.*

One of the biggest stumbling blocks to student success is lack of vocabulary knowledge. With low vocabulary, students fail multiple-choice tests and timed essay tests because they do not understand some (or all) of the words used in the questions. Their writing also lacks the sophistication that a larger vocabulary would bring.

Vocabulary learning permeates this entire textbook. Most of the exercises in this chapter test the students' knowledge of definitions — a necessary first step in vocabulary expansion — however, it must be noted that this is just the first step. Students must learn how to recognize and write about how these words, rhetorical devices, and stylistic elements are used by authors to add meaning, tone, or create an effect or purpose for writing. Lastly, students must also learn to apply these words, rhetorical devices, and stylistic elements in their own writing. These last two goals need to be emphasized in all assignments all year(s) long.

A glossary of terms that need to be learning in any honors English class can be found in both the *Practical Guide to the Advanced Placement (AP) English Language and Composition Examination* and the *Practical Guide to the Advanced Placement (AP) English Literature and Composition Examination* textbooks.

Some of the other contests review other concepts of English comprehension and composition.

Following are some of the ways that students have used the presentations defined in the first paragraph to engage the class in learning more creatively.

Exercise One

"Family Feud"

Directions: The class should be divided into two teams. One person from each team comes to the front and faces each other. A tennis ball (or some other object) is placed on a table between them. When the games hostess reads the question, the first person to grab the tennis ball gets to answer the question.

This portion can be also be accomplished by having each individual put a golf ball or throw soft darts, or ___ to determine who is eligible to answer the question. Each team member should have a chance to act in the individual role.

If an incorrect response is given, the opponent may answer. If the individual opponent gives an incorrect response the teams may attempt to answer in an alternating manner. If no one answers correctly, the hostess provides the answer. Each correct answer is worth one point. The team with the most points wins.

This game can be modified for upper level students by awarding an additional five points for any individual or team member who can give a correct example of the device. For example:

Personification — "The fog comes on little cat feet. It sits looking over city . . . and then moves on." Carl Sandburg

Here are the definitions for the contest. Students are to guess the word being defined.

Definition One:
A concept or value that can not be seen (love, honor, courage) which the writer usually tries to illustrate by comparing it metaphorically to a known concrete object.

Definition Two:
The process (including physical description, dialogue, thoughts and feelings, actions, or effect on others) by which the writer reveals the personalitoes of the people in the work.

Definition Three:
Usually written to reaffirm or finally state the thesis.

Definition Four:
Word choice used by the author to persuade, or to portray tone, purpose, or effect.

Definition Five:
A brief, clever, and usually memorable statement.

Definition Six:
A chosen arrangement of words that creates a pleasant sound.

Definition Seven:
A figure of speech used by the author to overexaggerate or overstate something to create a certain effect.

Definition Eight:
A literary device used to imply a discrepancy between what is said and what is meant.

Definition Nine:
A skillful handling of diction and syntax, used by the author to convey tone, purpose, or effect.

Definition Ten:
A comparison in which an unknown concept or an abstract idea is illustrated by comparing it directly to a known concrete object.

Definition Eleven:
The person telling the story.

Definition Twelve:
The process of arranging evidence to support a thesis.

Definition Thirteen:
A figure of speech that adds ambiguity by combining contradictory terms (cheerfully vindictive, living dead, etc.).

Definition Fourteen:
A statement or situation that appears contradictory but is true.

Definition Fifteen:
The Latin name for an appeal to the emotions used in an argument.

Definition Sixteen:
A fugure of speech in which inanimate objects are given animate qualities.

Definition Seventeen:
A device used by a writer to emphasize an important character trait, to reinforce a story's theme, to highlight the speaker's attitude, or to focus the reader's attention on a person, place, or thing.

Definition Eighteen:
Anything that represents something in a typical way.

Definition Nineteen:
The central idesa or the writer's view.

Definition Twenty:
The arrangement of words into sentences used by the author to convey tone, purpose, or effect.

Definition Twenty-one:
A statement that says less than what is means.

Definition Twenty-two:
References to literary, artistic, scientific, or historical people, places, or things.

Definition Twenty-three:
A story or poem in which the characters, settings, and events stand for other people or events or for abstract ideas or qualities.

Definition Twenty-four:
Assertions made based on a logical presentation of facts and statistics combined with an believable appeal to the emotions.

Definition Twenty-five:
A categorical statement made by the author, speaker, narrator, or character which generalize an opinion usually about human nature.

Definition Twenty-six:
The author's state of mind or point of view toward himself/ herself or another person, place, or thing.

Definition Twenty-seven:
The tension created in a story by the struggle or outcome of the struggle.

Definition Twenty-eight:
Language that is intended to be literal, has a dictionary meaning, and emphasizes an objective tone.

Definition Twenty-nine:
Language that is intended to have an implied meaning.

Definition Thirty:
The influence felt by the reader or listener as a result of the use of such rhetorical strategies as arguments, assumptions, attitudes, contrast, diction, imagery, ot repetition.

Definition Thirty-one:

A form of logical thinking used to analyze the author's reliability or credibility.

Definition Thirty-two:

A literary technique in which the author gives hints about future events.

Definition Thirty-three:

Diction describing the five senses.

Definition Thirty-four:

To restate the content of a work in your own words.

Definition Thirty-five:

The point of view or attitude created by the author's manipulation of language.

Definition Thirty-six:

The reason for writing the essay — usually based on the effect the writer wants to have on the audience.

Definition Thirty-sseven

A literary device in which a question is asked that requires no answer but usually provokes thought.

Definition Thirty-eight:

A word that means the same as another word.

Definition Thirty-nine:

A play upon words based on the multiple meanings of words.

Game Over!

Exercise Two

"The Memory Game"

Directions: Write the following three items (name of a rhetorical device, definition of the same rhetorical device, and an example of the same rhetorical device) on separate note cards. Then place them, face down, on the desk.

The class should be divided into two teams. One at a time, a student tries to match all three items by lifting up three cards so all can see, If they do not match the student places the card, face down, in the same place. The team with the best memory will be able to make the most matches and win. Here are the items to be copied on note cards:

Rhetorical Device:
Hyperbole

Definition:
An exaggeration made not to be taken literally but for the sake of emphasis.

Example:
"In a trice(which in Bangladesch, is two and a half hours) we were back in the hired cab, whereupon the Dkaka traffic, which normally doesn't move, quit doing even that." PJ O'Rourke

----

Rhetorical Device:
Assonance

Definition:
The similarity or repetition of a vowel sound in two or more words.

Example:
"I was napping and so gently you came rapping, and so faintly you came tapping. . ."   Edgar Allen Poe

----

Rhetorical Device:
Apostrophe

Definition:
Addressing someone or something not present.

Example:
"O Captain, my Captain."   Walt Whitman

Rhetorical Device:
Rhetorical Question

Definition:
A question asked solely to produce an effect — not to elicit a
reply.

Example:
"Are women persons?   Susan B. Anthony

Rhetorical Device:
Alliteration

Definition:
Repition of the intial letter or sound in two or more words.

Example:
"I stood there wondering, fearing, doubting, dreaming dreams
no mortal ever dared to dream before."   Edgar Allen Poe

Rhetorical Device:
Irony

Definition:
Saying something and meaning another; an occurence which is contrary to what is expected.

Example:
"Do not weep maiden, for war is kind."   Stephen Crane

Rhetorical Device:
Simile

Definition:
An indirect comparison between two unrelated things, indicating a likeness between attributes found in both things.

Example:
"By him, as by chain'd shot, whole ranks to die; he is the tyrant pike, our hearts the fry."   John Donne

---

Rhetorical Device:
Antithesis

Definition:
A balancing or contrasting of one term against another,

Example:
"It was the best of times, it was the worst of times."
                                        Charles Dickens

Rhetorical Device:
Metaphor

Definition:
A direct comparison between two unlike things.

Example:
"I would be pleased if this book . . . pointed the way to some odd, forsaken place that makes the tuning fork beneath your breastbone hum." Barton Sutter

----

Rhetorical Device:
Parallelism

Definition:
The repetition of similar beginnings to create balanced expressions. This is done when the writer wants to express a pair or series of ideas. Making each item parallel — making each item look alike grammatically — provides emphasis and establishes rhythm and balance.

Example:
"Let every nation know, whether it wishes us well or ill, that we shall pay any price, bear any burden, meet any hard ship, support any friend, oppose any foe to assure the survival and the success of liberty."   John F. Kennedy

----

Make more memory game cards by using example that appear in Chapters Two and Three for the following:

From Chapter Two "Diction" use puns, oxymoron, litotes, imagery (sights, sounds, and smells), etc.

From Chgapter Three "Syntax" use cumulative sentence, periodic sentence, inverted sentence, short and simple sentence, participle, gerund, subordinate clause, infinitive, etc.

Exercise Three

"Jeopardy"

Directions: Pick five categories from the many listed below. Write the categories on the board in a chart like the one below. Divide the class into two teams. Each tream picks one category. The hostess reads the answer and the teams have to state the question that would go with the answer. The team that finishes with the most points wins. The correct questions to these answers are in the *Teacher's Guide to The School House Books (AP) Writer.*

Quotes from Essays	English Terms I	English Terms II	Tone Words	Essay Writing
100	100	100	100	100
200	200	200	200	200
300	300	300	300	300
400	400	400	400	400
500	500	500	500	500

Here are the answers. The correct questions can be found in the *Teacher's Guide to The Schoold House Books (AP) Writer.*

"Quotes from Essays"

100   "I see a young Negro boy .. sitting on a step in front of a vermin-infested apartment in Harlem."

200   "Tis some visitor," I muttered, "tapping at my chamber door — only this and nothing more."

300   "I cannot think I was a very dangerous character in any of these aspects, but in all of them I carried the same warning on my back."

400   "Every man carries about him a touchstone, if he will make use of it, to distinguish substantial gold from superficial glitterings, truth from appearance."

500   "We want to start from scratch and words don't; which is the thing that matters — matters over and over again."

"English Terms I"

100   The use of ridicule, sarcasm, irony, etc., to expose or attack the follies of himan nature.

200   A reference to someone or something that is known from history, literature, religion, politics, sports, science , or some other branch of culture.

300   "One of the four major form or modes of writing in which the writer attempts to explain something.

400   A feeling of uncertainty and suspense about what will happen next in a story.

500   A style of writing that reveals the inner (and often chaotic) inner workings of a writer's mind.

"English Terms II"

100   The use of sounds that echo trheir sense.

200   "The series of related events of the story; sometimes called the storyline.

300   A relatively short story that teaches a moral.

400   A technique by which the writer suggest two or more conflicting meanings.

500   The use of pleasant, polite, and harmless-sounding expressions to mark harsh, rude, or infamous thoughts.

"Tone Words"

100   A longing, usually sentimental, to experience a past time.

200   Easily broken or dsamaged.

300   Lewd or uncontrolled. Has the same name as a Chinese food.

400   Having conflicting feelings about something.

500   Expressing excessive emotion in an unrestrained manner.

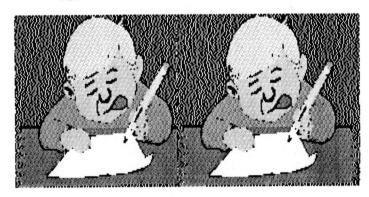

"Essay Writing"

100   This sentence, coming near the end of the introduc-
       tion (to guide the organization of the essay) and, com-
       ing at the beginning of the conclusion (to reveal a dis-
       covery made by the close reading of the passage) must
       show your conclusion about the realtionship between
       the author's manipulation of language and his creation
       of attitude, purpose, or effect.

200   The introduction to any timed question should be short
       and should never repeat this verbatim.

300   The correct process to record evidence - to quote and
       explain in the same sentence.

400   To achieve the highest scores, an essay answer must
       explore this aspect of the question.

500   To achieve the highest scores, the conclusion of the
       essay must have this.

FINAL JEOPARDY

A stylistic or rhetorical device which places two items side by
side or close together to convey tone or create an effect.

Exercise Four

"Word Scrabble"

Directions: Divide the class into two teams. Write the following scrambled words on the board one at a time. Each team
has a reasonable amount of time to unscrabble the word. If
they are stumped or get the wrong answer, the other team can
guess. Each right answer is worth one point. The team with
the most number of points at the end wins. Here are the
scrambled words. The answers can be found in the *Teacher's
Guide to The Schoold House Books (AP) Writer.*

tcatzreachrianio
tilhrcrae
hoste
oynry
mtpoenaoioao
csioconlun
pboelhyer
pitxjatunioos

Exercise Five

"Wheel of Fortune"

Directions: Split into three groups. Each team member has a chance to spin, select consonants, or buy a vowel. A vowel is worth 100 points. If an incorrect consonant or vowel is requested, the next team spins. When the right word is guessed, an extra 100 points will be awarded if a correct definition of author is given. Here are the categories and words:

Style:
R E A L I S M

Definitiuon: A literary style developed in the 19th Century that attempts to portray life accurately, without idealizing or romantizing it.
S A T I R E

Definition: A type of writing which makes fun of human weakness, vice, or folly in order to bring about change.

English Terms:
P L A U S I B I L I T Y

An element of literary judgment which determines the believ-ability of the work.

N O N   S E Q U I T U R S

Definition: Faulty conclusions about causal relationships.

Titles:

I STAND HERE IRONINING

Author: Tillie Olsen

ADAM BEDE

Author: George Eliot

BONUS ROUND

Pick five consonants and one vowel.

Phrase:

ONCE UPON A TIME

Exercise Six

Other Words:

Directions: Divide the class into teams of four. Write the following words on the board one at a time. The object is to create as many other words as possible from the word on the board. Here are the words:

Juxtaposition

Characterization

Answers can be found in the *Teacher's Guide to The Schoold House Books (AP) Writer.*

Exercise Seven

Synonyms:

Directions: Divide the class into teams of four. Write the following words on the board one at a time. The object is to write as many synonyms as possible for the word on the board. After 10 to 20 minutes, each group reads their words. If any other group has the same word, they each have to cross it off. The team with the most original, but correct synonyms, wins. Here are the words:

Big
Cold
Happy
Heated
Light
Mad

Answers can be found in the *Teacher's Guide to The School House Books (AP) Writer.*

Exercise Seven

Another Word:

Directions: Divide the class into teams of four. Write the following words and definitions on the board one at a time. The object is to define the original word and to guess the word that is defined and can be created with some of the letters from the original word. Any team member may raise their hand to answer. The first group to answer correctly wins a point. Here are the words:

What is the defintion of **"quadruple?"**
Using some of the letters in the word **"quadruple,"** find a four letter word that means "lack of refinement."

What is the defintion of **"confoundedl?"**
Using some of the letters in the word **"confounded,"** find a five letter word that means "to have gotten by searching."

What is the defintion of **"bolster?"**
Using some of the letters in the word **"bolster,"** find a five letter word that means "took without the owner's permission

What is the defintion of **"tottering?"**
Using some of the letters in the word **"tottering,"** find a four
letter word that means "to give forth a resonant sound."

What is the defintion of **"avaricious?"**
Using some of the letters in the word **"avaricious,"** find a seven
letter word that means "many-sided; versatile; or characterized by variety."

What is the defintion of **"chicanery?"**
Using some of the letters in the word **"chicanery,"** find a five
letter word that means "a place or position specially suited to
one person."

What is the defintion of **"contrast?"**
Using some of the letters in the word **"contrast,"** find a five
letter word that means "an entertainment at which a person
undergoes severe but playful criticism."

What is the defintion of **"conclusion?"**
Using some of the letters in the word **"conclusion,"** find a seven
letter word that means "an group of people assembled to deliberate, consult, or give advice."

What is the defintion of **"confessional?"**
Using some of the letters in the word **"confessional,"** find a six
letter word that means "to add zest or interest to something."

What is the defintion of **"connotative?"**
Using some of the letters in the word **"connotative,"** find an
eight letter word that means "a system used to write down
important information."

What is the defintion of **"purpose?"**
Using some of the letters in the word **"purpose,"** find a five
letter word that means "a spoken or written language with a
rhetorical structure."

What is the defintion of **"compare?"**
Using some of the letters in the word **"compare,"** find a four letter word that means "a mature female horse."

What is the defintion of **"conscience?"**
Using some of the letters in the word **"conscience,"** find a five letter word that means "inasmuch as; because."

What is the defintion of **"persuasive?"**
Using some of the letters in the word **"persuasive,"** find a five letter word that means "outstanding."

What is the defintion of **"natural?"**
Using some of the letters in the word **"natural,"** find a four letter word that means "an animal stunted in size compared to the rest of the litter."

What is the defintion of **"conveniently?"**
Using some of the letters in the word **"persuasive,"** find a four letter word that means "to hide."

What is the defintion of **"variable?"**
Using some of the letters in the word **"variable,"** find a six letter word that means "workable, likely to have real meaning."

What is the defintion of **"consideration?"**
Using some of the letters in the word **"consideration,"** find a six letter word that means "a nearly extinct vulture found in the mountains of Southern California."

Answers can be found in the *Teacher's Guide to The Schoold House Books (AP) Writer.*

Other Suggestions:

1. Play Hangman
2. Make a Word Find
3. Make a Crossword Puzzle
4. Play Pictionary with English Concepts, phrases, etc.

CHAPTER Ten:

An Extended Writing Project

Chapter Ten: An Extended Writing Project

A Term Paper Project that addresses Ambiguity

Most of the essay questions in both English Literature and English Language classrooms deal with ambiguity — issues that have more than two different interpretations. To earn the highest scores, the students need to explore that complexity in their essays. This extended assignment helps students deal with this all important concept.

This extended writing project includes selecting an abstract issue that affects today's students; surveying the information available on the issue by reading or viewing selections written or produced by people from the AP Suggested Reading List that have an opinion on the topic; and developing an eventual personal stance on that issue.

NOTE: It is expected that each student will have read widely — a minimum of six hundred pages — to develop a legitimate stance on the issue.

These selections should also include a variety of formats (autobiographies, debates, documentaries, editorials, essays, speeches, interviews, journal articles, novels, poems, etc.), and a variety of viewpoints on the same issue.

After taking notes to interpret, evaluate, and analyze the various viewpoints found, a ten-page paper is expected.

An Overview of the Steps:

It is very important to set up a schedule and meet deadlines when writing a longer paper. The following is a suggested schedule of deadlines:

The Assignment: Select an issue that affects today's students. Survey the information available on the issue by reading selections written by people from the AP suggested reading list that have an opinion on your topic. These selections should include a variety of formats (autobiographies, debates, documentaries, editorials, essays, speeches, interviews, journal articles, novels, poems, etc.) and a variety of viewpoints on the same issue. Take notes to interpret, evaluate, and analyze the various viewpoints found. Then write a ten page, 3,000 word paper which analyzes how the authors selected manipulate the language to develop their stance(s). In the end the student should have developed an original, defendable position.

Time: Eight weeks

To complete the assignment, the student will meet the following deadlines;

1. Select a topic appropriate to the assignment that has a minimum of six longer sources which represent varying viewpoints on the same issue. This is to be accomplished one week after the assignment starts.

2. Complete a Working Bibliography within the first week.

3. Read, research, think, evaluate and take notes. This will be checked weekly for a six week period.

4. Create a working outline by shuffling the notecards into piles which reveal a structural organization. This will be checked four weeks after the assignment starts.

5. Develop a thesis that advances your own stance. This is to be accomplished five weeks after the assignment starts.

6. Write a rough draft based on the outline and thesis. This rough draft should include parenthetical citations utilizing the MLA format. This is to be completed six weeks after the assignment starts.

7. Edit each others' papers in the seventh week comliant to the grading checklist provided.

8. Revise to make a final copy. This will include respectively: a title page, a formal outline, the text, and a bibliography. This will be due at the end of eight weeks.

Step One: Selecting a Topic

Select an issue that affects today's students. State this topic as a question that can be answered through research. Note: This question must be ambiguous enough to have more than one legitimate viewpoint. Look for quotations on the internet to accomplish step one. Many addresses can be discovered, but two of the best I've found are:

www.cyber-nation.com
AND/OR
www.quoteland.com

To select a topic from either of the two addresses on
the preceding page:
A. Click on quotations by topic or subject.
B. Click on a topic of interest. In this very prelimi-
nary stage, it is important to find key words that
reveal differing viewpoints. For instance,
1. Some synonyms for "independence" are:
individuality, unusualness, etc.
2. Some antonyms for "independence" are:
conformity, routine, convention, tradition,
commonness, ritual, routine, congruity, fash-
ionable, habit, obedience, etc.

Some important quotes that help to verbalize this topic into a
question are:

"Independence I have long considered as the grand blessing
of life, the basis of every virtue; and independence I will ever
secure by contracting my wants, though I were to live on a
barren heath."   Mary Wollstonecraft

"Imitation is suicide."   Ralph Waldo Emerson

"Whatever crushes individuality is despotism, no matter what
name it is called."   John Stewart Mill

"We are discreet sheep; we wait to see how the drove is going,
and then go with the drove."   Mark Twain

"Traditions are the guide posts driven deep in our subconscious
minds. The most powerful ones are those we can't even describe and aren't even aware of."
          Ellen Goodman

"Every generation laughs at the old fashions, but religiously
follows the new."   Henry David Thoreau

     "There is no calamity which a great nation can invite
which equals that which follows a supine submission to wrong
and injustice and the consequent loss of national self-respect
and honor, beneath which are shielded and defended a people's
safety and greatness."   Grover Cleveland

"Without the aid of prejudice and custom, I should not be able to find my way across the room."

William Hazlitt

Verbalizing an issue which indicates an important conflict for today's young adult for these choices would be something to do with Tradition vs. Independence. Reading the above quotes should help form a question, like the following, that would begin to address the complexity of the issue: When should we be Independent, and when should we follow the guideposts of tradition?

Here are some other issues that students have developed into papers:

What is the most effective means of instituting change? Can equality be achieved through non-violent means? Are recent equality standards fair? Is prejudice more powerful than equality? Does money really matter in today's society? What are the effects of love? Is love worth the pain? What is a good friend? How does courage form a basis for what a person becomes? How does honesty fit in a society of deception? How important is it to be virtuous? Is honesty always the best policy? What is society's perception of beauty? What are the effects of power? Who really runs the government? Are all politicians corrupt? What is society's perception of beauty? What is the value of the mind? What is the connection between freedom and responsibility? Is the future calculated by choice, fate, or both? To what extent must we conform? What makes an artists and a work of art great? Being the holder of so many important attributes, we would all like to think we possess the power to control our own minds, but do we? How does society view intelligence? Will honesty get you ahead in life?

Then scroll down searching the various quotations to find five to ten authors that are listed on this internet page that also appear on the AP Suggested Reading List.

Step Two: Locating, Evaluating, Using and Documenting Sources

Find longer sources written on the issue selected by the authors selected. Type in the authors name on a search engine. Scroll down, clicking on a source that lists a bibliography of your author's works.

A good internet source can be found at
> A. Type in Author's name on netsearch OR
> B. Type in www. teleport. com / ~ groves / names.htm
> C. Click on the letter representing the last name of your author
> D. Every home page available on-line will be listed. Click on the one that seems most appropriate.
> E. Print or check out source from list.

All the conventional library sources should be used as well.

MLA Documentation Style

We will be using the MLA style manual for research paper documentation. As a writer you will be responsible for applying the MLA style consistently to your paper from beginning to end. Following is a partial list of the rules for parenthetic references and Works Cited Entries that specifically apply to the Argument paper. For a more complete text, refer to the MLA Handbook for Writers of Research Papers.

Works Cited

You are expected to have a "Works Cited" page at the end of your paper. Cite all sources on this page using the following format. If certain items do not apply or are not available, simply skip those and go on to the next item.

Works Cited Entries: Books, Pamphlets, CD-Rom, etc.

Author's surname, first name. "Title of article, document, essay, etc." <u>Title of book, anthology, multivolume work, reference book, pamphlet, CD-Rom</u>, etc. Vol. 2. Ed. First name followed by surname. 3rd ed. City, State of publisher: Name of Publisher, most recent copyright date. page numbers.

Works Cited Entries:
Magazines, Newspapers, Interviews, Letters, Records, Videocassettes, etc,

Author's surname, first name. Letter. Address to ___. "Title of magazine or newspaper article, interview, or letter." By the name of the interviewer. Interview. Cartoon. Title of magazine or newspaper. List the letters LP if it is a recording. Videocassette. Movie. Map. Date listed as 4 April 1998: page numbers of article.

Works Cited Entries:
Computer Network Sources

Author's surname, first name. "Title of the article or document." Title of the journal, newsletter, conference, document, file, etc. Type of publication, volume number, issue numbe, or other identifying number (year or date of publication): number of pages or paragraphs if given/ or n.pag. On-line. Name of computer network. Date of access. Available: specify electronic address.

Works Cited Entries:
Non-print Sources

Author's or Singer's surname, first name. "Title of the Document, Cartoon, Radio Program, Segment of a TV Program." Title of the Song, Audiocassette, Movie, Filmstrip, Map, Newspaper, TV Program, etc. Dir. First name surname. Perf. Actor's (Actress's) First Name Surname. Type of non-print source - CD-ROM. LP. Videocassette. Cartoon. Address. Place of production: Publisher, Record Company, Movie Studio, or Producer, Date.

Other Modifications:
1. If two or three authors are listed, list them in the order chosen on the book's title page. Begin the first with author's surname, first name. Separate the two or three names with a

comma. Enter the second and third names as First name followed by surname.

2. If more than three authors are listed, list the first author only as author's surname, first name followed by a comma and et. al.

3. If you cite two or more books by the same author, list the books alphabetically by title with the authors surname, first name on the first book. For each additional entry by the same author, substitute three hyphens for the author's name.

4. The author may be listed as a corporate group such as United State. Department of Labor. Bureau of Statistics.

Parenthetical Citations

You are required to give credit for your sources of information by using parenthetical citations within the body of your paper. This can be done in any of the following manners:

1. List the author's name and page number in parentheses after each quote or paraphrase used.

2. List the author's name, Title of Source, and page number within the sentence of the text after each quote or paraphrase used.

3. Use any combination of the first two choices after each quote or paraphrase used.

The extensive list of sources following page has been used successfully by AP students in the past.

Works Cited

Angelou, Maya. Excerpt from *I Know Why the Caged Bird Sings* in *The Lively Art of Writing*. Ed. Cosmo F. Ferrara. 3rd Edition. New York, NY: Random House, 1989. 281-284.

Aristotle. *Politics*. London: Harvard University Press, 1977.

Atwood, Margaret. *Wilderness Tips*. New York: Doubleday, 1991.

Bacon, Francis. "The Advancement of Learning." *Great Books of the Western World*. Ed. Robert Hutchins. Chicago, Illinois: University of Chicago, 1952.

- - -. *The Complete Essays of Francis Bacon*. New York: Washington Square Press, 1963.

Baldwin, James. "The Creative Process." Creative America. 1962.

Bate, Walter Jackson. *Coleridge.* New York: The MacMillan Company, 1968.

Beck, Sanderson. "Thoreau's Civil Disobedience." On-line. Internet. 26 January 1997. Available: http//www.west.net/~brck/w16-thoreau.html

Beck, Sanderson. "The Pacifism of Bertrand Russell." On-line. Internet. 26 January 1997. Available: http//www.west.net/~brck/w24-russell.html

Bronowski, Jacob. *Identity of Man.* Heinemann, 1965.

Buckley Jr., William F. *Up From Liberalism.* New York: Stein and Day, 1984.

Carlyle, Thomas. *The French Revolution.* New York: The Heritage Press, 1956.

Churchill, Winston S. *Memories and Adventures.* New York: Weidenfeld and Nicolson, 1989.

Crane, Stephen. *Maggie: A Girl of the Streets.* New York: Bantam Books, 1986.

Dillard, Annie. *An American Childhood.* New York: Harper and Row, 1974.

- - - . "Annie Dillard Quotes." Two Pages. On-line. Internet. 12 September 1998. Available: http: //www.chesco.com/~artman/dillard.html

- - - . Pilgrim at Tinker Creek. New York: Harper and Row, 1974.

- - - . Teaching a Stone to Talk. New York: Harper and Row, 1982.

Einstein, Albert. *Ideas and Opinions.* New York, Crown Publishers, Inc., 1954.

Emerson, Ralph Waldo. "Essays: Second Series, Character." Essays and Lectures. New York, NY: Library of Congress, 1983. 493-509.

- - - . "Essays: First Series, Friendship." *The Essays of Ralph Waldo Emerson.* Cambridge, MA: The President and Fellows of Harvard College, 1987. 111-128.

- - - . Self-Reliance - 1841. Essay. Sixteen pages. On-line. Internet. 30 October 1998. Available: http: // www.nidlink.com/~bobhard/reliance.html

Fitzgerald, F. Scott. *The Great Gatsby.* New York: MacMillan Publishing Company, 1980.

Gray, Francine du Plessix. "On Friendship." *The Contemporary Essay.* Ed. Donald Hall. Boston: Bedford Books of St. Martin's Press, 1995. 198-203.

Hemingway, Ernest. *The Complete Hemingway Letters Collection.* Albany, New York: Sampton and Winston, Inc., 1984.

Jefferson, Thomas. "Inaugural Address." Speech. Seven pages. On-line. Internet. 30 October 1998. Available: http // www.columbia.edu / acis / bartleby / inaugral / pres 16.html

- - -. "Politics and Government: Freedom of Religion." List of Quotations. Eight pages. On-Line. Internet. 7 October 1998. Available: http: // text. virginia. edu / Jefferson / quotations / Jeff 1650. htm.

Keller, Helen. "Helen Keller's Speech." One Page. On-Line. Internet. June 30, 1925. Available: http: // www.uark.edu/ALADDIN/flions/hk.html

Kennedy, John Fitzgerald. "Address to the General Court of the Commonwealth of Massachusetts." Speech. 9 January 1961. three pages. On-line. Netscape Navigator 3.0. Available: http//www.cs.umb.edu/ jfklibrary/j010961.htm

King, Coretta Scott. *The Words of Martin Luther King, Jr.* New York: Newmarket Press, 1964.

King, Martin Luther. "I Have a Dream" Speech. On-Line. Internet. 21 September, 1998. Available: http:// www. ups.edu/history/afamhis/essays/dream.txt

Lewis, Thomas. *Late Night Thoughts on Listening to Mahler's Ninth Symphony.* New York: Viking Press, 1973.

Lincoln, Abraham. "Gettysburg Address." Speech. Two pages. On-line. Internet. 19 October 1998 Available: http:// gettysburg . com / visitor / booklet / bat / address . htm

Locke, John. *Of Civil Government, Second Treatise.* Chicago, IL: Henry Regnery Company, 1955.

Malcolm X. *The Autobiography of Malcolm X.* New York: Grove Press, Inc., 1965.

- - -. "Letter from Mecca." Three pages. On-line. Internet. 20 October 1998. Available: http://members.aol.com/ klove0l/meccaltr.htm

Mencken, Henry Louis. *A Choice of Days.* New York: Random House Publications, 1980.

- - -. "Hymn to the Truth." Prejudice: Sixth Series. On-line. Internet. Available: http://physserv.physics.wis.edu/ shalzi/mencken/hymn-to-the-truth/

Merton, Thomas. *Ghandi on Violence.* New York: New Directions Publishing, 1965.

Miller, Arthur. *The Crucible.* New York: Penguin Books, 1976.

More, Thomas. *Utopia.*

O'Rourke, P. J. *Give War a Chance.* New York: Atlantic Monthly Press, 1992.

Paine, Thomas. "The Crisis." *American Issues.* Ed. Charles M. Dollar and Gary W. Reichard. New York: Glencoe/ McGraw-Hill, 1994. 76 - 81.

- - -. "Common Sense." On-line. Internet. 7 February 1997. Available: http// odur.let.rug.nl / ~usa / d / 1776-1800 / pain e/ cm / senseo2.html

Roosevelt, Franklin. "The Four Freedoms." Speech. Seven pages. On-line. Internet. 6 January 1941. Avilable: http // www.libertynet.org / edcivic / fdr. html

Safire, William. *Lend Me Your Ears Great Speeches in American History.*

Sagen, Carl. *Billions and Billions.* New York: Random House, 1997.

- - -. Broca's Brain. New York: Random House, Inc.

- - -. The Dragons of Eden. New York: Random House, Inc., 1977.

Tennyson, Alfred Lord. *The Charge of the Light Brigade.* New York: Golden Press, 1964.

Thoreau, Henry David. "Civil Disobedience." On-Line. Internet. 1 January 1997. Available: Http// sunsite.berkley.edu/literature/thoreau/ civil disobedience

- - -. Walden. New York: Penguin Books, 1960.

Truman, Harry S. "Inaugural Address." Speech. Fifteen pages. On-line. Internet. 30 October 1998. Available: http // www.columbia.edu / acis / bartleby / inaugral / pres 53.html

Twain, Mark. *The Adventures of Huckleberry Finn.* UAS: Permabound, 1988.

- - -. "Mental Telegraphy." *The Complete Essays of Mark Twain.* Garden City, NY: Doubleday and Company, Inc., 1963. 71-76.

- - -. Directory of Maxims and Quotations. List of Quotes. Three pages. On-line. Internet. 26 September 1998. Available: http: // www.tarleton.edu/ activities/pages/facultypages/schmidt/truth.html

Vidal, Gore. *1876.* New York: Random House, 1976.

Viorst, Judith. "Friends, Good Friends — and Such Good
      Friends." *The MacMillan Reader.* Eds. Judith Nadell,
      John Langan, and Linda McMeniman. New York:
      NY:Macmillan Publishing Company, 1993. 290-295.
Weinberg, Arthur and Lila Weinburg. *Instead of Violence.* New
      York: Grossman Publishers, 1963.
Wilde, Oscar. *The Picture of Dorian Gray.* New York: Doubleday
      and Company, Inc., 1960.

Step Three: Notetaking

Survey the information available on the issue by reading or
viewing selections written by people from the AP Suggested
Reading List that have an opinion on your topic. These selection should include a variety formats (editorials, speeches, debates, interviews, documentaries, journal articles, etc.) and
viewpoints on the same issue.

Source Analysis

Answer the following questions to determine if the source is a
good source:

1. Is the source extensive enough so that the writer's ideas
can be understood fully?
2. Does the writer have a position or opinion on the issue/
topic that can be used in your study?
3. Is the writer's position acknowledged explicitly or implicitly?

All sources used in this term paper must have some sort of
argument. That is, they must have a claim — an opinion, assertion, idea, judgment, or point of view — that the speaker or
writer wants the reader of listener to accept; and they must
have support — emotional reasons such as shared beliefs, assumptions, and values, as well as logical evidence such as facts,
statistics, and authorities — that give the listener or reader a
basis for accepting the writer's or speaker's assertion. Any
argument must be tested for appropriateness, believability,
consistency, and completeness. The following questions can
be asked to evaluate the logic and emotional appeals of the
argument used in each source.

4. Does the writer bias the presentation with unacknowledged shaping of the information to match a position?

5. What are the writer's credentials (experience, training, or education relating to the topic/issue)?

6. Does the writer use unclear language or ideas?

NOTE: Based on the answers to the above questions, if you decide that the source is good enough to use in your paper, immediatey add the source to your working bibliography. Also, this sort of verification of each source has to be incorporated into the text of your final paper.

Content Analysis

List the following information for each source:

1. Type of Material (print, interview, TV documentary, etc. -

2. How did the format limit and/or aid in the effective presentation of the material? Give specific examples.

3. Who are the intended readers of this selection, and how do you know?

4. What effect does the targeting of certain groups of readers have on how the information is presented? Give specific examples.

5. What is the main view point of the selection?

6. What logical appeals are made?

    A. Does the author, speaker, or presenter represent the important opposing arguments fairly?

    B. Does the author, speaker, or presenter use specific examples , detailed description, quotations from authorities, facts, statistics, etc.

    C. Does the author, speaker, or presenter make us of amplification (widening of perspectives through analogies, comparisons, or other aspects of experience)?

7. What emotional appeals are made?

    A. Does the author arouse desires useful to the persuader's purpose and demonstrate how these desires can be satisfied by acceptance of the persuader's assertion (proposition or proposal or claim)?

    B. Does the author's summary include an arousal of indignation for the opponent's view, and an arousal of sympathy for the speaker/writer's view?

C. Be aware of illogical fallacies which are based on appeals to traditions, desires, hatreds, prejudices, etc.

5. What attempts are made to establish the writer's credentials ?

A. Does the writer use a reasonable tone, treating the opponent with respect by avoiding such things as illogical statements or inflammatory language?

B. Does the writer have some relevant experience with the issue?

C. Does the writer seem to have any prejudicial attitudes, sentiments, or stereotypes?

D. Does the writer make an attempt to embody some evidence of personal knowledge of the subject, good will toward the reader/audience, good sense, perspective, taste in judgment, or disinterest in personal benefit?

E. Note the features of the writer's style: sentences or vocabulary which was effective, too simple, or too difficult . . . Where was the writing clear? Where was it difficult to track? Where was the language appropriate or inappropriate for the intended audience?

6. Did the article change or modify your initial position on the subject?

Step Four: Outlining the Term Paper

I. Introduction

A. Begin with an appropriate quote, a startling statement, a question or a challenging series of questions, a humorous story, an attention-getting incident or illustration, an immediate issue or challenge, a reference to something related to the issue, a generalization about the topic or subject, etc. that attracts the attention of the readers.

B. Establish a focus for your paper by establishing the importance of your selected issue.

C. State several questions that will be considered, researched, and partially answered.

II. The Body

A. Viewpoint Number One- One paragraph or a blend of paragraphs that have more than one source that share the same viewpoint.

1. What is the first possible viewpoint on this issue?

2. List the selections that express that viewpoint.

3. List the main arguments given for that viewpoint.

4. List any unstated assumptions that the supporters of this viewpoint share, and back up your conclusions with specific evidence.

B. Viewpoint Number Two- One paragraph or a blend of paragraphs that have more than one source that share the same viewpoint.

1. What is the second possible viewpoint on this issue?

2. List the selections that express that viewpoint.

3. List the main arguments given for that viewpoint.

4. List any unstated assumptions that the supporters of this viewpoint share, and back up your conclusions with specific evidence.

B. Viewpoint Number Three- One paragraph or a blend of paragraphs that have more than one source that share the same viewpoint.

1. What is the third possible viewpoint on this issue?

2. List the selections that express that viewpoint.

3. List the main arguments given for that viewpoint.

4. List any unstated assumptions that the supporters of this viewpoint share, and back up your conclusions with specific evidence.

III. Conclusions
    A. List the points on which the various points agree.
        1. List the first type of supporting evidence.
        2. List the second type of supporting evidence. Etc.
    B. List the points on which the various points disagree.
        1. List the first type of supporting evidence.
        2. List the second type of supporting evidence. Etc.
    C. What viewpoints or information are missing?
        1. Explain why these views are not given by any of the selections
        2. Explain what effect this omission has

Step Five: Writing the First Draft

Writing can begin as soon as enough information has been gathered to make an outline. Begin where you can. Writing is a process of discovery. As your ideas begin to take shape, I suggest either writing the different paragraphs on separate sheets of paper or scrolling up and down on the word processor. Decide where the information you are reading goes, scroll up or down to find the appropriate paragraph and add the information.

Step Six: Proofreading and Revising the First Draft

Look for common mistakes (sentence fragment, run-on, comma omission after a long introductory phrase, commas omitted around nonessential elements, pronoun-antecedent agreement, shift in person, subject-verb agreement, shift in verb tense, faulty parallelism, etc.)

Revise content as new reading dictates. Make sure your paper stays focused. Keep your organization clear. Make sure the reader can see a clearly established design.

Always look for ways to create maturity . See the previous chapters on diction and syntax for help here.

Good Writing has concreteness, freshness, coherence, and correctness.

Step Seven: Writing the Final Draft

Include the following parts:

1. Title Page
  A. Make an original title for your paper. Place this in the center of the page.
  B. Place name, class, period, and date submitted at the bottom of the page.
II. Outline.
  A. Begin with your thesis statement.
  B. Roman numeral I begins the first body paragraph with a statement of the first viewpopint. Complete the rest of the outline following the suggestions for writing an outline written previously on step four.

III. The text, double spaced throughout, including parenthetical citations.

!V. Works Cited Page

Use the checklist on the following pages
as a guide for grading.

Checklist for the Writing Process Grade for the Extended Argument Term Paper

Check each item listed below that was completed by the due date agreed upon. The first check is made by the student and the second check is made by the teacher. The check made by the teacher is the final determination for this grade.
NOTE: In this system, one wrong is an A, two wrong is a B, three wrong is a C, four wrong is a D.

___-___1. A topic appropriate to the assignment was selected one week after the assignment started.

___-___2. A "working bibliography" was completed one week after the assignment started.

___-___3. The student's note cards (checked each week for six weeks) reflected a growth in reading, thinking, and evaluating.

___-___4. The student's note cards revealed three differing viewpoints and was shuffled to create an outline four weeks after the assignment started.

___-___5. A thesis was developed by the student that advanced a personal stance on the same issue five weeks after the assignment started.

___-___6. Although gaps may still be evident, a rough draft, based on the outline and thesis, was completed at the end of six weeks.

___-___7. The rough draft, at the end of six weeks, included the proper parenthetical citations in MLA format.

___-___8. A proper editing process for at least one other student was completed at the end of seven weeks.

___-___9. A final copy (including title page, formal outline, body with parenthetical citations, and a works cited page) was completed at the end of eight weeks.

MAXIMUM SCORE RESULTS: Student _____
MAXIMUM SCORE RESULTS: Teacher _____

STEP 2: Check each item below which accurately describes how the student failed to meet the deadline. (The student should check column one. The teacher should check column two):

___-___1. A topic was selected but it was not proven to be researchable because six longer sources could not be found that represented varying viewpoints on the same issue.

___-___2. Although a "working bibliography" was started, it did not include the necessary minimum of six longer sources, or the documentation did not follow appropriate MLA form.

___-___3. The student failed to produce new note cards at three different check points.

-___-___4. The writer either has not researched enough, read enough, or has not been able to find three differing viewpoints by the end of four weeks.

___-___5. The writer was not able to take a side on the issue after five weeks and therefore could not focus the research toward a desirable conclusion.

___-___6. The rough draft was either too incomplete to count, or lacking a clear organization.

___-___7. The rough draft may be missing some necessary parenthetical citations or are written improperly.

___-___8. The student may not have had the rough draft completed in time to qualify for this stage, or the editing itself may have been little more than "Good job, Joe!"

___-___9. The final copy was ready but the computer crashed, the printer failed, etc.

RESULTS:

Student: _____ - _____ = _____
            Step 1 Score   Step 2 Score

Teacher: _____ - _____ = _____
            Step 1 Score   Step 2 Score

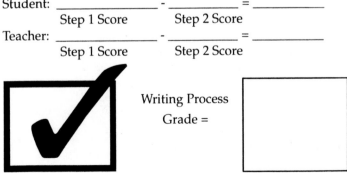

Writing Process
Grade =

Checklist for Content - Grade for the Extended Argument

STEP 1:   Check each item listed below which accurately describes the positive aspects of the term paper being graded. Add one point for each item checked from the list. This side describes the basic requirements for a well-written essay. The student should check column one. The teacher should check column two.   **NOTE: In this system, one wrong is an A, two wrong is a B, three wrong is a C, four wrong is a D.**

___-___1. The writer has written a clearly stated, significant thesis that is appropriately adapted to the assignment, reader, and writer.

___-___2. The writer appropriately introduces the subject, attracts the reader's attention, sets the tone, and ends with a thesis.

___-___3. This writer supports the discussion of each viewpoint with strong evidence (examples, illustrations, quotations, statistics, facts, definitions, etc.)

___-___4. This writer supports the discussion of each personal observation, experience, or reading with evidence that is unified, specific, accurate, adequate, and representative.

___-___5. The writer's reasoning is valid, adapted to the reader, documented or otherwise attributed clearly.

___-___6. The writer has balanced the argument with some appropriate appeals to emotions.

___-___7. The diction / sentence structure of this essay communicates a clear message.

___-___8. The organization of this essay aids in communicating a clear message.

___-___9. The grammar aids in communicating a clear message.

MAXIMUM SCORE RESULTS: Student _____
MAXIMUM SCORE RESULTS: Teacher _____

Practice Test One:

Section 1 Multiple-Choice

Time — One Hour — One class period

Directions: This part consists of selections from prose works and questions on their content, form, and style. After reading each passage, choose the best answer to each question and completely fill in the corresponding oval on the answer sheet.
Note: Pay particular attention to the focus of the questions that contain the words NOT, LEAST, or EXCEPT.

Questions 1 - 15. Carefully read the following passage before you choose your answers.

The world, with its Wealth of Nations, supply-and-demand and such like, has of late days been terribly inattentive to that question of work and wages. We will not say, the poor world has retrograded even here: we will say rather, the world has been rushing on with such fiery animation to get work and ever more work done, it has had no time to think of dividing the wages; and has merely left **them** to be scrambled for by the law of the stronger, law of supply-and-demand, law of Laissez-faire, and other idle laws and un-laws, — saying, in its dire haste to get the work done, "That is well enough!" And now the world will have to pause a little, and take up that **other side of the problem**, and in right earnest strive for some solution of that. For it has become pressing. What is the use of your spun shirts? They hang there by the million unsalable; and here, by the million, are diligent bare backs that can get no hold of them. Shirts are useful for covering human backs; useless otherwise, an unbearable mockery otherwise. You have fallen terribly behind with that side of the problem! Manchester Insurrections, French Revolutions, and thousandfold **phenomena** great and small, announce loudly that you must bring it forward a little again. Never till now, in the history of an

Earth which to this hour nowhere refuses to grow corn if you will plough it, to yield shirts if you will spin and weave in it, did the mere manual two-handed worker (however it may fare with other workers) cry in vain for such 'wages' as he means by 'fair wages, 'namely food and warmth! The Godlike could not and can not be paid; but the Earthly always could.

Gurth, a mere swineherd, born thrall of Cedric the Saxon, tended pigs in the wood, and did get some pairings of the pork. Why, the four-footed worker has already got   all that this two-handed one is clamoring for! How often must I remind you? There is not a horse in England, able and willing to work, but has due food and lodging; and goes about sleek-coated, satisfied in heart. And you say, It is impossible. Brothers, I answer, if for you it be impossible, what is to become of you? It is impossible for us to believe it to be impossible. The human brain, looking at these sleek English horses, refuses to believe in such impossibility of English men. Do you depart quickly; clear the ways soon, lest worst befall. We for our share do purpose, with full view of the enormous difficulty, with total disbelief in the impossibility, to endeavor while life is in us, and to die endeavoring, we and our sons, till we attain it or have all died and ended.

1. This first paragraph infers that the World has neglected to
        (A) divide the wages
        (B) supply the demand
        (C) strengthen the law
        (D) idle the law
        (E) work more
2. The antecedent of "them" (line seven) is the
        (A) World
        (B) law of supply-and-demand
        (D) law of the stronger
        (C) dividing the wages
        (E) un-laws
3. The "other side of the problem," first mentioned in line twelve, is poor
        (A) work
        (B) workers
        (C) supply
        (D) wages
        (E) laws

4. Starting in line fourteen, Carlyle describes spun shirts that "hang there by the million unsalable; and here, by the million, are diligent bare backs that can get no hold of them." He illustrates this common irony by using

    (A) repetition

    (B) juxtaposition of ideas

    (C) extended simile

    (D) cause and effect organization

    (E) positive diction

5. "They hang there by the million unsalable; and here, by the million, are diligent bare backs that can get no hold of them" is an example of

    (A) understatement

    (B) oxymoron   (D) hyperbole

    (C) allusion   (E) litotes

6. The phrase "Shirts are for covering human backs; useless otherwise, an unbearable mockery otherwise" is an example of all the following EXCEPT:

    (A) assertion

    (B) premise   (D) generalization

    (C) allusion   (E) assumption

7. The word "phenomena" in line 20 is synonymous with all the following EXCEPT:

    (A) French Revolutions

    (B) Manchester Insurrections

    (C) a remarkable person

    (D) thousandfold occurrences

    (E) great events

8. By fair wages Carlyle meant

    (A) more money

    (B) better animals

    (C) food and shelter

    (D) food and warmth

    (E) sleek-coated horses

9. The "Godlike" referred to in this passage were all the following EXCEPT:

    (A) the manual worker

    (B) the two-handed worker

    (C) the Earthly

    (D) the mere worker

    (E) bare backs.

10. Carlyle proves his point beginning in the second paragraph with an extended analogy between man and

(A) animal

(B) wages   (D) shirts

(C) work   (E) earth

11. When Carlyle says "The human brain, looking at these sleek English horses, refuses to believe in such impossibility of English men," he is making an appeal to the reader's

(A) logos

(B) pathos   (D) modesty

(C) ethos   (E) reality

12. Which of the following best describes the action Carlyle wants the reader to take?

(A) "And now the world will have to pause a little, and take up that other side of the problem. . ."

(B) "Shirts are useful for covering human backs; useless otherwise . . . ."

(C) Never till now . . . did the mere manual two-handed worker . . . cry in vain for such 'wages' as he means by 'fair . . . .' "

(D) "It is impossible for us to believe it impossible."

(E) "We for our share do purpose . . . to endeavor while life is in us . . . til we attain it."

13. The predominant stylistic device used by Carlyle to convince the reader to take action is

(A) ironic analogies

(B) authorial asides

(C) citations from well-know authorities

(D) circular reasoning

(E) red herring arguments

14. In this passage, Carlyle maintains a tone most accurately described as

(A) melancholy and inactive

(B) remote and disinterested

(C) needful and intolerant

(D) elevated and informal

(E) elevated and praising

15. All EXCEPT one of the following topics are addressed in this passage:

(A) work

(B) wages   (D) warmth

(C) food   (E) freedom

Questions 16-29. Carefully read the following passage before you choose your answers.

Among the several **artifices** which are put in practice by poets to fill the minds of an audience with terror, the first place is due to **thunder and lightning,** which are often made use of at the descending of a god or at the rising of a ghost, at the vanishing of a devil or at the death of a tyrant. I have known a bell introduced into several tragedies with good effect . . . but there is nothing which delights and terrifies our English theater so much as a ghost, especially when he appears in a bloody shirt. A specter has often saved a play though he has done nothing but stalked across the stage, or rose through a cleft of it and sunk again without speaking one word. There may be a **proper season** for these several terrors; and when they only come in as aids and assistances to the poet, they are not only to be excused, but to be applauded. . . .

For the moving of pity, our principal machine is the handkerchief; and indeed in our common tragedies, we should not know very often that the persons are in distress by anything they say, if they did not from time to time apply their handkerchiefs to their eyes. Far be it from me to think of banishing this instrument of sorrow from the stage; I know a tragedy could not subsist without it: All that I would contend for is to keep it from being misapplied. In a word, I would have the actor's tongue sympathize with his eyes.

A disconsolate mother with a child in her hand has frequently drawn compassion from the audience, and has therefore gained a place in several tragedies. A modern writer, that observed how this had took in other plays, being resolved to double the distress and melt his audience twice as much . . . brought a princess upon the stage with a little boy in one hand and a little girl in the other. This too had a very good effect. A third poet, being resolved to outwrite all his predecessors, a few years age introduced three children with great success. And, as I am informed, a young gentleman, who is fully determined to break the most obdurate hearts, has a tragedy by him where the first person that appears upon the stage is an afflicted widow in her mourning-weeds with half a dozen fatherless children attending her. . . . Thus several incidents that are beautiful in a good writer become ridiculous by falling into the hands of a bad one. But among all our methods of moving pity or terror, there is none so absurd and barbarous, and what more exposes us to the contempt and ridicule of our neigh-bors, than that dreadful butchering of one another that is so frequent upon the English stage. To delight in seeing men stabbed poisoned, racked, or impaled is certainly the sign of a cruel temper. . . .

It is indeed very odd to see our stage strewn with car-casses in the last scene of a tragedy; and to observe in the wardrobe of the playhouse several daggers, poniards, wheels, bowls for poison, and many other instruments of death. . . . To give my opinion upon this case; the fact ought not to have been represented but to have been told if there was any occa-sion for it.

16. The word "artifices," as used in this passage, is synony-mous with all BUT one of the following:
 (A) machine
 (B) instrument
 (C) trick
 (D) person
 (E) tactic

17. The phrases "thunder and lightning, which are often made use of at the descending of a god or at the rising of a ghost, at the vanishing of a devil or at the death of a tyrant" is an ex-ample of creating what type of sentence structure?
 (A) parallel
 (B) compound
 (C) simple
 (D) tight, simple
 (E) compound-complex

18. This passage is addressing what genre of literature?
 (A) comedies
 (B) tragedies
 (C) novels
 (D) short stories
 (E) poems

19. All BUT one of the following artifices is mentioned in para-graph one:
 (A) thunder
 (B) lightning
 (C) handkerchiefs
 (D) ghosts
 (E) bells

20. Which statement by Addison indicates the "proper season" for these artifices?

    (A) when the "actor's tongue (does not) sympathize with his eyes"

    (B) "when they only come in as aids and assistances to the poet"

    (C) when the poet needs to show that "the persons are in distress"

    (D) when the poet is "fully determined to break the most obdurate hearts"

    (E) when the poet wants "to fill the minds of an audience with terror"

21. The topic of paragraph one is:

    (A) terror (B) sorrow

    (C) humor

    (D) pity

    (E) laughter

22. In the first paragraph, the author's attitude toward those who use artifices can be best described as

    (A) suspicious

    (B) critical

    (C) incredulous

    (D) admirable

    (E) uncertain

23. The topic of paragraph two is:

    (A) terror

    (B) sorrow

    (C) humor

    (D) pity

    (E) laughter

24. Beginning in third paragraph, Addison shifts his emphasis from praising artifices used in the proper way to

    (A) satirizing bad writers' use of artifices through his use of hyperbole

    (B) illustrating good writers' use of artifices through his use of imagery

    (C) exposing good writers' use of artifices through his use of similes

    (D) defining bad writers by their lack of artifices through his use of litotes

    (E) praising artifices used in the improper way

25. When Addison uses the word "poet" he means:
    (A) essayist
    (B) dramatist
    (C) diarist
    (D) biographer
    (E) critic

26. All of the following words show Addison's disapproval EXCEPT:
    (A) absurd
    (B) barbarous
    (C) assistance
    (D) impaled
    (E) racked

27. Addison's use of the word "carcasses" in the last paragraph conveys a tone of
    (A) indifference
    (B) disgust
    (C) difference
    (D) ambivalence
    (E) disinterest

28. A poniard is all of the following EXCEPT
    (A) an instrument of death
    (B) a dagger
    (C) a knife
    (D) a medicinal instrument
    (E) and instrument of torture

29. Which of the following best describes the pattern of the author's discussion?
    (A) statement of fact followed by tentative assumptions
    (B) description of theory followed by exceptions to the theory
    (C) general statement followed by more general statements
    (D) forceful argumentation followed by concession to opponents
    (E) presentation of a problem followed by resolution of the problem

Questions 30 - 42. Carefully read the following letter before you choose your answers.

London, March 6, O. S. 1747

Dear Boy,

Whatever you do will always affect me, very sensibly, one way or another; and I am now most agreeably affected by two letters, which I have lately seen from Lausanne, up on your subject; the one was from Madame St. Germain, the other from Monsieur Pampigny; they both give so good an account of you, that I thought myself obliged, in justice both to them and you, to let you know it.

Those who deserve a good character ought to have the satisfaction of knowing that they have it, both as reward and as encouragement. They write that you are not only de-crotte, but tolerably well bred; and that English crust of awkward bashfulness, shyness, and roughness (of which, by the bye, you had your share) is pretty well rubbed off. I am most heartily glad of it, for, as I have often told you, those lesser talents, of an engaging, insinuating manner, an easy good breeding, a genteel behavior, and address, are of infinitely more advantage than they are generally thought to be, especially here in England.

Virtue and learning, like gold, have their intrinsic value; but if they are not polished, they certainly lose a great deal of their lustre, and even polished brass will pass upon more people than rough gold.

What a number of sins does the cheerful, easy good-breeding of the French frequently cover! Many of them want common sense, many more common learning; but in general, they make up so much, by their manner for those defects, that, frequently, they pass undiscovered.

I have often said, and do think, that a Frenchman, who, with a fund of virtue, learning, and good sense, has the manners and good-breeding of his country, is the perfection of human nature. This perfection you may, if you please, and I hope you will, arrive at.

You know what virtue is: you may have it if you will; it is in every man's power; and miserable is the man who has it not. Good-sense God has given you. Learning you already possess enough of, to have, in a reasonable time, all that a man need have. With this, you are thrown out early into the world where it will be your own fault if you do not acquire all the other accomplishments necessary to complete and adorn your character.

You will do well to make your compliments to Madame St. Germain and Monsieur Pampigny; and tell them how sensible you are of their partiality to you, in the advantageous testimonies which, you are informed, they have given you here.

Adieu! Continue to deserve such testimonies; and then you will not only deserve, but enjoy, my truest affection.

30. The word "sensibly" (line one) in the context of the passage is most nearly synonymous with
    (A) ethically
    (B) logically
    (C) emotionally
    (D) practically
    (E) rationally

31. The antecedent of "one" in line four is
    (A) letter
    (B) subject
    (C) feeling
    (D) Monsieur Pampigny
    (E) Madame St. Germain

32. In the context of the sentence in line eleven, the author probably intends the word "decrotte" to mean
    (A) unsoiled or free of contamination
    (B) covered in ink
    (C) decorative
    (D) lined with crusty material
    (E) offensive

33. When Chesterfield equates his son's former "bashfulness, shyness, and roughness" to an "English crust," he is employing the use of a
    (A) simile
    (B) metaphor
    (C) juxtaposition
    (D) personification
    (E) post hoc fallacy

34. One predominant characteristic of Lord Chesterfield's style, based on this letter, is his overuse of

    (A) onomatopoeia

    (B) oxymoron

    (C) commas

    (D) repetition

    (E) dialect

35. The relationship between Lord Chesterfield and his illegitimate son appears to be

    (A) overly loving

    (B) distantly praising

    (C) excessively deceitful

    (D) extremely caring

    (E) overwhelmingly admonishing

36. In paragraph three the author seems to make a rhetorical shift from praise to

    (A) instruction

    (B) comfort

    (C) damnation

    (D) cruelty

    (E) ignorance

37. The sentence, "Many of them want common sense, many more common learning. . ." is an example of

    (A) a loose sentence

    (B) parallel construction

    (C) periodic construction

    (D) complex construction

    (E) simple sentence

38. Qualities which Lord Chesterfield wants his son to obtain include all the following EXCEPT:

    (A) virtue

    (B) learning

    (C) good sense

    (D) perfection

    (E) good breeding

39. The purpose of Lord Chesterfield's letter seems to be to do all of the following EXCEPT:

    (A) let his son know he is proud of him

    (B) give his son encouragement

    (C) reward his son

    (D) reproach his bad behavior

    (E) let him know he is praiseworthy

40. In the sentence, "Good sense God has given you," Carlyle employs what type of syntax?

      (A) normal order

      (B) inversion

      (C) Subject first

      (D) transition

      (E) coherence

41. The tone of the overall passage can be best described as

      (A) sincere

      (B) remote

      (C) uninterested

      D) piousness

      (E) repugnant

42. The effect that this letter would have on his son can be best described as

      (A) rewarding confusion

      (B) supernatural confusion

      (C) awesome acceptance

      (D) apathetic isolation

      (E) disinterested apathy

Questions 43-55. Carefully read the following essay before you choose your answers.

After damning politicians up hill and down dale for many years, as rogues and vagabonds, frauds and scoundrels, I sometimes suspect that, like everyone else, I often expect too much from them. Though faith and confidence are more or less foreign to my nature, I not infrequently find myself looking to them to be able, diligent, candid, and even honest. Plainly enough, that is too large an order, as anyone must realize who reflects upon the manner in which they reach public office. They seldom if ever get there by merit alone, at least in democratic states. Sometimes, to be sure, it happens, but only by a kind of miracle. They are chosen normally for quite different reasons, the chief of which is simply their power to impress and enchant the intellectually underprivileged. It is a talent like any other, and when it is exercised by a radio crooner, a movie actor or a bishop, it even takes on a certain austere and sorry respectability. But it is obviously not identical with a capacity for the intricate problems of statecraft.

Those problems demand for their solution -- when they are soluble at all, which is not often -- a high degree of technical proficiency and with it should go an **adamantine** kind of integrity, for the temptations of a public official are almost as cruel as those of a glamour girl or a **dipsomaniac.** But we train a man for facing them, not by locking him up in a monastery and stuffing him with wisdom and virtue, but by turning him loose on the stump. If he is a smart fellow, which he usually is, he quickly discovers there that **hooey** pleases the boobs a great deal more than sense. Indeed, he finds that sense really disquiets and alarms them -- that it makes them, at best, intolerably uncomfortable, just as a tight collar makes them uncomfortable, or a speck of dust in the eye, or the thought of Hell. The truth, to the overwhelming majority of mankind, is indistinguishable from a headache.

After trying a few shots of **it** on his customers, the **larval statesman** concludes sadly that it must hurt them, and after that he taps a more humane keg and in a little while the whole audience is singing "Glory, glory, hallelujah, "and when the returns come in the candidate is on his way to the White House.

I hope no one will mistake this brief account of the

political process under democracy for exaggeration. It is almost literally true. . . . I happen to be acquainted . . . with
nearly all the gentlemen, both Democrats and Republicans,
who are currently itching for the Presidency. . . and I testify
freely that. . . . The worst of them is a great deal better company than most generals in the army, or writers of murder
mysteries . . . and the best is a really superior and delightful
man -- full of sound knowledge . . . and quite as honest as an
American can be without being clapped a madhouse. He . . .
(just) has not been caught yet.

43. Mencken begins with
     (A) an incidence damnation
     (B) concessions to opposing views
     (C) a solution to the problems that demand attention
     (D) a bridge connecting analogous and homologous
          similarities
     (E) a contrast between good and bad politicians
44. Mencken has problems with most politicians because he
expects them to be all of the following EXCEPT:
     (A) rogues
     (B) vagabonds
     (C) frauds
     (D) protagonists
     (E) scoundrels
45. According to the author, politicians get into office by all of
he following EXCEPT:
     (A) They have a power to impress the intellectually
          underprivileged.
     (B) They have a power to enchant the voting public.
     (C) They carry a certain austere and sorry
          respectability.
     (D) They have a capacity for the intricate problems of
          statehood.
     (E) They have a high degree of charm.

46. The word "adamantine" (line 20) in the context of the passage means all but one of the following:

      (A) unbreakable

      (B) unbending,

      (C) yielding

      (D) adamant

      (E) unrelenting

47. The word "dipsomaniac" (line 22) in the context of the passage means

      (A) alcoholic

      (B) glamorous

      (C) overwhelming

      (D) maddening

      (E) enterprising

48. Mencken gets the reader to identify with him by referring to those who like politicians as all of the following EXCEPT:

      (A) boobs

      (B) intellectually depraved

      (C) those who love "hooey"

      (D) those who shout "Glory, glory, hallelujah"

      (E) those who respect diligence and honesty

49. Mencken helps the reader define "hooey" by juxtaposing "hooey" with all BUT one of the following opposite words:

      (A) "truth"

      (B) "sense"

      (C) "exaggeration"

      (D) "knowledge"

      (E) "wisdom"

50. The sentence in lines 27-31, " Indeed, he finds that sense really disquiets and alarms them -- that it makes them, at best, intolerably uncomfortable, just as a tight collar makes them uncomfortable, or a speck of dust in the eye, or the thought of Hell" employs the use of a

      (A) metaphor

      (B) hyperbole

      (C) simile

      (D) oxymoron

      (E) allusion

51. The next sentence (lines 31-32), "The truth, to the overwhelming majority of mankind, is indistinguishable from a
headache," employs the use of a
>   (A) metaphor
>   (B) onomatopoeia
>   (C) simile
>   (D) oxymoron
>   (E) allusion

52. When Mencken calls the politician a "larval" statesman,
he is making a metaphor to equate the statesman with all BUT
one of the following:
>   (A) a maggot
>   (B) a worm
>   (C) a caterpillar
>   (D) a butterfly
>   (E) a grub

53. The antecedent of "it" (line 33) most literally refers to
>   (A) "truth"
>   (B) "sense"
>   (C) "exaggeration"
>   (D) "knowledge"
>   (E) "wisdom"

54. In this passage, the author maintains a tone most accurately
described as
>   (A) unbiased
>   (B) indifferent
>   (C) incredulous
>   (D) critical
>   (E) uncertain

55. As he defines the essence of "The Politician," H. L. Mencken
employs all BUT one of the following rhetorical strategies:
>   (A) examples
>   (B) an extended definition
>   (C) description
>   (D) brief narratives
>   (E) appeals to authority

END OF SECTION I

IF YOU FINISH BEFORE TIME IS CALLED, YOU MAY
CHECK YOUR WORK ON THIS SECTION.
DO NOT GO ON TO SECTION II UNTIL YOU ARE
TOLD TO DO SO.

Practice Test Two:

Section 1
Multiple-
Choice

Time — 1 hour

Directions: This part consists of selections from prose works and questions on their content, form, and style. After reading each passage, choose the best answer to each question and completely fill in the corresponding oval on the answer sheet. Note: Pay particular attention to the requirement of the questions that contain the words NOT, LEAST, or EXCEPT.

Questions 1 - 15. Read the following passage from *Discovering Poetry* by Elizabeth Drew carefully before you choose your answers.

We are accustomed to speak of such lines of poetry as "magical," and indeed they do bring a **revelation** with them. But it is not a revelation of anything supernatural, but a revelation of the natural power lying prisoned in words; a power which the poet can release. R. L. Stevens, writing about style, makes an extraordinary statement about language. "The sister arts," he says, "enjoy the use of a plastic and ductile material, like the modeler's clay; literature alone is condemned to work in **mosaic** with finite and quite rigid words." Finite and rigid seem old epithets for a conscious stylist to apply to words. For words are not mere collections of letters of the alphabet, with the finite meaning and rigid shape: nor are they mere audible syllables of loveliness or ugliness. **They** are the storehouse of innumerable traditional and individual associations, which **awaken** to life at their sight and sound, and which give their beauty and their power. And it is because of this power in words that the **emotional** experiences in poetry, although they can never be as acute as those of actual living, are possessed of greater resonance and **reverberation**.

There are certain words which are inseparable from

the idea of poetry. We cannot think of the nightingale or the rose, of love or sleep or death, of the moon and the sea, of the hills and the wind, of gold and silver, of woods and wild flowers, without a rush of poetic emotion and poetic coloring. *The horns of Elfland faintly blowing,* besides all the melody of its liquid and labial letters, is haunted with all the mystery of fairyland and all the adventure of the chase--remote, half-heard, and mingled together to create an effect as enchanting as it is imponderable. And *mighty poets in their misery dead* conveys talk that can be evoked of nobility, grandeur and beauty by the words "mighty poets," with all that is added to them by the juxtaposition of the full body of the words "misery" and "dead."

1. The word "revelation" (line 2) is most synonymous with
     (A) divulgence
     (B) concealment
     (C) veiling
     (D) cover-up
     (E) hiding
2. The primary technique used in lines five through nine is
     (A) generalization
     (B) dramatic irony
     (C) allusion
     (D) satire
     (E) hyperbole
3.   Drew claims that "literature alone is condemned to work in mosaic with finite and quite rigid words. . . . " In context, what does "mosaic" (line nine) mean?
     (A) any of several diseases of plants
     (B) humiliation in feeling
     (C) a signal on a bugle or a drum given at a fixed time
     (D) continuous photographic representations
     (E) a returning to a more modern state
4. The antecedent of "they" (line thirteen) is:
     (A) literature
     (B) words
     (C) ductile material
     (D) syllables
     (E) infinity

5. The words "awaken" (line fifteen) and "emotional" (line seventeen) are used by Drew to show
    (A) a release of power and beauty
    (B) poetry's possessiveness
    (C) how poetry is factual
    (D) how the sister arts are superior
    (E) how redundant words can be

6. The word "reverberation" (line nineteen) is most synonymous with all of the following EXCEPT:
    (A) echoes
    (B) stillness
    (C) sounds
    (D) rebounds
    (E) resonance

7. In lines 20-23, Drew makes use of
    (A) syllogisms
    (B) ambiguous references
    (C) exaggerations
    (D) parallelism
    (E) hyperboles

8. All of the following have been described by Drew as creating "a rush of poetic emotion and coloring" (line 24) EXCEPT:
    (A) epithets
    (B) nightingale
    (C) rose
    (D) love
    (E) moon

9. Drew describes words to be all of the following EXCEPT
    (A) emotional
    (B) labial
    (C) haunted
    (D) melodious
    (E) insignificant

10. The phrase "enchanting as it is imponderable" (lines 28-29) means charming yet ___ (All of the following EXCEPT)
    (A) ambiguous
    (B) implicit
    (C) indefinite
    (D) nebulous
    (E) repulsive

11. Line 25 and line 29 are in italics because

    (A) they are quotes from typical lines from the sister arts

    (B) they are quotes from typical lines of poetry

    (C) Drew wanted to break up the monotony of her essay

    (D) they are an allusion to her favorite novel

    (E) they are her own creations

12. Which statement best describes the attitude Drew wants to convey?

    (A) "They are the storehouse of innumerable traditional and individual associations."

    (B) "It is a revelation . . . of the natural power lying imprisoned in words, a power which a poet can release."

    (C) "Finite and rigid seem odd epithets for a conscious stylist."

    (D) "We are accustomed to speak of such lines of poetry . . . and . . . bring a revelation with them."

    (E) "The sister arts . . . enjoy the use of plastic and ductile material."

13. The tone of the passage can best be described as

    (A) melodramatic

    (B) overly sentimental

    (C) intellectually assessing

    (D) warily detached

    (E) indifferent

14. The development of this passage is based, in part, on

    (A) many abstract generalizations

    (B) circular reasoning

    (C) red herring argument

    (D) elaborately structured metaphors

    (E) several rhetorical shifts

15. Drew makes most use of all of the following types of sentence structure EXCEPT

    (A) tight, simple sentences

    (B) parallel structure

    (C) loose sentences

    (D) complex sentences

    (E) periodic sentences

Questions 16-25. Carefully read the following passage from Sir Thomas More's *Utopia* (1516) before you choose your answers.

No other crimes carry fixed penalties; the senate sets specific penalties for each particular misdeed, as it is considered atrocious or **venial**. Husbands chastise their wives and parents their children, unless the offense is so serious that public punishment seems to be in the public interest. Generally, the gravest crimes are punished by slavery, for they think this deters offenders just as much as instant capital punishment, and is more beneficial to the state. Slaves, moreover, are permanent and visible reminders that crime does not pay. If the slaves rebel against their condition, then, like savage beasts which neither bars nor chains can tame, they are put instantly to death. But if they are patient, they are not left altogether without hope. When subdued by long hardships, if they show by behavior that they regret the crime more than the punishment, their slavery is lightened or **remitted** altogether, sometimes by the prince's pardon. . . .

They do not allow divorce except for adultery or insufferable waywardness on the part of either spouse. The injured person is given permission to change spouses by the Senate, but the guilty party is considered **disreputable** and for the rest of his life is forbidden to remarry. They do not allow a husband to put away his wife against her will because of some bodily misfortune. They consider it a matter of cruelty and disloyalty to desert one's spouse when most in need of comfort, especially in old age (which is itself really a sickness, since it brings sickness in its train). It happens occasionally that when a married couple can not agree well together and when they have found other persons with whom they hope to live more happily, they separate by mutual consent and contract new marriages, but only with the consent of the senate. Such divorces are not allowed unless the senators and their wives have made careful inquiry into the grounds for it. They allow **them** unwillingly, for they know that it weakens the love of married couples to leave the door open to easy new marriages. They punish adulterers with the severest bondage. If both parties are married, they are divorced, and the injured persons may be married to one another or to someone else. But if either of the injured parties continues to love the undeserving spouse, then the couple may continue to live together in marriage, pro

314 Practice Test Two

viding the innocent person is willing to share in the labor to which bondmen are condemned. Sometimes it happens that the repentance of the guilty person so moves the prince to pity that he grants both of them freedom once more. If anyone commits adultery a second time, his punishment is death. A man who tries to seduce a woman is subject to the same penalties as if he had actually done it. They think that crime attempted is as bad as one committed, and that failure should not confer advantages on a criminal who did all he could to succeed.

16. The word "remitted" (line fifteen) is most synonymous
with   (A) prolonged
         (B) devised
         (C) executed
         (D) darkened
         (E) repealed
17. The word "disreputable" (line twenty)) was chosen because it connotes a state of being
         (A) free
         (B) full of repute
         (C) shameful
         (D) clean-cut
         (E) exemplary
18. The antecedent of "them" (line 32) is
         (A) senators
         (B) them
         (C) wives
         (D) divorces
         (E) grounds
19. Which of the following could be considered a weakness of this passage?
         (A) the overuse of the word "they"
         (B) the overuse of semicolons
         (C) lines 34-49
         (D) the misuse of subordinate clauses
         (E) the choice of vocabulary that is too simplistic for
                the purpose

20. The overall tone of the passage can be best described as
    (A) overly emotional
    (B) intimidating
    (C) disheartening
    (D) melodramatic
    (E) sad

21. The person who regulates the behavior of the individuals in More's society is called a
    (A) ruler
    (B) tsar
    (C) president
    (D) prince
    (E) king

22. According to the author, a "utopian" (perfect) society can be created if all of the following are true EXCEPT:
    (A) Individual freedoms are guaranteed.
    (B) It is considered a matter of cruelty and disloyalty to desert one's spouse.
    (C) No "easy" new marriages are granted.
    (D) Injured parties continue to love their spouse.
    (E) Two adulteries are punishable by death.

23. The author's attitude toward a spouse who commits adultery for the second time can best be described as
    (A) compassionate
    (B) indifferent
    (C) stringent
    (D) ambiguous
    (E) sympathetic

24. More draws contrast in this excerpt between all of the following EXCEPT
    (A) private and public punishment
    (B) husbands and wives
    (C) old and new marriages
    (D) governmental and personal rulings
    (E) innocent and guilty people

25. Judging by the passage, the author was probably a
    (A) teacher of English
    (B) romantic moviegoer
    (C) completely insane
    (D) modern journalist
    (E) idealistic politician

You are now half through with the test.

Check your time!!!

You should have 30 mnutes left to finish.

Make any necessary adjustments in time that you need to make.

Good luck the rest of the way!

<u>Questions 26-38.</u> Read the following passage from Thomas Jefferson's inaugural address "Political Toleration" carefully before you choose your answers.

During the contest of opinion through which we have passed, the animation of discussions and of exertions has sometimes worn an aspect which might impose on strangers, unused to think freely and to speak and to write what they think; but this being now decided by the voice of the nation, announced according to the rules of the constitution, all will, of course, arrange themselves under the will of the law, and unite in common efforts for the common good.

All, too, will bear in mind this sacred principle, that, though the will of the majority is, in all cases, to prevail, that will, to be rightful, must be reasonable; that the minority possess their equal rights, which equal laws must protect, and to violate which would be oppression. Let us then, fellow citizens, unite with one heart and one mind.

Let us restore to social intercourse that harmony and affection, without which liberty, and even life itself, are but dreary things; and let us reflect, that, having banished from our land that religious intolerance under which mankind so long bled and suffered, we have gained little if we countenance a political intolerance as despot, as wicked, and capable of as bitter and bloody persecutions. . . .

I know, indeed, that some honest men fear that a republican government can not be strong; that this government is not strong enough. But would the honest patriot, the full tide of successful experiment, abandon a government which has so far kept us free and firm, on the theoretic and visionary fear that this government, the world's best hope, may, by possibility, want energy to preserve itself? I trust not; I believe this, on the contrary, the strongest government on earth. I believe it to be the only one where every man, at the call of the law would fly to the standard of the law, and would meet invasions of the public order as his own personal concern.

Sometimes it is said that man can not be trusted with the government of himself. Can he, then, be trusted with the government of others, or have we found angels, in the form of kings, to govern him? Let history answer this question. Let us, then, with courage and confidence, pursue our own federal and republican principles; our attachment to union and representative government.

318 Practice Test Two

26. The "contest of opinion" that Jefferson refers to in line one
is   (A) the Civil War
       (B) The Korean War
       (C) the Revolutionary War
       (D) World War I
       (E) World War II

27. According to Thomas Jefferson, now that the majority has
decided upon a new Constitution, all should arrange themselves under the will of
       (A) man
       (B) the law
       (C) the majority
       (D) religion
       (E) the press

28. In the first paragraph (lines 1-8), Jefferson describes the
new government as
       (A) the voice of the nation
       (B) the ruler of the land
       (C) a strange but honest arrangement
       (D) an opinionated group of people
       (E) a lesser of two evils

29. Jefferson defines the function of the government in the
second paragraph (lines nine through fourteen) as including
all of the following EXCEPT:
       (A) the minority possess equal rights
       (B) equal laws will protect against oppression
       (C) the laws will be reasonable
       (D) oppressors will be accepted
       (E) citizens need to unite with one heart

30. The purpose of paragraph two is to:
             I. include the rights of the minority
             II. make the concept of equality clear
             III. convince the majority that they rule
       (A) I only
       (B) II only
       (C) III only
       (D) I and III only
       (E) I and II only

31. Jefferson states in paragraph three (lines fifteen through twenty-one) that life itself is dreary without
(A) love and happiness
(B) religion and morality
(C) harmony and affection
(D) joy and sorrow
(E) glitz and glamor

32. When Jefferson refers to the recent battles in which Americans "so long bled and suffered" (lines 18-19), he is making what kind of appeal?
I. Logos II. Pathos III. Ethos
(A) I only
(B) II only
(C) III only
(D) I and II only
(E) II and III only

33. The word "despot" (line twenty) is understood to mean all BUT one of the following:
(A) wicked
(B) independent
(C) tyrannical
(D) autocratic
(E) authoritative

34. Jefferson states in paragraph three (lines fifteen through twenty-one) that since we have "banished . . . that religious intolerance under which we long bled and suffered," we would lose everything if we now become
(A) politically intolerant
(B) socially intolerant
(C) tolerant of all religions
(D) happy with all social events
(E) totally confident in one government

35. What rhetorical device does Jefferson use in paragraph four (lines 22-32)?
(A) red herring argument
(B) circular reasoning
(C) concessions to opposing points of view
(D) appeals to authority
(E) inductive reasoning

36. When Jefferson calls our government "the world's best hope" (line 27), he is making use of what stylistic device?

    (A) simile

    (B) oxymoron

    (C) onomatopoeia

    (D) alliteration

    (E) metaphor

37. In the fifth paragraph (lines 33-39), when Jefferson asks if "man can not be trusted with the government of himself, can he, then, be trusted with the government of others," how does he answer his own question?

    (A) Yes, but people need to be watched.

    (B) No, so a President needs a veto power.

    (C) No, so we should not trust politicians.

    (D) History will provide the answer.

    (E) No one knows.

38. The rhetorical mode chosen by Jefferson in this passage is

    (A) persuasion

    (B) exposition

    (C) cause and effect

    (D) description

    (E) narration

Questions 39-50. Read the passage from "The Indian Juggler" by William Hazlitt carefully before answering the following questions.

Coming forward and seating himself on the ground, in his white dress and tightened turban, the chief of the Indian jugglers begins with tossing up two brass balls, which is what any of us could do, and concludes by keeping up four at the same time, which is what none of us could do to save our lives, not if we were to take our whole lives to do it in.

Is it then a trifling power we see at work, or is it not something next to miraculous? It is the utmost stretch of human ingenuity . . . .

To conceive of this extraordinary dexterity, distracts the imagination and makes admiration breathless. Yet it costs nothing to the performer, any more than if it were a mere mechanical deception with which he had nothing to do, but to watch and laugh at the astonishment of the spectators. A single error of a hair's breadth, of the smallest conceivable portion of time, would be fatal; the precision of the movements must be like a mathematical truth; their rapidity is like lightning.

To catch four balls in succession, in less than a second of time, and deliver them back so as to return with seeming consciousness to the hand again; to make them revolve around him at certain intervals, like the planets in their spheres; to make them chase each other like sparkles off a tire, or shoot up like flowers or meteors; to throw them behind his back, and twine them round his neck like ribbons, or like serpents; to do what appears an impossibility, and to do it with all the ease, the grace, the carelessness imaginable; to laugh at, to play with the glittering mockeries, to follow them with his eyes as if he could fascinate them with its lambent fire, or as if he had only to see that they kept time with the music on the stage. It is skill surmounting difficulty, and beauty triumphing over skill. It seems as if the difficulty, once mastered, naturally resolved itself into ease and grace, and as if, to be overcome at all, it must be overcome without an effort. The smallest awkwardness or want of pliancy or self-possession would stop the whole process. It is the work of witchcraft, and yet sport for children.

39. The admiring tone of the passage is created by Hazlitt's choice of all BUT one of the following words.
    - (A) trifling
    - (B) miraculous
    - (C) ingenuity
    - (D) extraordinary (E) breathless.

40. In relationship to the passage as a whole, the first two paragraphs function in which of the following ways?
    - I. It establishes the scene for the action described.
    - II. It conveys a mood which is contrasted with the rest of the passage.
    - III. It establishes the author's attitude toward the subject later described.
    - (A) I only
    - (B) II only
    - (C) III only
    - (D) I and II
    - (E) I and III

41. In paragraph three, the author admires a certain aspect of the Indian's juggling. This aspect of admiration can best be determined by Hazlitt's choice of what word?
    - (A) "precision"
    - (B) "movements"
    - (C) "like"
    - (D) "breadth"
    - (E) "truth"

42. In the last sentence of paragraph three, the figure of lightning is used as a simile for
    - (A) time
    - (B) truth
    - (C) power
    - (D) precision
    - (E) rapidity

43. What is chasing each other in paragraph four?
    - (A) sparkles
    - (B) flowers
    - (C) meteors
    - (D) ribbons
    - (E) four balls

44. All of the following statements describe Hazlitt's admiration of the Indian's juggling EXCEPT:
   - (A) "To conceive of this extraordinary dexterity, distracts the imagination and makes admiration breathless"
   - (B) "It is the work of witchcraft, and yet the sport for children"
   - (C) "It is skill surmounting difficulty, and beauty triumphing over self"
   - (D) "Coming forward and seating himself on the ground, in his white dress and tightened turban, the chief of the Indian jugglers begins with tossing up two brass balls . . ."
   - (E) "It seems as if the difficulty, once mastered, naturally resolved itself into ease and grace"

45. All BUT one of the following contrasts are made by Hazlitt
   - (A) what any of us could do and what none of us could do
   - (B) to do what appears an impossibility and to do it with ease
   - (C) grace and carelessness
   - (D) skill and beauty
   - (E) witchcraft and sport for children

46. The rhetorical strategy of the last paragraph is to
   - (A) use the events of one individual life to generalize about another
   - (B) stimulate the reader's attention by progressively expanding the focus of attention
   - (C) arouse expectations about a character which is finally proven false
   - (D) convince the reader of the speaker's wisdom by disproving opposing points of view
   - (E) appear initially uncertain about matters on which a stand is taken at the end

47. Juggling is described with adjectives that seem to
   - (A) emphasize its texture
   - (B) criticize its aesthetic qualities
   - (C) give it heroic dimensions
   - (D) make it trifling
   - (E) make it seem harmless

48. All of the following contribute to the effect of the last sentence EXCEPT

      (A) catch four balls in succession

      (B) extraordinary dexterity

      (C) makes admiration breathless

      (D) white dress and tightened turban

      (E) mere mechanical deception

49. Hazlitt describes juggling as being like all of the following EXCEPT

      (A) planets in their spheres

      (B) sparkles of tire

      (C) lightning

      (D) lambent fire

      (E) serpents

50. Hazlitt's style can be best described as

      (A) abstract and illusive

      (B) disjointed and effusive

      (C) informal and descriptive

      (D) complex and pedantic

      (E) symbolic and terse

END OF SECTION I, PRACTICE TEST TWO

IF YOU FINISH BEFORE TIME IS CALLED, YOU
MAY CHECK YOUR WORK ON THIS SECTION.

DO NOT GO ON TO SECTION II UNTIL
YOU ARE TOLD TO DO SO

Practice Test Three:

General Instructions

SECTION I — Time — 1 hour

<u>Directions:</u> This section consists of selections from literary works and questions on their content, form, and style. After reading each passage or poem, choose the best answer to each question and fill in the corresponding oval on the answer sheet. <u>Note:</u> Pay particular attention to the requirement of questions that contain the words NOT, LEAST, or EXCEPT.

<u>Question 1-16</u>: Read the following poem "Ode on a Grecian Urn" by John Keats carefully before choosing your answers.

1

Thou still unravished bride of quietness,
    Thou foster-child of silence and slow time,
Sylvan historian, who canst thus express
    A flowery tale more sweetly than rhyme:
What leaf-fringed legend haunts about thy shape   (5)
    Of Deities or mortals, or of both
        In Tempe or the dales of Arcady?
What men or gods are these? What maidens loath?
What mad pursuit? What struggle to escape?
        What pipes and timbrels? What wild ecstasy?

2

Heard melodies are sweet, but those unheard   (11)
    Are sweeter; therefore, ye soft pipes, play on;
Not to the sensual ear, but, more endeared,
    Pipe to the spirit ditties of no tone:
Fair youth, beneath the trees, thou canst not leave   (15)
    Thy song, nor ever can those trees be bare;
        Bold lover, never, never canst thou kiss,
Though winning near the goal — yet, do not grieve;
    She cannot fade, though thou hast not thy bliss,
        Forever wilt thou love, and she be fair!   (20)

3

Ah, happy, happy boughs! that cannot shed
    Your leaves, nor ever bid the spring adieu;
And, happy melodist, unwearied,
    For ever piping songs, for ever new;
More happy love! More happy, happy love!   (25)
        Forever warm and still to be enjoyed,
            Forever painting, and forever young;
All breathing human passion far above,
    That leaves a heart high-sorrowful and cloyed,
        A burning forehead, and a parched tongue.

4

Who are these coming to the sacrifice?   (31)
    To what green altar, O mysterious priest,
Leadest thou that heifer lowing at the skies,
    And all her silken flanks with garlands drest?
What little town by river or sea shore,   (35)
    Or mountain-built with peaceful citadel,
        Is emptied of this folk, this pious morn?
And, little town, thy streets for evermore
    Will silent be; and not a soul to tell
        Why thou art desolate, can e'er return.   (40)

5

O Attic shape! Fair attitude! with brede
    Of marble men and maidens overwrought,
With forest branches and the trodden weed;
    Thou, silent form, dost tease us out of thought
As doth eternity: Cold Pastoral!   (45)
    When old age shall this generation waste,
        Thou shalt remain, in midst of other woe
Than ours, a friend to man, to whom thou sayst,
    "Beauty is truth, truth beauty" — that is all
        Ye know on earth, and all ye need to know.

1. The speaker seems to be absorbed in the beginning with the powerful presence of this beautiful urn who "canst thus express a flowery tale more sweetly than our rhyme." This attitude is created by the poet's choice of all of the following EXCEPT: (A) "unravished bride"
    (B) "foster-child"   (D) "leaf-fringed legend"
    (C) "sylvan historian"   (E) "men or gods"

2. The speaker's excitement is also created by which of the following constructions?
    (A) One question characterized by periodic form and balance.
    (B) One question including a series of pleasant, idealized images.
    (C) One compound-complex sentence.
    (D) A series of exclamatory statements.
    (E) A series of short and quickly stated questions.

3. The speaker is also intrigued that life on the urn is suspended or "frozen" in time. All of the following words or phrases describe this arrested aspect of time EXCEPT:
    (A) "quietness"
    (B) "silence and slow time"
    (C) "who canst thus express"
    (D) "nor ever can these trees be bare"
    (E) "never, never canst thou kiss"

4. All of the following scenes are sculptured on Keats's imaginary urn EXCEPT:
    (A) Young lovers in flight
    (B) Young lovers in pursuit
    (C) A pastoral piper under spring foliage
    (D) An idyllic marriage with pipes and timbrels
    (E) The quiet celebration of communal pieties

5. In the context of line three, the word "sylvan" can best be interpreted to mean
    (A) Rusty
    (B) Pastoral   (D) Vulgar
    (C) Crude   (E) Sophisticated

6. In line 7, Keats make use of which of the following?
    (A) Allusion
    (B) Oxymoron   (D) Apostrophe
    (C) Understatement   (E) Metaphysical conceit

7. Which of the following statements best answer why Keats felt that the urn could tell a flowery tale better than his poetry?

 (A) A "leaf-fringed legend haunts about thy shape"

 (B) "Heard melodies are sweet, but those unheard/ Are sweeter."

 (C) The urn has "Fair youth, beneath the trees"

 (D) The woman on the urn is able to stay "forever young"

 (E) A picture paints a thousand words

8. Which of the following words illustrate the poetic license taken by poets to create the wanted rhythm?

 (A) "loath"

 (B) "ditties"   (D) "canst"

 (C) "e'er"   (E) "brede"

9. Keats likes the spirit ditties of no tone because they appeal better to the

 (A) Imagination

 (B) Sensual   (D) Sense of touch

 (C) Sense of sight   (E) Sense of sound

10. The image of trees who could never lose their leaves is an example of what figure of speech?

 (A) Simile

 (B) Paradox   (D) Analogy

 (C) Metaphor   (E) Apostrophe

11. Which of the following describes the speaker's state at the end of stanza three?

 (A) He feels mean-spirited and full of vengeance.

 (B) He is amused but cynical.

 (C) He has become disinterested and detached.

 (D) He is wearied with excess.

 (E) He has a new-found enthusiasm and hope.

12. The third stanza has been criticized as badly written because Keats used happy and forever too many times. However, he did this because he wanted to emulate the effect this urn has on the speaker at this point. Which of the following best describes this effect?

 I. All restraints are abandoned here to live in a forever happy world.

 II. The speaker is so excited he is making no sense.

 III. Keats wishes to emphasize the speaker's state of immortal happiness.

(A) I only (B) II only (C) III only (D) I and II (E) II and III.

13. A change in attitude can be seen in Keats's use of which phrase?

(A) "High-sorrowful and cloyed"
(B) "Breathing human passion"
(C) "A burning forehead"
(D) "A parching tongue"
(E) "Cold Pastoral"

14. In this poem, Keats reflects on all of the following EX-CEPT: (A) Religion

(B) Love
(C) Nature
(D) Escape
(E) Revenge

15. The speaker characterizes the life illustrated on the urn as

(A) Immortal and unchanging
(B) Happy and forever
(C) Mad and insane
(D) Contented and smug
(E) Pleasant and easygoing

16. All of the following are possible interpretations of the ambiguous ending "Beauty is truth -- truth beauty" EXCEPT:

(A) Keats preferred the beauty of the urn to the changing reality of life.
(B) This statement characterizes the search for beauty that typifies most Romantic writing.
(C) This statement is a universal and profound metaphysical proposition.
(D) This statement is simply nonsense.
(E) This is an overstatement uttered in the course of a dramatic dialogue.

Question 17 - 26. Read the following poem "I Died for Beauty — But was Scarce" by Emily Dickinson carefully before choosing your answers.

> I died for Beauty — but was scarce
> Adjusted in the Tomb
> When one who died for Truth, was lain
> In an adjoining Room —
>
> (5) He questioned softly "Why I failed?"
> "For Beauty," I replied —
> "And I — for Truth — Themself are One —
> We Brethren, are," He said —
>
> And so, as Kinsmen, met at Night —
> (10) We talked between the Rooms —
> Until the Moss had reached our lips —
> And covered up — our names —

17. Lines 1, 3, 5, 7, 9, and 11 are written in iambic
    (A) Trimeter
    (B) tetrameter   (D) hexameter
    (C) pentameter   (E) heptameter

18. Lines 2, 4, 6, 8, 10, and 12 are written in iambic
    (A) Trimeter
    (B) tetrameter   (D) hexameter
    (C) pentameter   (E) heptameter

19. Each quatrain has a rhyme scheme of
    (A) abca
    (B) aabb   (D) abcb
    (C) abab   (E) abca

20. Slant rhyme occurs in   I. Stanza 1
                           II. Stanza 2
                           III. Stanza 3
(A) I only (B) II only (C) III only (D) II and III (E) I, II, III.

21. The two speakers are "Brethern" because they both feel that "Beauty is truth, truth beauty." If Emily Dickinson is one speaker, who might be her "brethern"?
    (A) Geoffrey Chaucer
    (B) John Keats   (D) Anne Bradstreet
    (C) Alexander Pope   (E) John Donne

22. Slant rhyme is employed by Emily Dickinson to emphasize meaning by making which word stand out?

    (A) scarce

    (B) Truth   (D) Tomb

    (C) Beauty   (E) Names

23. All of the following are possible interpretations of the ambiguous idea "Beauty is truth -- truth beauty" EXCEPT:

    (A) Dickinson preferred the beauty to the changing reality of life.

    (B) This statement characterizes the search for beauty that typifies most Romantic writing.

    (C) This statement is a universal and profound metaphysical proposition.

    (D) This statement is simply nonsense.

    (E) This is an overstatement uttered in the course of a dramatic dialogue.

24. In the third stanza, moss literally may be growing in the cemetery setting of the poem, covering up the names, but figuratively, moss is also a metaphor for what?

    (A) Summer

    (B) Time   (D) Death

    (C) Age   (E) Life

25. Based on the beginning and ending lines of this poem, Dickinson's tone is

    (A) Pessimistic

    (B) Optimistic   (D) Tremulous

    (C) Indifferent   (E) Care-free

26. Which of the following best describes the poem as a whole?

    (A) An amusing satire on the excessive interest in Beauty and Truth

    (B) A poetic expression of the need for love to give meaning to life

    (C) A concisely written poem about the ambiguity of Beauty and Truth

    (D) A personal meditation on human courage in the face of death

    (E) A lyrical celebration of the importance of humanity's search for Beauty and Truth

Questions 27 - 40. Read the following passage from "The Artifices of Tragedy" by Joseph Addison carefully before you choose your answers.

Among the several **artifices** which are put in practice by poets to fill the minds of an audience with terror, the first place is due to **thunder and lightning,** which are often made use of at the descending of a god or at the rising of a ghost, at the vanishing of a devil or at the death of a tyrant. I have known a bell introduced into several tragedies with good effect . . . but there is nothing which delights and terrifies our English theater so much as a ghost, especially when he appears in a bloody shirt. A specter has often saved a play though he has done nothing but stalked across the stage, or rose through a cleft of it and sunk again without speaking one word. There may be a **proper season** for these several terrors; and when they only come in as aids and assistances to the poet, they are not only to be excused, but to be applauded. . . .

For the moving of pity, our principal machine is the handkerchief; and indeed in our common tragedies, we should not know very often that the persons are in distress by anything they say, if they did not from time to time apply their handkerchiefs to their eyes. Far be it from me to think of banishing this instrument of sorrow from the stage; I know a tragedy could not subsist without it: All that I would contend for is to keep it from being misapplied. In a word, I would have the actor's tongue sympathize with his eyes.

A disconsolate mother with a child in her hand has frequently drawn compassion from the audience, and has therefore gained a place in several tragedies. A modern writer, that observed how this had took in other plays, being resolved to double the distress and melt his audience twice as much . . . brought a princess upon the stage with a little boy in one hand and a little girl in the other. This too had a very good effect. A third poet, being resolved to outwrite all his predecessors, a few years age introduced three children with great success. And, as I am informed, a young gentleman, who is fully determined to break the most obdurate hearts, has a tragedy by him where the first person that appears upon the stage is an afflicted widow in her mourning-weeds with half a dozen fatherless children attending her. . . . Thus several incidents that are beautiful in a good writer become ridiculous by falling into the hands of a bad one. But among all our methods of moving pity or terror, there is none so absurd and barbarous, and what more exposes us to the contempt and ridicule of our neighbors, than that dreadful butchering of one another that is so frequent upon the English stage. To delight in seeing men stabbed poisoned, racked, or impaled is certainly the sign of a cruel temper. . . .

It is indeed very odd to see our stage strewn with carcasses in the last scene of a tragedy; and to observe in the wardrobe of the playhouse several daggers, poniards, wheels, bowls for poison, and many other instruments of death. . . . To give my opinion upon this case; the fact ought not to have been represented but to have been told if there was any occasion for it.

27. The word "artifices," as used in this passage, is synonymous with all BUT one of the following:

(A) machine

(B) instrument   (D) person

(C) trick   (E) tactic

28. The phrases "thunder and lightning, which are often made use of at the descending of a god or at the rising of a ghost, at the vanishing of a devil or at the death of a tyrant" is an example of creating what type of sentence structure?

(A) parallel

(B) compound   (D) tight, simple

(C) simple   (E) compound-complex

29. This passage is addressing what genre of literature?

(A) comedies

(B) tragedies   (D) short stories

(C) novels   (E) poems

30. All BUT one of the following artifices is mentioned in paragraph one:

(A) thunder

(B) lightning   (D) ghosts

(C) handkerchiefs   (E) bells

31. Which statement by Addison indicates the "proper season" for these artifices?
- (A) when the "actor's tongue (does not) sympathize with his eyes"
- (B) when they only come in as aids and assistances to the poet"
- (C) when the poet needs to show that "the persons are in distress"
- (D) when the poet is "fully determined to break the most obdurate heart
- (E) when the poet wants "to fill the minds of the audience with terror"

32. The topic of paragraph one is:
- (A) terror
- (B) sorrow
- (C) humor
- (D) pity
- (E) sadness

33. In the first paragraph, the author's attitude toward those who use artifices can be best described as
- (A) suspicious
- (B) critical
- (C) incredulous
- (D) admirable
- (E) uncertain

34. The topic of paragraph two is:
- (A) terror
- (B) sorrow
- (C) humor
- (D) pity
- (E) sadness

35. Beginning in third paragraph, Addison shifts his emphasis of praising artifices used in the proper way to
- (A) satirizing bad writers' use of artifices through his use of hyperbole
- (B) illustrating good writers' use of artifices through his use of imagery
- (C) exposing good writers' use of artifices through his use of similes
- (D) defining bad writers by their lack of artifices through his use of litotes
- (E) praising artifices used in the improper way

36. When Addison uses the word "poet" he means:
- (A) essayist
- (B) dramatist
- (C) diarist
- (D) biographer
- (E) critic

37. All of the following words show Addison's disapproval EXCEPT:

    (A) absurd

    (B) barbarous   (D) impaled

    (C) assistance   (E) racked

38. Addison use of the word "carcasses" in the last paragraph conveys a tone of

    (A) indifference

    (B) disgust   (D) ambivalence

    (C) difference   (E) disinterest

39. A poniard is all of the following EXCEPT

    (A) an instrument of death

    (B) a dagger   (D) a medicinal instrument

    (C) a knife   (E) an instrument of torture

40. Which of the following best describes the pattern of the author's discussion?

    (A) statement of fact followed by tentative assumptions

    (B) description of theory followed by exceptions to the theory

    (C) general statement followed by more general statements

    (D) forceful argumentation followed by concession to opponents

    (E) presentation of a problem followed by resolution of the problem

Questions 41 - 50. Read the following passage from Nathaniel Hawthorne's *The Scarlet Latter* carefully before you choose your answers.

Hester Prynne's term of confinement was now at an end. Her prison door was thrown open and she came forth into the sunshine, which, falling on all alike, seemed, to her sick and morbid heart, as if meant for no other purpose than to reveal the scarlet letter on her breast. Perhaps there was a more real torture in her first unattended footsteps from the threshold of the prison than even in the procession and spectacle that have been described, where she was made the common **infamy** at which all mankind was summoned to point its finger. Then, she was supported by an unnatural tension of the nerves and by all the combative energy of her character, which enabled her to convert the scene into a kind of **lurid** triumph.... The very law which condemned her — a giant of

stern features, but with vigor to support, as well as to annihilate, in his iron arm — had held her up through the terrible
ordeal of her **ignominy**. But now, with this unattended walk
from the prison door, began the daily custom; and she must
either sustain and carry it forward by the ordinary resources
of her character, or sink beneath it. She could no longer bor-
row from the future to bear her present grief. Tomorrow would
bring its own trial with it; so would the next day; and so
would the next; each its own trial, and yet the very same that
was now so unutterably grievous to be borne. The days of the
far off future would toil onward; still with the same burden
for her to take up and bear along with her, but never to fling
down; for the accumulating days and added years would pile
up their misery upon the heap of shame. Throughout them
all, giving up her individuality, she would become the general
symbol at which the preacher and moralist might point, and
in which they might vivify and embody their images of
woman's frailty and sinful passion. Thus, the young would be
taught to look at her ... as the figure, the body, the reality of sin.

41. Why does Hester have a "sick and morbid heart" (line 4)?
    (A) She hates the public
    (B) She has cardiovascular problems
    (C) She is experiencing guilt and confinement
    (D) The prison has made her sick.
    (E) She knows her husband is waiting

42. The phrase "the sunshine . . . (was) falling forth. . . as if
meant . . . to reveal the scarlet letter on her breast" in lines 3 - 5
is an example of what figure of speech?
    (A) Personification
    (B) Allusion   (D) Simile
    (C) Metaphor   (E) Alliteration

43. The word "infamy" in line 9 of the above passage describes
Hester as being a symbol of all but one the following:
    (A) shame
    (B) goodness   (D) wickedness
    (C) scandal   (E) atrocity

44. In lines 1 - 10 of this passage, what is going through Hester's
head?   (A) She feels everything is against her.
    (B) She thinks she must be crazy.
    (C) She is glad everything is finally over.
    (D) She is glad she is free at last.
    (E) She can't wait to get home.

45. In line 12 of the above passage "lurid" means all but one f the following:

    (A) Pale

    (B) Sensational   (D) Racy

    (C) Yellow   (E) Exciting

46. The phrase "The very law which condemned her -- a giant of stern features, but with vigor to support, as well as to annihilate, in his iron arm - " in lines 13 - 15 is an example of a

    (A) Personification

    (B) Allusion   (D) Simile

    (C) Metaphor   (E) Alliteration

47. In line 16 of the above passage "ignominy" means all but one of the following:

    (A) Honor

    (B) Shame   (D) Dishonor

    (C) Disgrace   (E) Scandal

48. What type of poetical device is Hawthorne using in the phrase "The days of the far off future would toil onward. . ." in lines 23 - 24?

    (A) Personification

    (B) Allusion   (D) Simile

    (C) Metaphor   (E) Alliteration

49. The last sentence of this passage, "Thus, the young would be taught to look at her ... as the figure, the body, the reality of sin. . . ." is an example of

    (A) Personification

    (B) Allusion   (D) Simile

    (C) Metaphor   (E) Alliteration

50. Hester's attitude in this passage can be best described as

    (A) fearful acceptance of the morbid Puritan punishment allotted her

    (B) reverence for God's people

    (C) self-satisfaction with the human dominion over humans

    (D) disgust with the evil that permeates Salem

    (E) scorn at the Puritan harshness

Glossary of Terms

used in the 1970 -- 1997
(AP) Advanced Placement
Examinations in

Language and
Composition
and
Literature and
Composition

• **Abstraction**

A concept or value that can not be seen (love, honor, courage, etc.) which the writer usually tries to illustrate by comparing it metaphorically to a known, concrete object. Sometimes this knowledge is hidden or esoteric because it is only known by or meant for a select few.

• **Ad hominem argument**

Attacking another person's argument by attacking the person rather than the issue. In the political arena this is called "mudslinging."

• **Adjectives**

Words that describe nouns. Look at these words when asked to address the author's use of diction.

• **Allegory**

A story or description that has a second meaning. This is portrayed by creating characters, setting, and/or events which represent (symbolize) abstract ideas.

• **Alliteration**

The repetition of initial consonant sounds.

• **Allusion**

References to literary, artistic, scientific, or historical people, places, or things.

• **Ambiguity (or Ambiguous References)**

The expression of an idea in such a way that more than one meaning is suggested. All AP essay passages have some ambiguity. To get the highest scores, students have to make reference to the multiple meanings seen in the passages.

• **Analogy**

A comparison of two things usually made by an author to show how something unfamiliar is like something widely known.

• **Anapest**

A metrical foot that has two unstressed syllables followed by one stressed syllable.

• **Anecdote**

A brief story used in an essay to illustrate a point.

• **Antagonist**

The force or person working against the protagonist. The villain is an antagonist.

• **Antithesis**

A statement in which direct opposites are contrasted in the same sentence. A contrast of ideas expressed in a grammatically balanced statement. "To err is human; to forgive, divine."

• **Antecedent**

The word for which the pronoun stands.

• **Aphorism**

A brief, sometimes clever saying that expresses a principle, truth or observation about life (see assertion).

• **Apostrophe**

A literary device in which the speaker directly addresses someone dead, someone missing, an abstract quality, or something nonhuman as if he/she/it were present. Example" "Ye knew him well, ye cliffs."

• **Approximate Rhyme**

Using words that have some sound correspondence, but the rhyme is not perfect.

• **Arguments**

Assertions made based on facts, statistics, logical or objective reasoning, hard evidence, etc.

• **Aside**

Private words, spoken by an actor to the audience, that are not meant to be heard by the other actors.

• **Assertion**

A categorical statement made by the author, speaker, narrator, or character which generalizes an opinion usually about human nature. A "for or against" stance taken by the writer of a personal essay (also called a proposition).

- **Attitude**

   The author's state of mind or point of view toward himself/herself or another person, place, or thing.
- **Assumption**

   An inference or conclusion, possibly based on evidence.
- **Authorial aside**

   Also called editorializing. When used in a fictional story, the author steps outside the story, speaking directly to the reader.
- **Balanced Sentence**

   Helps to characterize a writer's style, usually accompanied with a semicolon with a balanced number of words on each side.
- **Ballad Meter**

   A ballad is a fairly short story or poem that has some songlike qualities. A typical ballad stanza is a quatrain with the rhyme scheme abcb. The meter is primarily iambic.
- **Begging the Question**

   A persuasive fallacy in which the writer assumes the reader will automatically accept an assertion without proper support. Be aware of this with writers who use syllogisms or deductive reasoning to reach a conclusion.
- **Blank Verse**

   Poetry written in unrhymed iambic pentameter.
- **Cause and Effect Relationships**

   A dominant technique (also called rhetorical device) in which the author analyzes reasons for a chain of events. This causal analysis can also be the writer's main method of organization, or it can be one paragraph used to support a point in an essay developed through another pattern.
- **Characterization**

   The process by which the writer reveals the personalities of the people of the work.

- **Characterization**
  Revealed by:
  1. Direct author/poet statement: The author may use such direct diction as "cruel, conservative, deceitful, long-suffering," or "self-absorbed."
  2. Motivations: Some examples could include misguided altruisms, self-destructive ambition, self-conscious insecurity, financial considerations, or hypocritical tendencies.
  3. Physical Description
  4. Dialogue
  5. Thoughts and feelings
  6. Actions
  7. Effect on others, etc.
- **Chronology of Events**
  A method of organization usually used in narration in which the events are described as they happen. Flashbacks and flashforwards are sometimes used to interrupt the normal order.
- **Circular Reasoning**
  An error in persuasion which involves repeating the assertion endlessly without support.
- **Citations from Well-known Authorities**
  Persuasive device used to lend more credence to an assertion made.
- **Closed Couplet**
  Two consecutive lines of poetry that rhyme and present a completed thought.
- **Coherence**
  Having a clear connection among all the parts. This is achieved by using a clear organizational format and by providing appropriate connecting devices (transitions, bridging sentences, repeated words, synonyms, and conjunctions).
- **Comic Relief**
  Something said or done that provides a break from the seriousness of the story, poem, or play.
- **Compound Sentence**
  Two independent clauses connected by a conjunction.
- **Comparison and Contrast**
  Showing similarities and/or differences. The AP question usually asks for differences. The student is asked to make a judgment about the relative merits of the two passages. Which one is more effective?

- **Conceit**

  A juxtaposition that makes a surprising connection between two seemingly different things. T. S. Eliot is a modern poet known for his use of conceits.

- **Conclusion**

  Usually written to reaffirm or finally state the thesis. Other strategies used in the conclusion include expressing a final thought about a subject, summarizing main points, using a quotation, predicting an outcome, making an evaluation, or recommending a course of action.

- **Confessional Poetry**

  A modern term used to describe poetry that uses intimate and usually painful, disturbing, or sad material from the poet's life. Anne Sexton and Sylvia Plath are two modern Confessional poets.

- **Conflict**

  The tension created in the story by the struggle or outcome of the struggle — one of the narrative devices to address when analyzing the tone of the passage. Look for internal, as well as external conflict.

- **Connotative Language**

  Words which have implied meaning, emphasizing the feelings or subjectivity that surrounds the word. Denotative language, emphasizing the literal, dictionary meaning, is used to create an objective tone. Consider these aspects of words when analyzing how diction creates attitude, effect, or purpose.

- **Contrast**

  A literary technique in which the author examines two opposites (like the energy of youth and the infirmity of age, worldly possessions and democratic idealism, academic success and extracurricular activities, a speaker's sophistication and the student's naivete, or a group's smug views and the speaker's implied disapproval of them) to create an attitude, accomplish a purpose of effect or to make an assertion.

  Also, a rhetorical strategy which juxtaposes to unlike words together such as homologous and analogous, meaningful and meaningless, intrinsic and superficial, inheritance and convergence, intuition and imagination, etc. (See antithesis)

- **Control a Wide Range of the Elements of Writing**

  In mature writing, mature diction, varied syntax and effective paragraph organization combine to convey a clear and insightful evaluation, analysis, impression, or assertion.

- **Dactyl**

  A metrical foot with one stressed syllable followed by two unstressed syllables.

- **Deductive Reasoning**

  A form of logical thinking to analyze when one is asked to evaluate the persuasive devices used by the author. In deductive reasoning, general statements (**major premises**) believed to be true are applied to specific situations (**minor premises**). The result of deduction is a conclusion about a specific situation. This three step pattern is called a **syllogism**.

- **Defend, Challenge or Qualify**

  Present a logical argument "for" or "against" a certain decision; defend, challenge or qualify an assertion or the author's views.

- **Definition (extended)**

  A form of organization that emphasizes meanings. One means of organizing writing. For example, an abstract idea may be developed with a number of definitions of the idea.

- **Denotative Language**

  Denotative words have literal, dictionary meaning, emphasizing an objective tone. Connotative language has implied meaning, emphasizing the feelings or subjectivity that surrounds the word. Consider these aspects of words when analyzing how diction creates attitude, effect or purpose.

- **Description**

  Using vivid words to paint a picture of what the five senses are experiencing. The purpose of a descriptive essay is to create a **dominant impression** through the manipulation of details.

- **Diction**

  Word choice used by the author to persuade or to convey tone, purpose, or effect. This could be described as technical and abstruse, lofty and learned, pedestrian, colloquial, scientific, etc.

- **Dialogue**

  Conversation between people.
- **Didactic**

  A type of writing that is preachy or bossy.
- **Dilemma**

  A type of conflict in which both choices have some negative connotations.
- **Dramatic Monologue**

  A poem in which the speaker addresses one or more listeners who remain silent or whose replies are not revealed.
- **Dramatize**

  To act
- **Economy**

  A style of writing characterized by conciseness and brevity.
- **Effect**

  The influence or result of something, using such rhetorical strategies as arguments, assumptions, attitudes, contrast, diction, imagery, pacing, or repetition. This effect could include such results as to intensify the speaker's sense of the ridiculous, reveal the speaker's ___ attitude, emphasize the cynicism of ___, reduce ___ to the level of low comic characters, or to glamorize a character.

  Also, an impression created by the author's language choices which could be described as familiar reality imposed on an unfamiliar setting, sudden color in a former monochromatic scene, miraculous isolation in a hostile environment, ominous fragility in a threatening episode, supernatural inspiration of creative thought.
- **Either - or Fallacy**

  Arguing that a complex situation can be simply explained in one of two ways.
- **End-stopped lines**

  Lines of poetry that end with punctuation marks.
- **Epigram**

  A brief, clever, and usually memorable statement. For example, "We think our fathers fools, so wise we grow, Our wiser sons, no doubt, will think us so."

  Alexander Pope

- **Ethos**
    A form of logical thinking used to analyze the author's reliability or credibility. Address this issue when asked to evaluate the persuasive devices used by the author. Writers establish their ethos by using moderate appeals to emotion, avoiding a hostile tone, and/or demonstrating overall knowledge of the subject. Good persuasive writing has a balance of ethos, logos and pathos.
- **Euphemism**
    Describing something distasteful in a positive way.
- **Euphony**
    A choice and arrangement of words that creates a pleasant sound.
- **Evidence**
    Used to lend support to the writer's thesis. Whether writing a personal essay or an analysis of a passage's style, good evidence must be unified, specific, accurate, adequate, and representative. This is another way of evaluating persuasive writing that uses inductive reasoning.
- **Experience**
    Evidence from your personal life that can be used to support a defend, challenge or qualify question. If the question does not specifically allow you to use evidence from your personal experience, observations and reading, do not do this.
- **Exposition**
    A type of writing, a mode, which explains . . .
- **Extended Figure**
    Any metaphor, simile, personification, or apostrophe that is developed through several lines or throughout the poem.
- **False Analogy**
    Makes the error of assuming that since two things are alike in some ways, they are alike in all ways.
- **Feelings**
    One purpose of a poem may be to convey emotions such as curiosity, contentment, remoteness, resignation, or foreboding.

•Figures of Speech

Imaginative comparisons (similes, metaphors, personification, etc.) used by the author to convey tone, purpose, or effect.

•Flashback

One aspect of narrative structure in which the writer goes back in time to reveal past history that is somehow important to the story.

•Foreshadowing

A literary technique in which the author gives hints about future events. Another aspect of narrative structure in which the author maintains interest by giving clues about future happenings.

•Foil

A character who contrasts with another character.

•Foot

A unit of meter that contains an arranged numbered of syllables. For instance, an anapestic foot contains two unstressed syllables followed by one stressed syllable. Other types of feet are called dactyl, iamb, spondee, and trochee.

•Form

The external pattern of the poem. Different types of form include continuous form (lines follow each other without formal grouping, breaking only at the end of a unit of meaning); stanzaic form; free verse; fixed form (the ballad, Terza Rima, etc.); and blank verse.

•Free Verse

Poetry that does not conform to a regular pattern of rhyme or rhythm. The words are arranged in lines but have no fixed meter.

•Grotesque

An element of Gothic Romanticism in which bizarre, fantastically ugly or absurd elements are somehow important to the overall effect of the poem or story.

- **Hasty Generalization**

  Making an unsound inductive inference based on insufficient, inadequate, unspecified evidence.
- **Heroic Couplet**

  Two consecutive lines of poetry that rhyme and are written in iambic pentameter.
- **Hyperbole**

  A figure of speech in which the author uses overexaggeration or overstatement to create a certain effect, accomplish a particular purpose or reveal an attitude.
- **Iamb**

  A metrical foot that has one unaccented syllable followed by one accented syllable.
- **Imagery**

  Diction describing the five senses (visual, tactile, auditory, olfactory, and emotional) used by the author to convey tone, purpose, or effect.
- **Inductive Reasoning**

  A form of logical reasoning which examines evidence before drawing a conclusion.
- **Internal Rhyme**

  Rhyme that occurs within a line of poetry.
- **Inverted Order**

  Reversing the normal subject-verb-complement order seen in a sentence. Poets sometimes change this order to conform to rhyme and rhythm patterns. Prose writers may change this order for emphasis.
- **Irony**

  A literary device used by prose writers/dramatists in which the writer implies a discrepancy between what is said and what is meant (verbal irony), between what happens and what is expected to happen (situational irony), or between what a character in a play thinks and what the audience knows to be true (dramatic irony).
- **Juxtaposition**

  Placing two persons, places, things or ideas next to each other to create an effect, reveal an attitude, or accomplish a purpose. Such juxtaposition could include a married couple, two types of religions, or such abstract ideas as virtue and youth, innocence and egotism, or wealth and poverty.

- **Litotes**

    See understatement.

- **Loose Sentence**

    Consists of usually more than two clauses or phrases which are connected together by a series of conjunctions (and, but, or). Writers may use this to make the essay less formal. Using too many loose sentences makes for a rambling essay.

- **Lyrical Poetry**

    A poem whose main purpose is to express the personal feelings or thoughts of the speaker rather than to tell a story.

- **Manipulation of Language**

    A skillful handling of diction and syntax, used by the author to convey tone, purpose, or effect.

- **Metaphysical Conceit (see Conceit)**

    So-called because they were used by the Metaphysical Poets of the seventeenth century, this type of conceit is especially startling, complex and ingenious.

- **Metaphor (extended or elaborate)**

    A direct comparison in which an unknown item is understood by directly comparing it to a known item Metaphors can be **directly stated** or **implied**. When it is developed throughout the poem or over several lines, it is called an **extended metaphor**. One that has been used too often is called a **dead metaphor**; one that compares things that are visually or imaginatively incompatible is called a **mixed metaphor**.

- **Meter**

    A set of stressed and unstressed syllables of a poetic line, carefully counted to conform to a regular pattern. Meter is described by the type of foot used (iambic, trochaic, dactylic, or anapestic) and the number of feet in each line (monometer, dimeter, trimeter, tetrameter, pentameter, hexameter, heptameter, or octometer). **Blank verse** is written in iambic pentameter because each foot has an unstressed syllable followed by a stressed syllable, and each line has five of these iambic feet.

- **Narrative Structure or Narrative Techniques**
  Using a chronology of events, plot, conflict, character-ization, setting, and other elements of storytelling to convey tone, purpose, or effect.
- **Narrator**
  The person telling the story. A narrator can be de-scribed as a participating observer who is partial to someone, a third person narrator who is aware of the main character's thoughts (central omniscient), a non-participating narrator who is unaware of the main character's thoughts (third person objective), a first person narrator who refers of himself in the third per-son, a third person narrator who reveals the thoughts of several characters (Omniscient).
- **Naturalism**
  A nineteenth-century literary movement that carried realism to a negative extreme. In naturalistic stories character outcomes are doomed by heredity and en-vironment.
- **Non Sequiturs**
  Faulty conclusions about causal relationships.
- **Objective**
  Without bias, neutral. You may have to interpret a description as being subjective or objective.
- **Observation**
  Evidence from your observations of society that can be used to support a defend, challenge or qualify ques-tion. If the question does not specifically allow you to use evidence from your personal experience, obser-vations and reading, do not do this.
- **Octave**
  An eight line poem, or the first eight lines of a Petrarchan sonnet.
- **One - Side - at - a - Time Method**
  One of two ways to organize a comparison-contrast essay. In this type of organization the writer would discuss all the points of one passage first, then discuss all the points of the other passage second, showing the differences between the two.
- **Onomatopoeia**
  The use of words that imitate the sounds they make.
- **Organization**
  The process of arranging evidence to support a thesis.

- **Organization** (continued)

  The type of organization used could be chronological, spatial, emphatic, simple to complex, definition, cause and effect, deductive, inductive, comparison and contrast, division and classification, examples, analogy, side-by-side, point-by-point, etc.

  The type of organization used may also be dictated by the mode of writing. The descriptive mode of writing may use a spatial organization. The narrative mode may use a chronological organization. The persuasive mode may use inductive or deductive reasoning. Or the modes may shift within the writing, offering a different organization (see rhetorical shift).

- **Oxymoron**

  A figure of speech that combines contradictory terms (cheerfully vindictive, jumbo shrimp, deafening silence, the living dead).

- **Pacing**

  The rate of movement (tempo) of a story may be slower with exposition or description, faster with dramatic incidence, etc.

- **Paradigm**

  A model, ideal or standard.

- **Paradox**

  A statement or situation that appears contradictory but is true. For instance, the mountains in a setting of a poem, may be both remote and oppressively present. Metaphysical and Cavalier poets of the 17th century made great use of paradoxes.

- **Parallel Syntax or Constructions**

  A stylistic technique in which items in a series are created with identical grammatical structures.

- **Paraphrase**

  To restate the content of the poem in prose.

- **Parody**

  A rewriting of a popularly recognized work to make fun of something. Rewriting *Little Red Riding Hood* in more "politically correct" language would be an example of a parody.

- **Pathos**

  Appeal to emotion.

- **Periodic Sentence**

  A sentence with a number of qualifying phrases placed in emphatic order (the most important idea is last.)
- **Personification**

  A figure of speech in which inanimate objects are given human qualities (The fog comes in on little cat feet).
- **Petrarchan or Italian Sonnet**

  A fourteen line poem organized in two segments: the octave (the first eight lines) and a sestet (the last six lines. The rhyme scheme is ABBA, CDCD, EFEF, GG. The other type of Sonnet is called an Elizabethan or Shakespearean Sonnet.
- **Perspective**

  The position chosen by the author to tell the story. This is formally known as first person, third person objective, limited omniscient, or omniscient. Some other ways of describing the perspectives that could be taken by the speaker to tell the story include an acquaintance of one of the characters in the story, or a chronicler of past events, or an uninvolved eye-witness, or a commentator on social trends, or a defender of a popular figure, etc.
- **Persuasion**

  Writing which appeals to the reader's emotions and value systems, encouraging the reader to adopt an attitude or change a position.
- **Plausibility**

  An element of literary judgment. Is the work BELIEV-ABLE? Whether the work is Romantic or Realistic, some element of believability must exist for reader empathy to occur.
- **Point - by - Point**

  One of two ways to organize a comparison-contrast essay. In this type of organization the writer would discuss one aspect of both passages, showing how this one aspect differs; then do the same for a second and third aspect, intertwining evidence from both passages in each paragraph.
- **Point of View**

  The tone or attitude created by the author's manipulation of language. ALSO SEE NARRATOR.
- **Post Hoc Fallacy**

  Erroneously concluding that one event caused another just because it came first.

•**Psychological Insight**

An ability to see the inner nature of things.

•**Pun**

A play upon words based on the multiple meanings of words. Puns are usually used to create humor, but can be a serious element in poetry as well.

•**Purpose**

The reason for writing an essay, usually based on the effect the writer wants to have on his or her audience. Some purposes could include: to describe a situation, characterize an era, portray an unusual character, depict an inequitable situation, comment on a popular assumption , arouse sympathy for a character, provide a contrary opinion, reinforce a concept, etc.

•**Quatrain**

A poem of four lines, or a stanza of four lines within a poem.

•**Questionable Authority**

Vague appeals to unsubstantiated authority revealed by such phrases as "studies show" and "experts claim." Good persuasive writing documents references to authority, specifically establishing credibility.

•**Reading**

References to particular writers, composers, or other artists that can be used to support a defend, challenge or qualify question. If the question does not specifically allow you to use evidence from your personal experience, observations and reading, do not do this.

•**Realism**

A literary style developed in the nineteenth century that attempts to portray life accurately, without idealizing or romanticizing it.

•**Red Herring Arguments**

Deliberate attempts to focus on a minor issue rather than addressing the main point.

•**Refrain**

A repeated word, phrase, or group of lines in poetry.

•**Relevance**

A free choice question may ask you to discuss how a work of literary merit written before 1900 relates to today's modern reader.

•Repetition

A device used by the writer to emphasize an important character trait, to reinforce the story's theme, to highlight the speaker's attitude, to provide a transition between paragraphs, to maintain an idea of persistence, or to focus the reader's attention on a certain person person, place, or thing.

•Resolution

The conclusion of a story.

•Rhetorical Purpose

The reason for the speaker's remarks, or a definition of the attitude that the author would like the reader to adopt.

•Rhetorical shift

The changing modes or patterns of organization within an essay. Some examples are the change from exposition to argument, from hypothesis to proof, from sympathetic narration to objective description, from descriptive narration to poetic meditation , from contemplative rumination to active participation, from personal reminiscence to objective exposition, from poetic rhapsody to minute description, from philosophical logic to scientific vigor, from speculation to generalization, or the change from profound meditation to cold reasoning. Some other structural shifts could include a digression from the main subject of the poem, a change from description to narration, counterargument to establish the speaker's credibility, metaphorical application of an image in the poem, or a simile for the relationship between two characters.

A rhetorical shift could also be a change in attitude, purpose, or effect seen in a literary work For example, a speaker's mode of expression may change from one of criticism to acceptance, homage to entreaty, rationality to enthusiasm, uncertainty to resolution, or languor to determination.

•Rhetorical Purpose

Reason for the speaker's remarks; or define the attitude that the author would like the reader to adopt.

•Rhetorical Structure

Any organizational device used by the author to convey tone, purpose, or effect. Such writing choices may include establishing a thesis, presenting a description, presenting a contrasting description, describing an expectation, posing a question and answering it, beginning a narrative and embellishing it, etc.

•**Rhetorical Strategy**

Writing choices made by the author to accomplish purpose. These may include such things as allowing the reader to form individual judgments, undercutting the speaker's statements with irony, imitating the language of a certain group of people, beginning and ending on a note of uncertainty, or contrasting the setting and its inhabitants. Rhetorical innovation is a mark of a good writer.

•**Rhetorical Question**

A literary device in which a question is asked that actually requires no answer.

•**Rime Royal**

A Chaucerian Stanza composed of seven lines written in iambic pentameter with a rhyme scheme of ababbcc.

•**Romanticism**

A literary movement that emphasizes intuition, imagination, and emotions over reason. Most romantics are outspoken in their love of nature and contempt for material things. Most romantics are concerned with the ideal rather than the real. An AP essay may ask you to address romantic diction or romantic atmosphere.

•**Satire**

A type of writing which makes fun of human weakness, vice, or folly in order to bring about change. Some ways to satirize include mingling the serious and the trivial indiscriminately, juxtaposing religious and political views, using repetition to exaggerate character weakness, vice, or folly, etc.

•**Selection and Presentation of specific detail**

Facts, circumstances, characteristics, techniques, etc., used by the author to convey tone, purpose, or effect.

•**Sestet**

Six lines of poetry (see Pterarchan sonnet).

- **Setting**

  The time and location of the story. The setting may be used by the writer to create conflict, atmosphere, mood, or character.

- **Shakespearean Sonnet**

  A fourteen line poem composed of three quatrains, followed by a rhyming couplet. The rhyme scheme is ABAB, CDCD, EFEF, GG.

- **Short, Simple Sentences**

  Three short sentences connected together by commas. Example: "I came, I saw, I conquered." Its brevity may make it emphatic.

- **Soliloquy**

  A long speech made by a character in a play while he/she is alone on stage.

- **Sound**

  An element to consider when analyzing poetry. For instance, how do sound devices add to the overall effect of the poem?

- **Spatial Organization**

  A method of organization used mainly in descriptions. The writer addresses everything in a certain area (space) before going on to another area.

- **Spenserian Stanza**

  A nine line stanza with the rhyme scheme ababbcbcc. The first eight lines are written in iambic pentameter and the last line is **alexandrine**—iambic hexameter. This form was created by Edmond Spenser and used by such poets as John Keats, Percy Byssche Shelly, Lord Byron, and Robert Burns.

- **Stereotypes**

  Anything that represents something in a typical way. Terms may be described as stereotypical.

- **Subjective**

  Full of feelings, biases, etc. You may have to interpret a description as being subjective or objective.

- **Subordinate Clause**

  A dependent clause beginning with a subordinating conjunction such as after, although, as, as if, as long as, as though, because, before, if, in order that, provided that, since, so that, than, though, unless, until, when, whenever, where, wherever, whether, while.

- **Syllogism**

  A method of developing the argument of a paragraph involving three steps—if a major premise is true and a minor premise is true, then a conclusion or prediction about the future can be made.

- **Symbol**

  A person, place or thing that represents something else . . . for instance, the whippoorwill in the poem could be presented as a symbol of death. . . a cross could be a symbol of the villager's plight, etc.

- **Synonym**

  A word that means the same as another word. You may have to pick a word that is synonymous with a word in the passage.

- **Syntax (Sentence Structure)**

  The arrangement of words into sentences, used by the author to convey tone, purpose, or effect. These can be described as simple, compound, or complex; argumentative, expository, interpretive or narrative; declarative, imperative, interrogative, or exclamatory.

- **Terza Rima**

  An interlocking, 3 line stanza form with the rhyme scheme aba bcb cdc ded, etc.

- **Theme**

  The central idea, usually by the writer of a work. Theme deals with the writer's view of the world which implicitly reveals some insight about human nature. A good way to start to define theme is to determine the subject of the work. Some subjects could include religious skepticism, emotional deprivation, hopeless deprivation, excessive wildness, or excessive wealth. A description of the passage and its general theme may include such definitions as a character analysis of two professional people which emphasizes the elements of idealism and selflessness that motivate them, or a narrative treatment of the conflicts inherent in the structure of social classes; etc.

- **Tone**

  The attitude created by the author's manipulation of language. AP passages dealing with tone are complex and ambiguous. To achieve highest marks on a tone essay, the writer has to define the tone in a specifically complex way.

•**Total Meaning**

>The entire experience communicated by the poem — the sensuous, emotional, intellectual, and imaginative.

•**Tragedy**

>A play in which the protagonist comes to an unhappy end. The main character is usually an honorable person whose downfall is caused by what Aristotle called a **tragic flaw** (an error in judgment or character weakness).

•**Transcendentalism**

>A nineteenth century movement in the Romantic tradition which believes that humans can rise above materialism to a higher happiness through simplicity and communion with nature.

•**Understatement (Litotes)**

>A statement that says less than what it means. These are often used to make an ironic point.

•**Wit**

>A quality of writing that combines cleverness with keen perception, especially in the writer's ability to state things that the reader has thought but not been able to express in words.

SCHOOL HOUSE BOOKS

Date ____-____-____   Purchase Order Number _____

SHIP TO: **BILL TO:**

_____   _____

Name of High School   Independent School District #

_____   _____

Contact Name   Contact Name or Department

_____   _____

Street Address / PO Box   Street Address / PO Box

_____   _____

City, State Zip   City, State Zip

For Credit Card Orders Call 1•877•376•7100

ITEM # PRODUCT	PRICE PER COPY	QUANTITY	TOTAL
4001 *A Practical AP Language Guide* (2nd ed.)	24.95	_____	_____
4002 AP LANGUAGE ANS/EXPLANATIONS	7.00	_____	_____
5001 *A Practical AP Literature Guide* (2nd ed.)	24.95	_____	_____
5002 AP LITERATURE ANS/EXPLANATIONS	7.00	_____	_____
6001 *School House Books* WRITER (1st ed.)	39.95	_____	_____
6002 *WRITER* Teacher's Guide	10.00	_____	_____

- -

SUBTOTAL   _____

Subtract 10% (20% for 5 or more books)   _____

SUBTOTAL   _____

Applicable Sales Tax (Any personal checks must
   include 6.5% sales tax. Schools are exempt.)   _____

SUBTOTAL   _____

Shipping & Handling ($7.00 Minimum,
7-25 items = $1.00 per item, Larger Orders= Cost)   _____

Please make check payable to:

School House Books
921 Pembina Trail
Detroit Lakes, MN 56501   TOTAL   _____